Common Core Curriculum: United States History, GRADES K–2

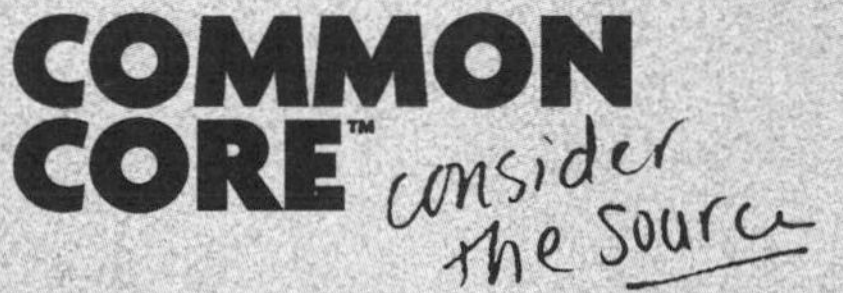

JB JOSSEY-BASS™
A Wiley Brand

Cover design by Chris Clary
Cover image: Statue of Liberty, © Diogo Salles

Published by Jossey-Bass
A Wiley Brand
One Montgomery Street, Suite 1200, San Francisco, CA 94104-4594 www.josseybass.com

Credits:
White Cloud, Head Chief of the Iowas by George Catlin | © Corbis
A Frigate - Dominic Serres © National Maritime Museum, Greenwich, London
George Washington by Gilbert Stuart | © Christie's Images/Corbis
Valley of the Yosemite by Albert Bierstadt | © Burstein Collection/CORBIS
President Reagan giving a speech at the Berlin Wall. Courtesy Ronald Reagan Library

Jossey-Bass books and products are available through most bookstores. To contact Jossey-Bass directly call our Customer Care Department within the U.S. at 800-956-7739, outside the U.S. at 317-572-3986, or fax 317-572-4002.

The content in this book also can be found online. See "The Alexandria Plan" at commoncore.org.

Wiley publishes in a variety of print and electronic formats and by print-on-demand. Some material included with standard print versions of this book may not be included in e-books or in print-on-demand. If this book refers to media such as a CD or DVD that is not included in the version you purchased, you may download this material at http://booksupport.wiley.com. For more information about Wiley products, visit www.wiley.com.

Library of Congress Cataloging-in-Publication Data

Common Core Curriculum: United States history, grades K-2/Common Core, Inc. – 1
pages cm. – (Common Core U.S. and world history)
Includes index.
ISBN 978-1-118-52626-2 (pbk.); ISBN 978-1-118-58335-7 (pdf); ISBN 978-1-118-58343-2 (epub)
1. United States–History–Study and teaching (Primary) 2. United States–History–Study and teaching (Primary)–Standards. I. Common Core, Inc.
LB1530.C66 2014
973.071–dc23

2013045497

Printed in the United States of America

FIRST EDITION

PB *Printing* 10 9 8 7 6 5 4 3 2 1

Contents

Introduction: How to Use the Alexandria Plan

The Alexandria Plan is Common Core's curriculum tool for teaching United States and world history. It is a strategic framework for identifying and using high-quality informational texts and narrative nonfiction to meet the expectations of the Common Core State Standards (CCSS) for English language arts (ELA) while also sharing essential historical knowledge with students in elementary school (kindergarten through fifth grade). These resources can be used in either the social studies block or the ELA block during the elementary school day. The curriculum helps teachers pose questions about texts covering a wide range of topics: from the caves at Lascaux to King Tut's tomb, Chief Joseph to Kubla Khan, and the birth of democracy to the fall of the Berlin Wall. These books tell stories that thrill students. Accompanying text-dependent questions (TDQs) will elevate student learning to a level that will help them master the new CCSS for English language arts (CCSS-ELA).

We call these curriculum materials the "Alexandria Plan" because we enjoy thinking about the role that they–and the teachers who use them–play in passing along important knowledge to future generations. In ancient Egypt, the Library of Alexandria, along with a museum, was part of a grand complex that sought to collect and catalog "all the knowledge in the world." It became a center of learning, attracting scholars, philosophers, scientists, and physicians from all corners of the earth. Though it fell to fire, the spirit of Alexandria remains. Some twenty-three hundred years later, a new library stands near the site of its ancient ancestor, and the story of Alexandria and its great library inspires our efforts to help teachers illuminate the future by inculcating in their students an understanding of the past.

The Alexandria Plan is the second in a suite of curriculum materials Common Core is developing to help educators implement the CCSS. In 2010, Common Core released its Curriculum Maps in English Language Arts. The Maps are a coherent sequence of thematic units, roughly six per grade level, for students in kindergarten through twelfth grade. Now known as the Wheatley Portfolio, these resources connect the skills delineated in the CCSS with suggested works of literature and informational texts and provide sample activities that teachers can use in the classroom to reinforce the standards. The Wheatley Portfolio will soon grow, with resources to help educators enact the instructional shifts while cultivating in students a love of excellent books–all based on featured anchor informational and literary texts, poetry, and the arts. In summer 2013, we began rolling out a comprehensive, K–12, CCSS-based mathematics curriculum known as Eureka Math, with embedded professional development. Please watch our website, commoncore.org, for future releases.

HOW WILL THE ALEXANDRIA PLAN HELP ME, MY SCHOOL, MY DISTRICT, OR MY STATE IMPLEMENT THE CCSS-ELA?

The CCSS-ELA emphasize the importance of literacy across the curriculum. Indeed, CCSS architect David Coleman has said, "There is no such thing as doing the nuts and bolts of reading in kindergarten through fifth grade without coherently developing knowledge in science, and history, and the arts–period." Unfortunately, research has illustrated that history is one in a group of core subjects that have been squeezed out of many classrooms. The Alexandria Plan guides educators through the process of reprioritizing the teaching of history in the classroom and will assist teachers in addressing key CCSS-ELA while also meeting state social studies standards.

HOW ARE THESE RESOURCES STRUCTURED?

The print editions of the Alexandria Plan, each organized by subject and grade span, present essential content knowledge in United States and world history. United States history is separated into eighteen eras, and so is world history. To make this knowledge accessible to students in elementary school, we established two grade spans: lower elementary (kindergarten through second grade) and upper elementary (third grade through fifth grade). Each book contains one subject area (United States or world history) as well as the resources for teaching to one grade span (lower or upper elementary). Learning expectations articulate the key ideas, events, facts, and figures to be understood by students in a particular grade span. Suggested anchor texts; text studies (comprising TDQs and exemplar student responses, and accompanied by performance assessments based on one or more featured anchor texts); and more select resources flesh out the content for each era. The following is a detailed breakdown of what is contained in a given era of the Alexandria Plan as well as in the accompanying collection of era summaries that provide additional historical content for teachers.

Overview

Each overview captures the essence of the history presented in a given era. The paragraph concludes with a brief description of what students will learn and be able to do after completing the associated text study.

Learning Expectations

This section describes what our teachers have identified as being appropriate and necessary for students to know in each grade span. It is this knowledge that students need to master so that they will be prepared for later grades. Teachers can break down the content indicated into grade-specific expectations that fit their classroom.

Suggested Anchor Texts

For each era of U.S. and world history, we provide a well-vetted list of suggested anchor texts that can be used to impart essential knowledge found in the "Era Summaries" and "Learning Expectations." So that educators can select the book that is best suited to their classroom, we provide text recommendations covering an array of topics in the era. These carefully curated selections include exceptional works of narrative nonfiction, informational texts, and historical fiction. The texts are rich in historical content, well written, fair in their presentation of history, and often beautifully illustrated, allowing for the development of text-dependent questions that illuminate both the historical content and the authors' and illustrators' craft. These texts may also serve as mentor texts for students' own writing.

Featured Anchor Text

Teacher-writers selected one or two of the suggested anchor texts to illuminate in a text study aimed at the higher end of a particular grade span. Although all of the suggested anchor texts are worth exploring with students, each featured anchor text captures a particularly pertinent aspect of the era in which it is featured. Occasionally, the featured anchor text is paired with a supporting text to provide additional content to support student understanding.

Text Study

Each text study provides teachers with detailed guidance about how to lead students through a close, patient reading of a featured anchor text. Using a carefully crafted sequence of TDQs, teachers can effectively guide students through a detailed reading of a complex text. The questions lead students to use evidence directly from the text to explain and support their answers. Such close reading leads students to absorb key historical knowledge while honing essential CCSS-ELA skills. Answers are provided for each question. These TDQs are followed by at least one comprehensive performance assessment for each study. Both the TDQs and the performance assessments require students to support conclusions or opinions about the text with specific text evidence.

Performance Assessments

Each text study is followed by at least one performance assessment that allows students to demonstrate (typically, through a CCSS-based writing assignment) their understanding of the key ideas, historical events, and figures discussed in the featured anchor text. These performance assessments flow naturally from the progression of TDQs about the featured anchor text. Suggestions of activities that can be used to extend or expand instruction, labeled as extensions, are often included.

Connections to Common Core State Standards for English Language Arts

Each text study also includes CCSS-ELA citations for nearly every one of the TDQs, performance assessments, and extensions, along with explanations of how each of these items helps address the CCSS-ELA. Please note that our citations for the standards follow the established CCSS format: strand.grade.number.

More Resources

We include a list of related resources, including works of historical fiction, art, poetry, music, primary sources, and multimedia resources, that teachers can incorporate into lessons, use to extend or enrich instruction, or simply use to build their own content knowledge. Teachers often ask for quality primary sources that they can use in elementary grades, so Common Core sought out engaging, relevant, and accessible primary sources for teachers and their students. Sources of essential geographic knowledge are also incorporated where appropriate. Like our suggested anchor text selections, these resources have been carefully curated to save teachers countless hours of searching for resources to extend students' knowledge of history.

Era Summaries

Each of the eras in the Alexandria Plan also contains a concise and compelling summary of the history of that era—all collected together at the end of each print edition—highlighting the people, events, places, and ideas that constitute essential knowledge for teachers to share with students. The content of the summaries was guided by exemplary state social studies standards, written by a historian with expert knowledge of those standards. Nationally recognized historians vetted each summary and meticulously reviewed them for accuracy. These easy-to-read summaries contain what college- and career-ready high school graduates should know about each era. The summaries also make it convenient for teachers to review the history of the era in preparation for lesson planning and deeper research.

HOW WERE ANCHOR TEXTS SELECTED?

Teacher-writers with decades of classroom experience reviewed hundreds of historical fiction, narrative nonfiction, and informational texts, selecting the most engaging and content-rich among them. Each anchor text conveys an essential aspect of the history addressed in the "Learning Expectations" for each era. The list of texts is neither comprehensive nor exhaustive. In other words, a text has not been selected for every aspect of the history contained in the era summaries, nor do we imagine that we have identified all of the great texts available that are relevant to an era. The list represents a great start—a set that we look forward to building over time.

We were looking for rigorous, accurate, well-written, and wonderfully illustrated texts, considering the following criteria:

- *The text should enliven historical events in ways that nurture children's innate curiosity.*

  We sought texts that bring to life the historical setting, events, and story being told. Although our focus was on the selection of complex, content-rich texts, we also recognized that the texts needed to be age appropriate. Much consideration was given to readability, and whenever possible, we have placed texts in appropriate grade bands, based on their Lexile level. Where Lexile levels may pose ostensible challenges for teachers, we have explained how teachers might approach instruction (for example, reading the text aloud or scaffolding the amount of text students are expected to read).

  In addition, we have geared our questions and answers to the upper level of each grade band. Teachers will have to use questions that are appropriate for their students and look to the answers provided as guides for where to lead students, building understanding over time. Teachers who have piloted these materials have often reported being surprised at how successfully students mine and appreciate these texts, even when the texts were at first considered "too hard." They have told us—and we believe—that it is important not to underestimate what students can do when they are presented with compelling, high-quality texts.

- *The text should make teaching more fun, by engaging the teacher in compelling history.*

  One of the key instructional shifts called for in teaching to the CCSS-ELA is the significant increase in the amount of time and attention students are asked to devote to evidence-based analysis of what they are reading. Instead of focusing on metacognitive reading strategies at the expense of content, teachers can now focus on the content of the text, confident that it lends itself well to the kind of analysis demanded in the CCSS-ELA, but also giving students a chance to immerse themselves in the content, making learning more interesting for students and teachers alike.

- *The text should serve, in its quality and complexity, as an exemplar for teaching the literacy skills defined in the CCSS-ELA.*

  The third criterion for text inclusion was that the text should be significantly complex enough to support the rich text study, including the focus on important English language arts standards. If the texts weren't well written and compelling, they simply would not lend themselves to the kind of analysis that the CCSS-ELA demand—and that teachers and students enjoy. These texts, by celebrated authors including Peter Sis and Diane Stanley, exhibit the power of narrative history, the efficacy of great illustrations, the effect of figurative language, and the strength of arguments that are supported with clear evidence.

HAS THE ALEXANDRIA PLAN BEEN PILOTED?

Yes, extensively. We asked teachers from rural, urban, charter, and private schools across the country to pilot a selection of the materials and to share their experience. Nearly one hundred teachers participated, including new teachers, National Board Certified teachers, and veterans who have been recognized by their respective districts for excellent teaching. Their generous feedback helped us both improve these materials and explain more clearly how to use the features of the curriculum. Rather than speak for them, here are two testimonials from pilot users:

> The Map made it very easy for the teacher by giving information about the book as well as historical information. The direction of the lesson was centered around the character of Christopher Columbus and the vocabulary used to describe him–*brave, studious, curious, patient, dreamer*. The students described Columbus and were able to defend their answers. I never really thought about the character of Columbus and all that he went through to make his dreams come true. He was a true leader. Our school is a "Leader in Me" school, and this lesson illustrated several of the habits (character traits) we want our students to exhibit.
>
> –Trudy Phelps, kindergarten teacher, Dolby Elementary School, Louisiana

> The text was the core of the social studies lesson. I worked from the text out. In most social studies lessons you start from the outside and move in. Students related to the characters and seemed to feel they were there. They simply had a better understanding of the history behind the text. The text, with a well-balanced set of questions, made the experience easier as they developed an understanding of the history.
>
> –Jayne Brown, kindergarten teacher, Avery's Creek Elementary School, North Carolina

WHY ARE THERE SO MANY TEXT-DEPENDENT QUESTIONS?

It is important to note that we do not expect teachers to ask *all* of the questions we've provided. Our rather exhaustive sets of questions are intended to support teachers in the scaffolding that will be necessary to meet the needs of all learners. Further, careful study of these questions, including how they are constructed, will help teachers craft text-dependent questions for other high-quality texts on their own. Indeed, the curriculum can be used as a professional development tool and as a means of understanding what is expected of students according to the CCSS-ELA. Please contact Common Core through commoncore.org if you would like to learn about our professional development services.

DOES THE ALEXANDRIA PLAN REQUIRE ME TO ADOPT A PARTICULAR METHOD OF INSTRUCTION?

No. The way teachers choose to prepare students to approach the study of a text depends on their teaching style and the needs of students. A teacher may choose to have students read short sections of text with a few assigned questions, preparing students to participate fully in discussion. Or a teacher may choose to have students work in pairs or small groups to read and to discuss questions, preparing to pull their ideas together for a rich whole-class seminar discussion. Or a teacher may want students to grapple with the text independently at first. During their first reading of the text, students might circle passages where they are confused and/or underline points that they thought were interesting. Students might annotate the reading selection with questions and notes. As the teacher circulates during the independent reading time, he or she might note themes of questions that students generate as they read. The teacher could then use the TDQs, as needed, to clarify misunderstandings and to go deeper into the text than the students were able to go on their own. We offer these questions for teachers to use as they see fit.

HOW CAN I SCAFFOLD UP TO A TEXT?

If a teacher wishes to use one of the suggested anchor texts but feels it is too difficult for his or her students, using more accessible texts to build background knowledge might be considered. This strategy involves reading aloud less challenging texts to prepare students to tackle the more difficult text. Following is an example of how to build skills and rigor up to the featured anchor text for U.S. era 11, *Abraham Lincoln: Lawyer, Leader, Legend* by Justine and Ron Fontes, recommended for lower elementary students.

At a Lexile level of 790L, this text is certainly at the upper range for the age level, and we are not suggesting that K–2 students read this book independently. Instead, we suggest that they follow along (with their own copy or using a document camera) as the teacher reads it aloud. Even still, it might be best to first introduce some of the vocabulary and concepts through easier books on the same topic, such as the following:

- *Abe Lincoln's Hat* by Martha Brenner: 330L
- *Mr. Lincoln's Whiskers* by Karen B. Winnick: 420L
- *Looking at Lincoln* by Maira Kalman: AD480L
- A. *Lincoln and Me* by Louise Borden: AD650L
- *When Abraham Talked to the Trees* by Elizabeth Van Steenwyk: 670L

Each of the books tells interesting stories about Abraham Lincoln as a person and a leader, creating a whole reservoir of background knowledge. This mounting knowledge arouses curiosity in the children, prompting a desire for more information. By the time the teacher is ready to share the more challenging *Abraham Lincoln: Lawyer, Leader, Legend*, the students know that Lincoln stored important things in his hat, grew whiskers because a young girl thought it would make him more dignified, stood tall to make hard decisions, and practiced his speeches on stumps in the woods. This background knowledge will make the complex text easier to understand.

Across Beringia: Original People of North America

(ca. 20,000 BCE to ca. 1600 CE)

GRADES: K, 1, 2

OVERVIEW

The first humans to settle on the American continents twenty thousand years ago eventually developed complex cultures with sophisticated political, economic, and religious systems. Native Americans adapted to very different landscapes and climates, from arctic to tropical, and this influenced all aspects of their behavior and customs. The featured anchor texts for this era, *Native Homes* and *The Discovery of the Americas: From Prehistory through the Age of Columbus*, explore how the first Americans lived. Students in lower elementary grades will report informed opinions on how native people lived. Upper elementary students will produce informed essays about the effect of European exploration on the native people of the Americas.

○ ○ ○

Interested in learning more about this time period? Read a more complete history in the "Era Summaries."

LEARNING EXPECTATIONS

Lower elementary: Students should be familiar with the major Native American cultural regions and civilizations—especially those cultures indigenous to what would become the United States, and to students' own state in particular. Students should understand the human impact of early European contact and conquest.

Upper elementary: Students should be aware of the tribal cultures and advanced civilizations that existed in the Americas before European contact. They should understand the environmental impact of both Native American and European arrivals, and the profound effects of European contact and conquest, both on indigenous civilizations and on Europe itself through the discovery of new foods and resources.

SUGGESTED ANCHOR TEXTS

Native Homes by Bobbie Kalman
Last Leaf First Snowflake to Fall by Leo Yerxa
Native North Americans: Dress, Eat, Write, and Play Just Like the Americans by Joe Fullman
Raven: A Trickster Tale from the Pacific Northwest by Gerald McDermott

FEATURED ANCHOR TEXT

NATIVE HOMES BY BOBBIE KALMAN

This book was selected because it explores Native American dwellings and presents each nation as a separate culture. Native American groups are organized by their geographic location, allowing students to see easily the relationship between environment and the development of culture. The book includes detailed illustrations and maps, sure to engage younger students, and provides an opportunity to highlight how text features help us learn about cultures different from our own.

TEXT STUDY

To answer the following text-dependent questions correctly, students must closely read an informational text. All of the text-dependent questions offer teachers an opportunity to support the Common Core State Standards for English language arts, especially in regard to how illustration and other features of an informational text may add to students' understanding of content. Each question requires that students note key details, ideas, and events and make connections among them (including comparing and contrasting information within the text about the various nations).

1. **Look closely at the map on page 5. What do you notice about the homes on the map?**

   Note: *The goal of this question is to invite students into the topic by focusing on visual representations of Native American homes, where they are, and what that might suggest about Native American cultures.*

   - There are different types of homes in different regions on the map.
   - Some homes are rounded, and some are more square shaped with peaked roofs.
   - The homes appear to be made of natural resources, such as animal skins in the Great Plains and wood in the Northeast.
   - There is a big difference between the iglu in the north and the chickee in the south.
   - The only tipis are in the Great Plains.

2. **According to the text on page 4, what is the meaning of the word *indigenous*?**
   - According to the context clue, the word *indigenous* is a word used to describe "first peoples."
   - The repetition of the word *native* in the following sentences lends a deeper understanding of the word.

3. **According to the text on page 4, what do native peoples of North America prefer to be called? Why?**
   - They prefer to be called by their particular nation's name rather than the more generic term *Native American.*

- They want to be called by their particular nation's name because each nation has its own language and culture.

4. **Why are there so many types of traditional Native American homes?**
   - The homes had to suit a particular group's surroundings and lifestyle, as well as the climate of the area where that group lived.
   - The homes were made from local natural resources. Different regions yielded different resources available for building homes.

5. **How does the third paragraph on page 4 help explain how native people in different regions built distinct homes?**
   - The author provides examples of a traditional dwelling from each area in North America. He explains how each dwelling is related to its climate and the natural resources in the area.
     - In the cool climates of the Northeast and Northwest, nations built large wooden homes using tree trunks.
     - In the warm and wet Southeast, homes were made without walls but with thatched roofs made of plants.

   Note: *After studying this text, students may gain deeper understanding by returning to the illustrated map on page 5. It would be interesting to challenge them to notice more about the traditional homes and their relationship to the environments in which the nations were located.*

6. **Study the two traditional types of dwellings in the illustrations on pages 6 and 7. What do you notice?**
   - The dwelling on page 6 looks similar to the pueblo picture on the map on page 5. It is a permanent dwelling in a dry, hot climate.
   - The dwellings on page 7 are tipis, made of animal skins. They are movable homes.

7. **According to the text on pages 6 and 7, why was it important for the Great Plains nation to be able to move?**
   - They were nomadic, moving from place to place to follow animal herds. They lived in a place where they had to rely on meat for food. They needed to be able to follow the buffalo during different seasons. The homes were light and easy to assemble in new locations.

8. **Why were the people in other nations able to build permanent homes?**
   - When nations lived in areas where there was good soil and a good water supply, people were able to settle down permanently. They were able to grow crops. Although they went on short hunting trips, they were able to stay in one place.

9. **According to the illustration on page 7, how did the people of the Great Plains nation carry the animals they killed in the hunt?**
   - They used dogs to pull the heavy loads.

   Note: *Explain to students that horses did not come to the Native Americans until the Europeans came to the New World. Prior to the Europeans' arrival, dogs were used.*

Note: *In an effort to "regionalize" the study for your own area, you might want to choose the pages that closely relate to a local Native American nation. Closely read the pages, asking students such questions as the following:*

- *What were the natural resources used for building this nation's homes?*
- *How did this nation's home design reflect the climate?*

- *How was the home a form of protection from weather and intruders?*
- *How did the home reflect the culture of the Native American nation?*

Explain the steps that were necessary to build the home. Ask students to study the illustration provided with the text to see how many details can add to their understanding of culture and lifestyle.

PERFORMANCE ASSESSMENTS

1. Tell the students to write an informative/explanatory paragraph about one of the homes discussed in the book.

2. Ask students to write an opinion sentence that describes which home they find most interesting and why.

EXTENSION

Help students find one legend or story that originates from one of the Native American nations whose homes they studied. Read the stories to the class, or have one of the students in the group read to the class, and discuss new learning of the culture gleaned from the details in each story.

CONNECTIONS TO COMMON CORE STATE STANDARDS FOR ENGLISH LANGUAGE ARTS

- Question 1 asks students to consider an illustrated map and glean key information from it (RI.K.1,7; RI.1.1,7; RI.2.1,7).
- Question 2 addresses the use of context clues to help determine the meaning of an important word (RI.K.4; RI.1.4; RI.2.4; L.K.4; L.1.4; L.2.4).
- Questions 3, 4, 7, and 8 focus on students' understanding of key details and ideas in the text, as well as connections among them (RI.K.1,2,3; RI.1.1,2,3; RI.2.1,2,3).
- Question 5 asks how details in the text relate to one another (RI.K.3,6; RI.1.3,6; RI.2.3,6).
- Questions 6 and 9 ask students to consider illustrations and glean key information from them (RI.K.1,7; RI.1.1,7; RI.2.1,7).
- The performance assessments require students to reread and summarize information about the Native American nations studied. They also offer students an opportunity to express an opinion about a Native American home and give a reason for that opinion (RI.K.9; RI.1.9; RI.2.9; W.K.1,2; W.1.1,2; W.2.1,2).
- The extension asks students to read related literary texts to build further understanding of a culture, read aloud to other students, summarize information orally for others in the class, and discuss that information as a group (RI.K.1,2,3; RI.1.1,2,3; RI.2.1,2,3; SL.K.1,2,6; SL.1.1,2,6; SL.2.1,2,6).

MORE RESOURCES

PRIMARY SOURCES

Native American fishing practices (Library of Congress)

Eskimo portrait (Library of Congress)

Eskimo arrowhead shapes (Library of Congress)

Mayan sun god (Metropolitan Museum of Art)

Pueblo mesa architecture (Denver Public Library)
Photo taken in 1899

POETRY AND MUSIC

Inuit throat singing, video (*National Geographic*)

ART AND ARCHITECTURE

Personal pendant, carved during the Ice Age (British Museum)

USEFUL WEBSITES

Native American legends organized by group name (First People)

Native American legends of the Northwest

Caribou migrating across the present Beringia (Encyclopedia Britannica)

Driven to Discover: Europeans Establish the New World

(Late 1400s to Late 1600s)

GRADES: K, 1, 2

OVERVIEW

Such explorers as Christopher Columbus, Hernán Cortés, and Amerigo Vespucci were compelled by the attraction of discovering the unknown. Their discoveries of the New World sparked intense competition between European kingdoms, even though journeys were fraught with peril. Still, the imperial nations were consumed by the desire to possess these new lands and their riches. The experiences of noted explorers and those who followed in their trails, and their complex relationships with native people, illustrate the beginnings of North American communities as we know them today. Reading *Follow the Dream: The Story of Christopher Columbus* or *Exploration and Conquest: The Americas after Columbus, 1500–1620* will give students the essential background on these global pioneers. Younger students will dissect Columbus's adventurous spirit, whereas older students will weigh the effects of Europeans' encounters with native people.

○ ○ ○

Interested in learning more about this time period? Read a more complete history in the "Era Summaries."

LEARNING EXPECTATIONS

Lower elementary: Students should understand that European explorers set out seeking "God, gold, and glory" (including the profits to be had from the spice trade). They should know that the Europeans found already peopled lands, met the native peoples with much tension, and settled the Americas for a variety of reasons.

Upper elementary: Students should understand the different aims of the major European empires in the Americas (particularly in the areas that would become the United States) and the consequences of those differing aims in their contact with indigenous peoples. They should understand that European settlers had different aims in different regions, contributing to the creation of very different new societies.

SUGGESTED ANCHOR TEXTS

Follow the Dream: The Story of Christopher Columbus by Peter Sis
Encounter by Jane Yolen
The Story of Columbus by Anita Ganeri

FEATURED ANCHOR TEXT

FOLLOW THE DREAM: THE STORY OF CHRISTOPHER COLUMBUS BY PETER SIS

This beautifully illustrated, fictionalized biography was selected because it tells the story of Columbus as a dreamer and adventurer. The story is told twice. It is told using breathtaking artwork and elegantly simple text.

TEXT STUDY

These text-dependent questions ask students to read closely, looking for text evidence in both the illustrations and the text. Students are asked not only to think deeply about the relationship between illustrations and text but also to compare and contrast illustrations in ways that allow them to examine character development and the unveiling of key concepts. The culminating performance assessment offers students a chance to reread closely and to focus on Columbus's important characteristics, which on their own, in a sense, tell his story. It also gives them an opportunity to write opinions using evidence from the text to support their assertions.

1. **After looking closely at the illustration and text on the title page, explain what the boy appears to be doing. Why do you think the author, who is also the illustrator, chose to illustrate the title page this way?**
   - The boy is looking out of a small doorway in a huge wall that seems to be part of a fort or a castle. All is blue outside the door.
   - The title, *Follow the Dream*, is also in blue.
   - The author probably wanted to "invite" us into the boy's mind, making us wonder what he is looking at, thinking about, and planning to do.

   Note: *Students could infer that the boy has a desire to step out of the walled area and into the blue to follow his dream.*
2. **Read the "Note to the Reader." How does this note help explain the artwork on the title page?**
   - Ancient maps showed Europe surrounded by high walls.
   - Columbus is the boy in the picture. He did not allow the walls to hold him back.
   - He went into the world and explored it; he followed his dream.
3. **Study the artwork and text on page 1. What can you tell about the city in the picture?**
   - The year is 1450.
   - The city is built near the water.
   - There are two lighthouses.
   - The city is bordered either by the sea or by a wall around the outside of the city.
   - The city is Genoa, Italy.

4. **According to the illustration and text on pages 2 and 3, what did Columbus's father do?**
   - In the illustration, his mother and father are weaving on a loom.
   - The text says that his father was a weaver.

   Note: *Teachers might discuss the word* weave *to ensure that students understand its meaning and—later on page 7—its figurative use. Students could practice making sentences with different nuances of the word* weave *and/or other words that have similarly simple literal and figurative meanings (see question 8).*
5. **Describe the cloth in the room with young Columbus as shown on page 4.**
   - It is blue and covered with stars.
   - It is not in the loom, but hanging from the top of it.
6. **In the same illustration on page 4, what is young Columbus doing? Why?**
   - Although he is sitting at the loom, Columbus isn't weaving. He is reading a book by candlelight.
   - The text suggests that Columbus isn't planning to be a weaver like his father, but that he is planning something different for his future.
7. **How does the cloth change from the illustration on page 4 to the illustration on page 5? Why do you think the author uses the cloth in this way?**
   - The blue cloth with stars is transformed from cloth hanging atop the loom to a sail on a boat. Columbus is still reading, sitting on the same bench, but now he is seated on a boat.
   - The blue background and stars on the cloth look like the night sky. This illustration shows that Columbus is "dreaming" of his future as a sailor.
   - The cloth becomes the sail of Columbus's boat, suggesting that Columbus will one day turn his dreams into action.
   - The text on page 5 says that Columbus is dreaming of faraway places described in a book by Marco Polo.

   Note: *Throughout the thirteenth century, Italian painters routinely painted ceilings blue with stars. This was a convention that was widely adopted and of which there remain many excellent examples. Its use here reinforces Columbus's Italian roots.*
8. **How does the author use the word *weaving* on page 7 differently than he does on page 3?**
   - On page 3, the text says that Columbus was expected to grow up to be a weaver like his father.
   - Here the author writes, "He kept weaving dreams of adventure and discovery."
   - This time the word *weaving* means that Columbus is planning something different, but that he is still "weaving" together two things: adventure and discovery.
9. **What was Columbus's plan?**
   - According to page 7, he planned to go to the "Orient" (like Marco Polo), but he would sail west across the Atlantic Ocean.
10. **How did Columbus prepare for his trip? What can you infer about Columbus's character from these preparations?**
    - According to page 8, he became an expert sailor and learned to read maps and navigate using the stars.
    - According to page 9, he traveled looking for a "sponsor": someone to provide ships, supplies, and the crew.

- According to page 12, he went to the king and queen of Spain to ask for ships. However, they said no to his request.
- According to page 14, he went again to the king and queen.
- According to pages 15 and 17, he waited six years, holding onto his dream. He then convinced Queen Isabella and King Ferdinand. They gave him three ships and ninety men for a crew.
- One might infer from this extensive effort that Columbus had determination, tenacity, and patience.

  Note: *Students might generate other, simpler words, of course, but teachers might use this as an opportunity to enhance students' vocabulary and help them recognize relationships between abstract nouns and adjectives* (determination *versus* determined, *and so on*).

11. **Study and describe the two illustrations on pages 18 and 19. How are they similar, and how are they different? What do we learn from each? Why do you think the author included both?**
    - Both illustrations show one of Columbus's ships in the center. The flags are flying from the tops of the masts.
    - The illustration on page 18 shows a cross-sectional view of the ship.
      - This helps the reader see how the Santa Maria was packed with food, water, and goods for trading. The Nina and the Pinta are also pictured in the brown sketch.
    - The illustration on page 19 shows the launch of the *Santa Maria* with full color. The ship is leaving from Spain.
    - We can see that the first illustration shows a "plan" for the ships—and what they are like inside—and the second illustration shows that the plan became a reality.
      - The author probably wanted to show the reader that Columbus followed through with his plan.
12. **How does the author describe the crew's fear?**
    - On page 20, the water is calm and the scene is peaceful. The text describes the sea as "calm" and says that "at first, it seemed the journey would be easy."

      Note: *Teachers might discuss the meaning of the word* seemed *to emphasize the contrast between this page and the next.*
    - On page 21, the water is full of waves. There are monsters in the sea and fearful creatures in the sky. The text says that "from the beginning, the crew was uneasy" in an "endless expanse of sea, with its unfamiliar birds and fish and seaweed," which "frightened them."
    - "They wanted to turn back," says the text.
13. **How did Columbus trick the crew into thinking they were not so far from home?**
    - According to page 22, he kept two different logs. On the one he showed the crew, the distances were shorter.

      Note: *Teachers might discuss the multiple meanings of the word* log *to clarify its use to refer to a record of distance on a journey.*
14. **What can you learn from the logs shown on pages 21 and 22?**
    - You can see how many miles the ship had traveled by each recorded date.
    - The weather and sailing conditions are recorded—the winds, the rain, the currents.
    - The logs note new sightings of animals—a whale, birds, porpoises, crab, and flying fish.
    - There are sketches of the clouds, the sea, the moon, and a shooting star.

15. **Why did Columbus assume he had arrived in Japan?**
    - Columbus was trying to sail west toward the Orient. Japan was part of the Orient.
    - Columbus's assumption is also mentioned on page 25, where it says that he thanked God for his arrival and expected to see the treasures of the Orient.
16. **What appears to have happened between the illustration on page 26 and the illustration on page 27?**
    - Time has passed.
        - Where there were once only ten people and Columbus on the shore of an island, there is now a class of children and a teacher looking up at a statue of Columbus.
        - There are now cars and high buildings.
        - The borders around the illustrations have changed from flying birds to more modern objects, such as a key, a radio, a camera, and a tennis shoe.
17. **What do we know that Columbus never really knew?**
    - Columbus had found a new continent, America.

PERFORMANCE ASSESSMENT

Work together to generate a list of Columbus's characteristics, such as, but not limited to, "adventuresome," "determined," or "persistent." Have each student choose a characteristic that he or she thinks best describes Columbus. Reread the text to allow students to gather text evidence for their chosen character quality.

Ask students to write an opinion paragraph describing their choice of characteristic. Support the students as needed as they gather sufficient text evidence to include in their paragraph. Students should write a sentence that states their opinion, provide two or three relevant reasons or details that support their opinion, use linking words, and offer a concluding statement. At earlier levels, students may draw or dictate their opinion and/or write a label, sentence, or series of related sentences. See standards for more details.

CONNECTIONS TO COMMON CORE STATE STANDARDS FOR ENGLISH LANGUAGE ARTS

- Question 1 asks students to examine both the text and the illustration on the title page of an informational text, helping them understand the function of each, and how these components work together to create an enticing title page (RI.K.5,7; RI.1.5,7; RI. 2.5,7).
- Question 2 not only reinforces students' understanding of the title page but also helps them to identify the author's purpose and even to recognize parallels between the author's experience and the experience of his subject (RI.K.5.1,5,7,8; RI.1.5.1,5,7,8; RI.2.5.1,5,7,8).
- Question 3 helps students glean key details about the content of the book from an illustration (RI.K.1,7; RI.1.1,7; RI. 2.1,7).
- Question 4 focuses on a key word that is essential to students' understanding of the subject's story; it also allows students to identify key details in an informational text using both an illustration and the text (RI.K.5.1,4,7; RI.1.5.1,4,7; RI.2.5.1,4,7).

- Questions 5, 6, and 14 ask students to identify key details in illustrations in an informational text (RI.K.1,7; RI.1.1,7; RI. 2.1,7).
    - Question 6 also encourages students to make connections between the text and an illustration, highlighting a key concept of the text.
- Question 7 encourages students to examine the relationship between two illustrations and the development of a key concept in this informational text. It also allows students to identify key details in an informational text using both illustration and text (RI.K.1,3,5,7; RI.1.1,3,5,7; RI.2.1,3,5,7).
- Building on question 2, question 8 asks students to recognize the figurative use of a word previously used literally in the text (RI.K.4,5; RI.1.4,5; RI.2.4,5; L.K.5; L.1.5; L.2.5).
- Question 9 prompts the explanation of an important detail in this informational text (RI.K.1,5; RI.1.1,5; RI.2.1,5).
- Question 10 prompts the explanation of key details, but also addresses character development in this fictionalized biography, highlighting the power of narrative history and fictionalized biography and offering teachers an opportunity to draw parallels between character development in literature and character development in a rich informational text. The question also presents an excellent opportunity for teachers to build students' inferring skills, enhance students' vocabulary, and focus on an essential grammatical concept (RI.K.1,2,3; RI.1.1,2,3; RI.2.1,2,3; RL.K.3; RL.1.3; RL.2.3; L.K.1; L.1.1; L.2.1).
- Building on question 10, question 11 asks students to describe and compare two illustrations, reinforcing their understanding of an essential concept in this informational text: that the subject was able to follow through and "make his dream come true" (RI.K.1,3,7; RI.1.1,3,7; RI.2.1,3,7).
- Questions 12 and 16 encourage students to examine illustrations and text closely to glean important comparisons and contrasts that reinforce understanding of details essential to the text (RI.K.1,2,3,7; RI.1.1,2,3,7; RI.2.1,2,3,7).
- Questions 13 and 17 each ask students to explain an important detail in this informational text (RI.K.1; RI.1.1; RI.2.1).
- Question 15 prompts students to make an inference and connect information from various parts of the text (RI.K.1,3; RI.1.1,3; RI.2.1,3).
- The performance assessment allows students to reread the text closely with a specific focus on characterization. Students must convey their opinion about one of the subject's characteristics using evidence from the text (RI.K.1,2,3; RI.1.1,2,3; RI.2.1,2,3; RL.K.3; RL.1.3; RL.2.3; W.K.1; W.1.1; W.2.1).
    - This assessment also prepares students for W.4.9, which begins in grade 4.

MORE RESOURCES

PRIMARY SOURCES

Items from a Spanish treasure ship (Library of Congress)

Four faces of Pocahontas (Smithsonian Source: Resources for Teaching American History)

1629 Seal of the Massachusetts Bay Colony (Smithsonian Source: Resources for Teaching American History)

Spanish settlement at St. Augustine, Florida (Library of Congress)

British gold coin used at Jamestown, Virginia (British Museum)

A *Briefe and True Report of the New Found Land of Virginia*, 1590 (Project Gutenberg)

Letter from Hernán Cortés to King Charles V, 1520 (Fordham University)

Photo of Christopher Columbus's handwritten notes on Marco Polo's *Le Livre des Merveilles*, 15th century (Wikipedia)

USEFUL WEBSITES

"What Was Columbus Thinking?"

National Endowment for the Humanities EDSITEment! lesson for grades 3 through 5 that can be adapted. The site contains links to terrific primary resources—for example, Columbus's letters, a Library of Congress exhibition on Columbus, and more.

"The Map That Named America" (Library of Congress)

Uniquely American: The Beginnings of a New Nationality

(1607 to Late 1600s)

GRADES: K, 1, 2

OVERVIEW

Great Britain was the most successful of the European nations to settle colonies in North America–but at first, it had its attention focused on matters closer to the home isles. Britain's colonies experimented with local self-government and popular power. When the British turned their thoughts back to North America and the profits they could reap, tension mounted between new North American ways of life and the interests of the mother country that sought to govern there. Through a close reading of *The First Thanksgiving*, students will develop an informed opinion about whether or not the benefits of life in the new colonies were worth the hardships. An informational text exploring the New England, mid-Atlantic, and southern colonies, *We the People: The Thirteen Colonies*, gives older students the essential background to facilitate multimedia presentations in which they compare and contrast regional differences in America.

○ ○ ○

Interested in learning more about this time period? Read a more complete history in the "Era Summaries."

LEARNING EXPECTATIONS

Lower elementary: Students should understand that different kinds of colonial societies arose in different regions in response to different circumstances and goals. They should understand that new and often unprecedented freedoms emerged for many colonists, even as slavery was introduced to the colonies.

Upper elementary: Students should be able to identify the basic cultural differences between the New England, mid-Atlantic, and southern colonies, and should understand the fundamental reasons why these regions emerged with such different ways of life. They should also understand the growing role of political and religious freedoms as well as slavery in the different regions.

SUGGESTED ANCHOR TEXTS

The First Thanksgiving by Linda Hayward
Samuel Eaton's Day: A Day in the Life of a Pilgrim Boy by Kate Waters
Sarah Morton's Day: A Day in the Life of a Pilgrim Girl by Kate Waters
Squanto's Journey: The Story of the First Thanksgiving by Joseph Bruchac
Tapenum's Day: A Wampanoag Indian Boy in Pilgrim Times by Kate Waters
Three Young Pilgrims by Cheryl Harness

FEATURED ANCHOR TEXT

THE FIRST THANKSGIVING BY LINDA HAYWARD

This book was selected because it tells the story of the journey and settling of the Plymouth colony in Massachusetts with accurate information and quality artwork, all supervised by the research staff of Plimoth Plantation. This informational text relates more details about the political and religious climate in England than do most books written for readers from this age group. The Native Americans play a major role in the account, which shows the important presence of the two groups through illustration and text, but finally shows Native American strength, generosity, and resourcefulness during this period of American history.

TEXT STUDY

The ability to answer the questions correctly depends on a close reading of the text. The questions help focus the students on the ways in which the author relates important historical details through illustration and text, nurturing students' ability to glean information from both. The questions help students recognize that point of view is significant in informational texts as well as in literary texts.

1. **According to page 4, where and when did this historic event begin?**
   - This historic event began in Plymouth, England, in 1620, where the Pilgrims were boarding a ship to travel abroad.
2. **According to the text on pages 8 and 9, why were the people on the *Mayflower* willing to risk their lives to sail to the New World?**
   - The king of England made it very difficult for them to worship as they wanted. He declared that everyone needed to worship according to his religion. The Pilgrims tried to meet in secret, and were reported by their neighbors. They had no religious freedom.
3. **According to page 10, to where were the Pilgrims sailing?**
   - The Pilgrims, having boarded the *Mayflower*, were sailing across the Atlantic Ocean from England to America.
4. **According to pages 11 through 14, what made the trip across the Atlantic Ocean so challenging?**
   - They had to leave everyone and everything they knew.
   - The ship was crowded with 102 passengers.
   - The ship was "cold and damp," it had no fresh water, and they had to eat the same meal every day.
   - There were huge storms at sea.

5. **According to pages 20 and 21, what were the Pilgrims looking for in a place to settle?**
   - They needed to find a place with a harbor.
   - They needed a source of fresh water.
   - They needed to be able to have fields for planting.
6. **What did the Pilgrims name their new home?**
   - The Pilgrims named their new settlement New Plymouth.

   Note: Students may notice that the place of origin and the destination had similar names. Probe for the reason why.
7. **According to the text on pages 22 through 29, what kinds of challenges did the Pilgrims face during their first winter in New Plymouth?**
   - The Pilgrims needed to build houses, and the weather was bad. It took "weeks to finish just one house."
   - There was little to eat. They had to eat food from the ship as well as "roots, wild birds, and shellfish."
   - They lived in fear of the Native Americans.
   - The weather was cold, with icy winds and freezing rain.
   - They felt "miserable and so alone!"
   - Many of the people were sick and then died: "By the end of the winter only half of the Pilgrims are still alive."
8. **How did the Pilgrims' opinions of the Native Americans change throughout the book? Cite evidence from the text to show how the Pilgrims' opinions changed.**
   - Pilgrims moved from fear of the unknown, based on warnings, to real fear of the Native Americans watching them.
     - On page 6, the text says that the Pilgrims had been warned that "Indians may attack them."
     - On page 17, the Pilgrims are said to be wondering about the Native Americans hiding in the forest.
     - On page 18, the texts says that the Pilgrims saw the Native Americans and frightened them away.
   - The Pilgrims then began guarding their settlement out of fear.
     - From the illustration on page 20 and the text on page 24, we know that the Pilgrims posted guards because they were still afraid and unsure, knowing the Native Americans were watching them.
   - The Pilgrims slowly showed that they wanted to trust the Native Americans and began to learn from them.
     - According to page 30, when Samoset walked into the settlement, the children were terrified, but the Pilgrims soon learned that he knew English and could answer many of their questions. They gave him gifts, and the text says they "wanted" to trust him.
     - According to page 32, Squanto, who also spoke English, moved onto the settlement and helped the Pilgrims learn to survive. He taught them to hunt, to find berries and herbs, and to plant corn by putting a fish into the ground with the seed to make the soil richer.
   - The Pilgrims tried to make friends with more of the Native Americans.
     - Page 34 describes how Squanto and Samoset told the Pilgrims of a Native American king named Massasoit.

- Massasoit and the Pilgrim governor showed respect to each other with bows and kisses.
- According to page 36, the Pilgrims and the Native Americans signed a peace treaty that was "kept for 54 years!"
- Page 40 describes the first Thanksgiving, at which Massasoit and ninety Native Americans came to enjoy a time of thanksgiving for the harvest. The Native Americans brought food to contribute, and they all ate together, celebrating for three days.

9. **Why was it important for the author (on page 37) to include the fact that none of the Pilgrims chose to go back on the *Mayflower* as it sailed back to England?**
   - The book is filled with descriptions of the difficulties that the Pilgrims encountered on the trip to the New World and during their settlement, but it also shows how the desire to worship freely must have been a strong enough reward to make them want to stay and work hard for their new life.

10. **Reread the first page and last page of the book. On page 4 of the text, how are the Pilgrims described? According to page 48, why is this group still remembered today?**
    - The Pilgrims are described as "too poor" and "too ordinary to ever be famous," yet they are still remembered four hundred years later.
    - The Pilgrims are remembered because Abraham Lincoln made Thanksgiving Day a national holiday.

PERFORMANCE ASSESSMENTS

1. Instruct students to write an opinion paragraph based on the following prompt:

- The Pilgrims faced huge challenges during their voyage and during their first winter in America. Do you think all of the hardships of settling in America were worth it for the Pilgrims? State your opinion clearly in a (topic) sentence. Support your opinion with strong evidence from the text. Write a concluding statement that restates your opinion.

At earlier levels, students may draw or dictate their opinion and/or write a sentence or series of related sentences. See standards for more details.

2. Have students read the historical fiction book *Tapenum's Day: A Wampanoag Indian Boy in Pilgrim Times* by Kate Waters or *Squanto's Journey: The Story of the First Thanksgiving* by Joseph Bruchac. Guide students back to the idea of the Pilgrims' fear of the unknown as they came to the New World. As a class, compare and contrast the experiences of the Native American protagonist and a Pilgrim child, possibly completing a graphic organizer, such as a T-chart or Venn diagram.

Discuss how accounts of the same events may differ when offered through different eyes. Using a chronological chart, work as a class to retrace the major events told in *The First Thanksgiving* from the Pilgrims' perspective. Challenge students to choose one of the events from the book to retell orally from a Wampanoag point of view. Using what they know about Tapenum from his story or about Squanto from a biography, students should write a narrative paragraph describing the event from his point of view. At earlier levels, students may draw or dictate their opinion and/or write a sentence or series of related sentences.

EXTENSION

Sort paragraphs written by students in the second performance assessment to create a chronological telling of the Pilgrims' arrival, first winter, and feast from a Wampanoag point of view.

CONNECTIONS TO COMMON CORE STATE STANDARDS FOR ENGLISH LANGUAGE ARTS

- Questions 1, 3, and 6 require students to answer basic questions about key details in the text (RI.K.1; RI.1.1; RI.2.1).
- Questions 2, 5, and 8 ask students to answer basic questions about key details or ideas in the text and to make connections among events (RI.K.1,2,3; RI.1.1,2,3; RI.2.1,2,3).
    - Question 8 also asks students to cite evidence from the text to support their claims.
- Questions 4 and 7 focus on key details in the text and ask students to trace a topic across paragraphs (RI.K.1,2; RI.1.1,2; RI.2.1,2).
- Question 9 draws attention to the author's craft—in this case, why she chose to include a certain detail that enhances students' understanding of one of the book's key concepts (RI.K.1,2,3,6; RI.1.1,2,3,6; RI.2.1,2,3,6).
- Question 10 also emphasizes the author's craft, encouraging students to reread certain sections for key details and helping them relate those details to important, enduring understandings about the Pilgrims (RI.K.1.2,3,6; RI.1.1.2,3,6; RI.2.1.2,3,6).
- The first performance assessment requires students to demonstrate understanding of what they have read by expressing an opinion about it, citing evidence from the text in support of that opinion (RI.K.1,2,3; RI.1.1,2,3; RI.2.1,2,3; W.K.1; W.1.1; W.2.1).
    - The first performance assessment also anticipates standard W.4.9, which begins in grade 4.
- The second performance assessment helps students understand that point of view matters in both literary and informational texts. It requires students to sequence events and retell what they have comprehended. Writing a narrative—from a particular point of view—allows students to demonstrate that they understand both the facts and the various perspectives of those involved in historical events (RI.K.1,2,3,6; RI.1.1,2,3,6; RI.2.1,2,3,6; W.K.1; W.1.1; W.2.1).
    - This performance assessment also anticipates standard W.4.9, which begins in grade 4.

MORE RESOURCES

HISTORICAL FICTION

The Courage of Sarah Noble by Alice Dalgliesh

PRIMARY SOURCES

Philadelphia before the American Revolution (Library of Congress)

African captives yoked in pairs (PBS: Africans in America)

Settlement and colonial life (Library of Congress: Pictorial Americana)

Dance instruction manual, 1711 (Library of Congress)

Instructions for the Virginia Colony, 1606 (University of Groningen)

Portrait of Cotton Mather, original 1728 (Smithsonian Institution)

USEFUL WEBSITES

Award-winning interactive activity whereby students learn about the first Thanksgiving from multiple perspectives (Plimoth Plantation)

Interactive map of New Amsterdam in 1660 superimposed over a map of Lower Manhattan in 2009 (WNET, New York Public Media)

UNITED STATES HISTORY, ERA 4

Taxation without Representation: Tension Mounts

(ca. 1660 to 1763)

GRADES: K, 1, 2

OVERVIEW

During the seventeenth century, Britain's international and domestic problems had caused it to let the colonies essentially rule themselves. But that soon changed: from 1660 to 1763, the British government stabilized and turned to the business of ruling the colonies—lucrative business, because the colonies had grown into profitable trading posts and commercial centers. Britain's expanded rule changed the colonists, laying the groundwork for some of the most important events in modern history. *If You Lived in Colonial Times* gives younger students a resource to explore what daily life in the colonies looked like; they can then select a topic that interests them to explore further. Older students can read *Making Thirteen Colonies: 1600–1740* to learn how regional differences in the British colonies spurred differing attitudes on slavery, prompting students to research the beginnings of America's "peculiar institution."

○ ○ ○

Interested in learning more about this time period? Read a more complete history in the "Era Summaries."

LEARNING EXPECTATIONS

Lower elementary: Students should understand that Britain began to want more benefit from its colonies in the seventeenth and eighteenth centuries and to take more notice of them, drawing Britain and the colonies more tightly together in a British Atlantic world—while also sowing the seeds of conflict over the colonies' rights.

Upper elementary: Students should understand the role of trade in tying Britain and the colonies together, and they should know that this closer relationship generated tension over local self-rule, even as the culture of the colonies became more British. Students should know that the colonies were drawn into wars for the empire, which showed their loyalty to Britain but also set the stage for new conflict over the wars' costs.

SUGGESTED ANCHOR TEXTS

If You Lived in Colonial Times by Ann McGovern
Our Colonial Year by Cheryl Harness
The Courage of Sarah Noble by Alice Dalgliesh

FEATURED ANCHOR TEXT

IF YOU LIVED IN COLONIAL TIMES BY ANN MCGOVERN

This book was selected because it describes life in colonial times and contains a large volume of well-organized information. Arranged in groups of topics (which are in question form), the text shows specifically how trade developed within the colonies and how trade took place across the Atlantic. Although this lesson focuses on trade, the text could be used to study other facets of colonial daily life.

TEXT STUDY

The text-dependent questions that follow give students a chance to learn important historical content about life in colonial America while also analyzing an informational text that is organized in a somewhat unusual way. Students must read closely to locate information and make connections between details and key concepts.

1. **Using the table of contents, answer the following questions: How is this text organized? Do you see a relationship among the questions within each group?**
   - This text is organized according to various series of questions.
   - The questions seem to be chunked together by category, such as appearance, schooling, medicine, Sundays, and so on.
2. **According to pages 6 and 7, when and where were "colonial times"? How do the text features help you understand the time and the place in history?**
   - The text describes colonial times as the period in history from "about seventy years after Columbus arrived in America" to the time when the thirteen colonies became the United States in 1776. The chart at the bottom of page 6 aids understanding because it shows this period on a basic timeline between the *Mayflower*'s landing and the thirteen colonies' becoming states.
   - The map on page 7 shows only the New England colonies, and the text clarifies that this book is only about these colonies. New England included the land that "became the states of Connecticut, Rhode Island, Massachusetts, New Hampshire, Vermont, and Maine."
3. **Referring back to the table of contents, where would we look to learn how people worked during colonial times?**
   - We would look under two different questions: "Did people work hard in colonial days?" on page 48 and "Who were the workers in a colonial town?" beginning on page 67.
4. **What is the main topic of pages 48 and 49: "Did people work hard in colonial days?" What are the key details that support the main topic?**
   - The main topic of these pages is stated in the first few sentences of this section. It was necessary for colonists to work hard because they had to make almost everything they used.

- Some examples of key supporting details are as follows:
  - People had to spin, weave, and knit the clothes they wore.
  - People had to grow, bake, or churn the food they ate.
  - People had to make the dishes they used to prepare and eat food.
  - People had to make their own homes for shelter, as well as their own furniture.
  - People even had to make their own soap and candles for cleanliness and light.

5. **According to pages 67 through 69, why did the colonists need cobblers, blacksmiths, and tanners?**
   - According to the text on page 67, the colonists needed cobblers to mend and make shoes. Because the colonists walked everywhere they went, their shoes wore out quickly.
   - According to page 68, the colonists needed blacksmiths because iron was important to the colonies. The blacksmith made iron shoes for horses and oxen as well as iron pots, nails, and tools. The blacksmith also acted as a dentist, pulling out teeth for people in pain.
   - According to page 69, the tanner's job was to make leather from animal skins. The colonists wore leather breeches, leather aprons, leather caps, and leather boots. They also used leather for buckets, saddles, and mugs.
6. **According to page 78, what did trading ships take away from the New England harbor?**
   - The ships took fish, corn, candles, and other goods to such places as other colonies along the Atlantic coast as well as England.
7. **According to the information you have read so far in this text, who provided the things that shipped from the New England harbor?**
   - The fishermen caught the fish, the farmers grew the corn, and candlemakers in the colonies made the candles.
8. **What came in on the ships that sailed into the New England harbor?**
   - According to page 79, cargo ships from England brought a fire engine, a shiny coach, a horse, new books, and mail for the people of New England. The ships also brought people who wanted to settle in New England. The ships also carried slaves from Africa "who were not glad to come."
9. **How does the building of a ship in colonial New England prove that colonists had to work together in the New World?**
   - According to page 80, many kinds of workers were required to build one ship.
     - "Lumbermen cut down the tall pine trees to make the tall masts for the ships."
     - "Carpenters built the wooden parts of the ships."
     - "Ropemakers made ropes for the ships."
     - "Sailmakers made the ships' sails."
     - "Blacksmiths made nails and anchors and other hardware for the ships."
     - "Coopers made barrels to hold food and drink for the long voyage."
     - "Sailors and captains sailed the ships."
   - The colonists' individual trades made it possible to provide the necessities for shipbuilding and all other aspects of colonial living. Because the colonists each had one or more specialties, it was also necessary to live in a community where goods and services could be traded among the colonists. The newly built ship sailing out of the port demonstrated how a community worked together.

PERFORMANCE ASSESSMENTS

1. Provide students with a chance to learn more about the New England colonies by using other parts of this text. Ask them to choose a question from the table of contents that is of interest to them, but that is not considered in this question set. Ask them to use the selected question and the first few sentences of the section to discover the main topic of the article. Require students to find the key details that support the main topic. Students should then write an informative/explanatory paragraph that introduces the topic, provides relevant supporting details, and has a concluding sentence. See standards for more details.

At earlier levels, students may draw or dictate their explanation and/or write a sentence or series of related sentences. To extend the individual learning into the whole community of learners, have students read their paragraph aloud to the other students.

2. Direct students to use the jobs listed in the book as a guide to create a colonial museum showing the work of the colonists. Students should research other jobs in a colonial village. Have students each choose or make one object to represent a trade and write a detailed informative/explanatory description of how the colonist did his or her job.

Have students write out the steps in a process. For example, a candle represents the work of a candlemaker. The student would write out the steps in making a candle and place those steps beside the candle in a display. At earlier levels, students may draw or dictate their explanation and/or write a label, sentence, or series of related sentences.

CONNECTIONS TO COMMON CORE STATE STANDARDS FOR ENGLISH LANGUAGE ARTS

- Questions 1, 2, and 3 ask students to use the features of an informational text (here, the table of contents, a timeline, and a map) to locate and make connections among key details and concepts (RI.K.1,2,3,5,7; RI.1.1,2,3,5,7; RI.2.1,2,3,5,7).
- Questions 4 and 5 give students a chance to see the relationship between a central message and its supporting details (RI.K.1,2,3; RI.1.1,2,3; RI.2.1,2,3).
  - Question 5 also asks students to locate evidence in a specific section of the text (RI.K.8; RI.1.8; RI.2.8).
- Questions 6, 7, and 8 require students to glean and/or explain essential details from the text (RI.K.1,2; RI.1.1,2; RI.2.1,2).
- Question 9 allows students to synthesize information from a number of places in the text to make a case about a key concept (RI.K.1,2,3,6,8; RI.1.1,2,3,6,8; RI.2.1,2,3,6,8).
- The first performance assessment gives students a chance to use informational text features on their own to identify and explain a main topic and supporting details. It also requires them to write an informative/explanatory paragraph that explains what they have learned. They are given practice in reading their paragraph aloud for others (RI.K.1,2,3,5; RI.1.1,2,3,5; RI.2.1,2,3,5; W.K.2; W.1.2; W.2.2; SL.K.1,6; SL.1.1,6; SL.2.1,6).
  - This task also prepares students for standard W.4.9, which begins at grade 4.
- The second performance assessment allows students to conduct research (a Common Core State Standards priority) about other aspects of colonial life in America and present their findings in an informative/explanatory paragraph (a "how-to" explanation) for the real purpose of creating a "museum" (RI.K.1,2,3; RI.1.1,2,3; RI.2.1,2,3; W.K.2; W.1.2; W.2.2)

MORE RESOURCES

PRIMARY SOURCES

Religion in 18th-century America (Library of Congress)

Geography and its impact on colonial life (Library of Congress: Teachers)

Map of British plantations in North America, 1755 to 1760 (Library of Congress)

George Washington's map accompanying his "Journal to the Ohio," 1754 (Library of Congress)

French and Indian War enlistment papers, 1760 (Smithsonian Institution)

USEFUL WEBSITE

Colonial Williamsburg crafts and trades (Colonial Williamsburg Foundation)

Independence: America Gains Its Freedom

(1763 to 1783)

GRADES: K, 1, 2

OVERVIEW

Britain expected the colonies to help pay for its costly wars abroad—and began taxing them to that end. Efforts to draw more revenue from the colonies outraged the Americans, who had no voice in the British Parliament. Escalating taxes were met with protest, boycotts, and rebellion. Eventually, the flames were fanned until they sparked revolution and full-blown war. *A Picture Book of Paul Revere* introduces younger students to one of America's first patriots and prompts a thoughtful analysis of how Paul Revere forever changed American history. Older students will explore the divisive issue of taxation as they read *A History of US: From Colonies to Country: 1735–1791*, and they will investigate primary sources to learn why paying taxes sparked the ire of colonists who had once pledged their loyalty to Britain.

○ ○ ○

Interested in learning more about this time period? Read a more complete history in the "Era Summaries."

LEARNING EXPECTATIONS

Lower elementary: Students should understand the concept of taking someone else's property without his or her agreement, and why that threatened many Americans. They should understand that Americans were willing to fight against outside control to protect their freedoms. Students should also know that many figures and events from the American Revolution are still remembered in modern holidays and popular culture.

Upper elementary: Students should understand the monetary needs that the French and Indian War created in Britain and the British decision to tax the colonies to help pay for the war. They should also understand both the concept of taxation without representation and why Americans responded so strongly to the new tax laws. They should know that the dispute over their freedoms was so serious that it led to war and independence. They should understand how difficult the fighting was and how determined many Americans were to protect their liberty.

SUGGESTED ANCHOR TEXTS

A Picture Book of Paul Revere by David A. Adler
American Revolution: A Non-Fiction Companion to Revolutionary War on Wednesday by Mary Pope Osborne
Boston Tea Party by Pamela Duncan Edwards
Revolutionary War on Wednesday by Mary Pope Osborne
The Ride: The Legend of Betsy Dowdy by Kitty Griffin

FEATURED ANCHOR TEXT

A PICTURE BOOK OF PAUL REVERE BY DAVID A. ADLER

This book was selected because it shows how the character of an important historical figure was built through life experiences prior to the time when his heroic actions were taken. Revere's patriotic actions exemplify the story of America's path to independence.

TEXT STUDY

Note: *Because there are no page numbers in this book, we will reference page 1 as the first page of text.*

The text-dependent questions present teachers with multiple opportunities to reinforce Common Core State Standards for English language arts expectations, including the ability to glean key details from an informational text (in this case, details about an important figure in American history and the Revolution in which he played a significant part).

1. **Look closely at the illustration on page 1 to gather information about the place where Revere was born. What do you see in the illustration, and what might you infer from those details?**
   - The buildings are close to a body of water, so it is a town by the sea or ocean.
   - There is a dock going out into the water.
   - There are ships close to the buildings, so it must be a harbor.
   - There are no leaves on the trees, so it is wintertime.
   - The buildings and ships are old-fashioned, so it must be a long time ago.
2. **What additional information about the setting of this biography can you learn from the text on page 1?**
   - Paul Revere lived near the edge of Boston Harbor, on Fish Street.
   - He lived in a small, crowded house.
   - He was born on January 1, 1735.
3. **The opening paragraph of the book, on page 1, says that Revere "was born in a small, crowded house . . . the second of [his parents'] nine children." What can we learn about Revere from this family description?**
   - The family was not wealthy, and they shared a small space. He was born into a family with one other sibling, and then seven more children were born.
   - He was not born into a wealthy family; they had many kids, and he lived in a small house.

4. **What can we learn about Revere from the description of his schooling on page 2?**
   - He learned manners in "infant school."
   - He went to an all-boys' school until he was thirteen to learn reading, writing, and basic arithmetic.
   - He had a basic education, just until age thirteen, and he knew manners.
5. **What can we learn about Revere from the description of his work on pages 3 and 4?**
   - After he finished school at thirteen, he went to work for his father in his silversmith shop.
   - When he was nineteen and his father died, he took over the silversmith shop to support his family.
   - We come to know that Revere learned the silversmith business and that he was responsible.
6. **What can we learn about Revere from his work as a bell ringer, described on page 3?**
   - Revere and six other boys formed a group to ring eight large bells at a church.
   - He enjoyed music and could work in a group.
7. **What do we learn about Revere's character from his involvement in the French and Indian War?**
   - Revere joined the Massachusetts regiment and stayed until he was sent home.
   - He was willing to join the war as a soldier, showing that he took responsibility for his country.
8. **What do we learn about Revere's character from the detailed description on pages 10 through 13 of his marriages and family?**
   - When he married, they moved into the small, crowded house with Revere's family. They added eight more children, two of whom died. Then Revere's wife died. He married again and had eight more children, three of whom died.
   - He had to learn to be a goldsmith, too, learning how to clean teeth and make false ones. He even fixed umbrellas for people.
   - Despite some sad events in his life, Revere worked very hard to provide for his large family.
9. **According to the text on page 15, Revere and the Sons of Liberty said, "No taxation without representation." What does that sentence mean?**
   - The British (English) soldiers were being paid for by taxes imposed on the colonies.

     Note: *Teachers may need to review the idea of taxes for students.*
   - The colonies did not have anyone in Britain to vote on whether they should be taxed.
   - The Sons of Liberty believed that taxation without representation was wrong. They believed that people who were not able to vote for a tax should not be expected to pay the tax.
10. **According to the text on page 16, what actually happened during the Boston Massacre?**
    - A group of colonists had a fight with British soldiers in Boston. The colonists threw snowballs, ice, wood, and coal. They called the soldiers "lobsters" and "bloody backs."
    - The soldiers fired back and killed five colonists.
11. **How did Revere tell a story of the Boston Massacre that was different from what actually happened, and why did he do it?**
    - He made an engraving showing all of the soldiers lined up and firing their guns at peaceful citizens.
    - He told a different story from what actually happened because he wanted to stir anger in the colonists against the British.

12. **According to the illustration and text on pages 18 and 19, what happened at Boston Harbor, and why did it happen?**
    - Details found in the illustration include the following:
        - There are people dressed as Native Americans. They are on boats and ships in the harbor.
        - The people are throwing boxes over the sides of a ship and dumping the contents into the water.
        - It is nighttime.
    - Details found in the text include the following:
        - Three ships from England were in Boston Harbor, loaded with tea.
        - The people of Boston were expected to pay a tax on the tea, but they refused.
        - On December 16, 1773, Revere and other Boston friends dressed as Native Americans and boarded three ships in Boston Harbor.
        - They broke 342 chests of tea and dumped them in the water.
        - Later, five thousand soldiers came to Boston to close the harbor until the colonists paid for the tea, but they never did pay for it.
13. **According to the illustrations and text on pages 21 through 23, how did Revere help the colonists at the beginning of the Revolutionary War?**
    - Revere, William Dawes, and Samuel Prescott rode horses to warn the colonists and Minutemen in Lexington and Concord that the British were going to attack.
    - The next day, the Minutemen were ready for the first battle of the Revolutionary War.
14. **According to page 24, why is July 4 an important date to Americans?**
    - The Declaration of Independence was signed on that date. Neither the British king nor Parliament ruled the thirteen colonies any longer. The colonies had become a collection of independent governments.
15. **How did Revere help during the Revolutionary War?**
    - He served as a lieutenant colonel in command of the Boston Harbor Fort at Castle Island.
    - He set up a mill to make gunpowder.
    - He made cannons.
    - He cut copper plates and printed paper money for the Massachusetts colony.

PERFORMANCE ASSESSMENTS

1. Have students write an informative/explanatory paragraph telling about one way that Revere helped his country. Students each should describe what he did in a sentence that introduces the topic, provide two or three relevant supporting details to support their choice, and include a concluding sentence that shows how one or more of Revere's actions supported his country. See standards for more details.

For example, students could write about his engraving of the Boston Massacre, his participation in the Boston Tea Party, his ride to warn the Minutemen, or his help during the Revolutionary War itself. At earlier levels, students may draw or dictate their explanation and/or write a label, sentence, or series of related sentences.

2. As a class, create an illustrated timeline depicting significant events of the American Revolution. Students should be sure to note how Revere was involved or not involved in each

major event, as described by the text. Discuss together his role as a citizen in a changing colony and country. For example, a timeline might include the following items:

- 1760s–Sons of Liberty, of which Revere was a member.
- March 1765–Stamp Act. Revere spoke out ("No taxation without representation"); he led protests.
- March 5, 1770–Boston Massacre. Revere made an engraving of the event to stir up hatred for the British.
- December 16, 1773–Boston Tea Party. Revere led a group of men in boarding the ships and dumping the tea.
- May 10, 1774–Arrival of five thousand British soldiers in Boston to close the harbor. Revere lived in Boston.
- April 18, 1775–British movement to attack the Minutemen. Revere warned the Minutemen during the night.
- July 3, 1776–Declaration of Independence. Revere was not involved in the signing.
- 1775 to 1783–American Revolution. Revere was a lieutenant colonel; he led the defense of the Boston Harbor Fort.

CONNECTIONS TO COMMON CORE STATE STANDARDS FOR ENGLISH LANGUAGE ARTS

- Question 1 helps students focus on what they can learn from illustrations in informational texts (RI.K.7; RI.1.7; RI.2.7).
- Questions 2 and 15 ask students to identify key details in the text (RI.K.1; RI.1.1; RI.2.1).
- Questions 3, 5, 7, 8, 11, 12, 13, and 14 all give students the chance to identify key details and main topics concerning Revere's life and its relationship to the American Revolution. Students must connect ideas and events across paragraphs and pages, often having to make inferences (RI.K.1,2,3,6; RI.1.1,2,3,6; RI.2.1,2,3,6)
    - Questions 12 and 13 also ask students to infer information from illustrations (RI.K.7; RI.1.7; RI.2.7).
    - It is also beneficial to point out the writer's effective characterization techniques in general and to note that good narrative history often contains strong characterization techniques that help readers understand the motivations, actions, and characteristics of important historical figures–and how they affect historical events (RL.K.3; RL.1.3; RL.2.3; RI.K.6; RI.1.6; RI.2.6).
- Questions 4, 6, and 10 focus on identification of key details in a biography of an important person's life (RI.K.1,2; RI.1.1,2; RI.2.1,2).
- Question 9 allows students to analyze the origin, meaning, and significance of an important historical phrase (RI.K.4; RI.1.4; RI.2.4; L.K.5; L.1.5; L.2.5).
- The first performance assessment gives students a chance to write an informative/explanatory paragraph that requires them to demonstrate understanding of essential historical information and cite evidence to support their assertions (RI.K.2; RI.1.2; RI.2.2).
- The second performance assessment asks students to sequence events described in an informational text, identify the role of an important historical figure in the events, and discuss orally the effect of the person's actions (RI.K.1,2,3; RI.1.1,2,3; RI.2.1,2,3; SL.K.1,4; SL.1.1,4; SL.2.1,4).

MORE RESOURCES

HISTORICAL FICTION

Sam the Minuteman by Nathaniel Benchley

PRIMARY SOURCES

Revolutionary War enlistment form (Library of Congress)

Broadside announcing the sale of slaves: 1769 (PBS: Africans in America)

Images from the Revolutionary War era (National Archives)

"No Stamp Act" teapot (Smithsonian Institution)

Paul Revere's artwork, used as war propaganda, 1770 (Gilder Lehrman Institute of American History)

ART AND ARCHITECTURE

Benjamin Franklin Urging the Claims of the American Colonies Before Louis XV (Smithsonian Institution)

Lithograph of the destruction of tea at Boston Harbor, 1846 (National Archives)

USEFUL WEBSITE

Revolutionary War timeline (UShistory.org)

UNITED STATES HISTORY, ERA 6

We the People: Building an American Republic

(1776 to 1789)

GRADES: K, 1, 2

OVERVIEW

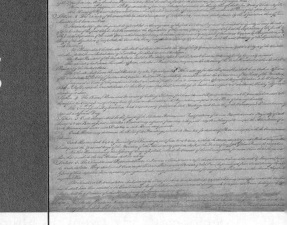

Americans fought a long and costly war to gain independence. After a decade of experimentation, they built a system that divided rights, duties, and responsibilities between the state governments and a new federal system. But the new Constitution left some questions unanswered, including the ultimate fate of slavery—an institution that would come to divide the nation. *D Is for Democracy: A Citizen's Alphabet* introduces younger students to the basic principles of our government and encourages them to write and illustrate examples of the importance of these principles. Older students will explore the drafting of the Constitution in *We the People: The Story of Our Constitution* and then synthesize what they've learned in a timeline that they can share with others.

○ ○ ○

Interested in learning more about this time period? Read a more complete history in the "Era Summaries."

LEARNING EXPECTATIONS

Lower elementary: Students should understand that American democracy took years of trial and error before the systems were developed as we know them today. They should also learn the basic role of citizens in our republic under the Constitution, and they should understand that a constitution lays out the basic rules for a system of government.

Upper elementary: Students should understand why the ideas of the American Revolution led the states to make Congress's powers so limited under the Articles of Confederation. They should then understand how different the Constitution's approach is, and why experience had changed so many minds about how powerful government needed to be. Students should learn how the Constitution lays out the structure of the U.S. government, how the different branches check and balance each other, and what fundamental rights are guaranteed by the Bill of Rights.

SUGGESTED ANCHOR TEXTS

D Is for Democracy: A Citizen's Alphabet by Elissa Grodin
Now and Ben: The Modern Inventions of Benjamin Franklin by Gene Barretta
Unite or Die: How Thirteen States Became a Nation by Jacqueline Jules

FEATURED ANCHOR TEXT

D IS FOR DEMOCRACY: A CITIZEN'S ALPHABET BY ELISSA GRODIN

This book was selected because it uses an alphabet book format to teach rich truths about democracy and citizenship. Although the deeper layers of the book can prove challenging even to upper elementary students, the ABCs are simple enough for lower elementary students to understand. The illustrations are intriguing, and the civics-related vocabulary is challenging.

TEXT STUDY

The text-dependent questions that follow address a number of priorities outlined by the Common Core State Standards. In particular, nearly all of them address the close relationship in this informational text between the illustrations and the words on the page.

1. **In the title of this book, what are the three key words letting you know what the book is about and how it is organized?**
   - The words are *democracy, citizen's*, and *alphabet*. It is a book about citizens in a democracy, and it is organized as an alphabet book.
2. **On the "A" page, what do you notice in the illustrations? How does the text help explain why the women are marching?**
   - In the illustrations, the women are marching for equal rights.
     - The clothes are old-fashioned.
     - The same figure from the cover (Uncle Sam) is marching with the crowd of women.
     - The women are carrying signs with such words as *demand, amendment, Constitution*, and *no slavery*.
     - The women have on ribbons with such words as *liberty, equality, suffragette, equal rights*, and *vote yes*.
   - From the text, we can learn that the women are marching for an amendment to the Constitution.
3. **According to the text on the "C" page, what might be happening in the illustration?**
   - Members of Congress are probably discussing ideas for new laws. It looks like a committee may be listening to one member's idea.

   Note: *In the fine print on the page, there is an explanation of Congress's role in government and how the committees work in the formation of new national laws.*
4. **Read the rhymes for the "D," "E," and "V" pages. Compare the text and illustrations on each of the pages. Tell how they are similar to and different from each other.**
   - In the text, "Democracy" is described as a system of government in which citizens can choose whom they vote for, and "Elections" take place when the citizens "Vote." All three words are about people voting and electing someone in a democracy.

- The first "D" and "E" illustrations show different eras of life: long ago and present day. The "D" illustration probably depicts a major election result, the "E" illustration a voting process in a school election.
- The "V" illustration also depicts the present day and introduces the idea of a vote for each person on a ballot.

  Note: *Encourage this kind of linking of ideas throughout the book, helping children see relationships between ideas.*

5. **Look closely at the illustration on the "F" page to see if you can find familiar faces. According to the rhyme, who are these people, and what did they do?**
   - Students may recognize George Washington and Benjamin Franklin in the illustration.
   - The text says that these men were called the "Founding Fathers" and that they wrote the U.S. Constitution.
6. **By looking closely at the fine print on the "G" page, what does the word *democracy* mean? Why is this word defined on the page for the word *Government*?**
   - The word *democracy* comes from Greek. *Demos* means people and *kratos* means power.
   - Our government is a democracy, and that means that people have the power.
7. **What does the illustration on the "I" page show? How does the text add to your understanding?**
   - The illustration shows people on board a boat looking at the Statue of Liberty. They look like they are very happy to be there, smiling, pointing, and waving their hats.
   - The text tells us that these people have left their homes to find a better life in America. This process of moving is called "Immigration."
8. **Compare the illustration on the front cover to the illustration on the "N" page. What do you notice in the illustrations, and how does the text add to your understanding of the location?**
   - The illustrations show pink flowers and Uncle Sam. The cover illustration shows a building and a pool. The "N" illustration shows a monument.
   - The text on the "N" page tells us that the place is the "Nation's capital" and the pink flowers are cherry blossoms.
   - The fine print explains that the city is named Washington, DC. Washington is named for our first president, and the District of Columbia is named for Christopher Columbus. It also names the monument in the illustration, the Washington Monument. The cherry trees depicted were a gift from the mayor of Tokyo, Japan, in 1912.
9. **According to the fine print on the "R" page, what are the three "R's" of religious freedom? How does the illustration support the text?**
   - The fine print says that these are the three R's of religious freedom:
     - "Rights" means every citizen has a right to choose his or her own religion.
     - "Respect" means we respect other people's choice of religion.
     - "Responsibility" means we have to be sure that we protect the religious freedom of others.
   - The illustration shows many different houses of worship. There is a church, a synagogue, a mosque, a cathedral, and an orthodox building.
10. **According to the illustration on the "S" page, how is the Senate organized?**
    - The Senate is made up of two elected representatives for every state.

11. On the "U" page, the author tells the reader about Uncle Sam. Who is he?

- According to the rhyme and the illustration, Uncle Sam was not a real person, but a cartoon.
- According to the fine print, Thomas Nast drew him in the 1800s as an emblem of a citizen in the United States. Uncle Sam was a patriotic figure that was used on war posters.

12. What is the main idea of the "W" page? How does the illustration help you to know?

- Although the letter W stands for *Washington*, the illustration shows seven other presidents. This page is really about presidents more than just about Washington.

13. According to the "Y" and "Z" pages, who should be involved in our country's government?

- Both pages focus on the word *You*. The author wants each citizen to be involved in the government.

PERFORMANCE ASSESSMENTS

1. Give students the following prompt:

- Write an informative/explanatory paragraph explaining why voting is an important part of being a citizen. Use text evidence to support your explanation. Start with a sentence that introduces the topic, provide two to three relevant supporting details from the text to support your explanation, and include a concluding sentence.

At earlier levels, students may draw or dictate their explanation and/or write a label, sentence, or series of related sentences. See standards for more details.

2. Create a class alphabet book about democracy. Students can choose to use the key word from each page or a related key word. (For example, students might want to have the letter P stand for *President* instead of *Political Party*.) Have each student write a paragraph that uses the key word correctly and explains its meaning, according to the following prompt:

- Start with a sentence that introduces the word, provide two to three examples of using the word correctly, and include a concluding sentence. Create a related illustration to accompany the paragraph.

At earlier levels, students may draw or dictate their explanation and/or write a label, sentence, or series of related sentences. See standards for more details.

You may publish the book in a multimedia presentation, with illustrations scanned onto slides or using photographs from throughout history. The American Memory Collection, Library of Congress, is a great resource: http://memory.loc.gov/ammem/index.html.

EXTENSIONS

1. This book provides a golden opportunity to study the way the author uses rhyme to communicate information. Spend time looking at the pattern of rhyming used by the author. Students could make collections of word pairs that rhyme and are connected by similar ideas. For example, *voices* and *choices* are two words connected to the idea of voters. Students could identify the words and then use them correctly in a sentence, such as "When we vote, we use our ballots as voices to make our choices."

2. As a class, read the anchor text again and create a then-and-now chart to help the students distinguish between the time when the U.S. government was created and the present day. Students should be able to see how Americans still enjoy the benefits of a well-articulated system of government.

CONNECTIONS TO COMMON CORE STATE STANDARDS FOR ENGLISH LANGUAGE ARTS

- Question 1 focuses on word choice. It asks students to think about how the author chose to organize the text, and why she did so in this way. And it brings key concepts into relief by focusing on the meanings of key words (RI.K.2,4,6; RI.1.2,4,6; RI.2.2,4,6).
- Questions 2 through 5 and questions 7, 8, 9, and 12 give students an opportunity to note the relationships between illustrations and text, as well as which key ideas and details are rendered through each or in combination. They help students understand the relationships between events, ideas, and/or concepts (RI.K.1,2,3,6,7; RI.1.1,2,3,6,7; RI.2.1,2,3,6,7).
- Questions 10 and 11 encourage close (re)reading and the practice of locating and inferring key details and main topics (RI.K.1,2; RI.1.1,2; RI.2.1,2).
- Question 13 asks students to identify a key detail (RI.K.1; RI.1.1; RI.2.1).
- The first performance assessment requires students to synthesize key details and other information from an informational text, as well as to write an informative/explanatory paragraph (RI.K.3,4,5,6,7; RI.1.3,4,5,6,7; RI.2.3,4,5,6,7; W.K.2,8; W.1.2,8; W.2.2,8).
    - This task also prepares students for standard W.4.9, which begins in grade 4.
- The second performance assessment gives students a chance to demonstrate understanding of key vocabulary from an informational text and the ability to write an informative/explanatory paragraph (RI.K.3,4,5,7; RI.1.3,4,5,7; RI.2.3,4,5,7; W.K.2,8; W.1.2,8; W.2.2,8).
    - This task also prepares students for standard W.4.9, which begins in grade 4.

MORE RESOURCES

HISTORICAL FICTION

Write On, Mercy! The Secret Life of Mercy Otis Warren by Gretchen Woefle

PRIMARY SOURCES

A *Tobacco Plantation*, 1788 (PBS: Africans in America)

U.S. thirty-dollar bill, printed in 1776 (Smithsonian Institution)

POETRY AND MUSIC

"An Ode for the 4th of July," 1788 (Library of Congress)

ART AND ARCHITECTURE

Sculpture of James Madison (Smithsonian Institution)

Miniature portrait of George Washington, painted in 1776 (National Portrait Gallery)

UNITED STATES HISTORY, ERA 7

Democracy Made Real: America Passes the Torch

(1789 to 1800)

GRADES: K, 1, 2

OVERVIEW

America's sights would soon shift to westward expansion. But first, the young nation and its fledgling government had to show that the new republic could govern effectively and that power could be transferred from one political party to another. The United States indeed created a working federal government, navigated a potentially poisonous party schism, and successfully handled the difficult election of 1800. *George Washington: Soldier, Hero, President* gives lower elementary students the biographical knowledge to persuade others that our first president was a great American. Upper elementary students will explore the ideological tension between the Founding Fathers in *The Revolutionary John Adams* and produce essays that evaluate both sides of an argument, paving the way for students' participation in debates about government that continue to this day.

○ ○ ○

Interested in learning more about this time period? Read a more complete history in the "Era Summaries."

LEARNING EXPECTATIONS

Lower elementary: Students should understand what a government is and why we need one. They should know what a constitution is and does, and how it lays out the basic rules that a government follows. Students can then understand not only the importance of George Washington in making the new government work but also Washington's iconic role in American culture. They should also understand that people quickly and inevitably split over what direction the new nation should take, resulting in political debate.

Upper elementary: Students should know that the Constitution left much unsaid, and that the first U.S. Congress and president were left to set up the actual government. They should understand Washington's central role in making the new system function in its early, formative stages. Students should also understand that the first party schism was sparked by different ideas about what kind of country the United States would be—either controlled, European-style, by the wealthy, who would help bolster U.S. military power, or based on a society of relatively equal farmers. Students should also recognize the great achievement of the new system in respecting elections and transferring power between the parties.

SUGGESTED ANCHOR TEXTS

George Washington: Soldier, Hero, President by Justine and Ron Fontes
Big George: How a Shy Boy Became President Washington by Anne Rockwell
George Washington and the General's Dog by Frank Murphy
George Washington's First Victory by Stephen Krensky
The House That George Built by Suzanne Slade
"Young George Washington," *Appleseeds*, February 2004

FEATURED ANCHOR TEXT

GEORGE WASHINGTON: SOLDIER, HERO, PRESIDENT BY JUSTINE AND RON FONTES

This book was selected because it is well illustrated with drawings, paintings, photographs of tools of the time, and maps. Students will be captivated by the fresh telling of the life of a well-known figure in American history. Various stories about Washington paint a picture of a purposeful life, demonstrating how everything he learned early on was useful to him as an adult and helped him serve the country he loved. The text also exhibits some features commonly found in informational texts (for example, a table of contents, chapters, illustrations, captions, a glossary, and an index) that make a significant amount of important historical information easier to digest. These features help very young students learn how informational texts are often organized.

TEXT STUDY

The following text-dependent questions offer many opportunities for teachers to support the Common Core State Standards for English language arts while teaching students about the significant role Washington played in establishing the American nation. The questions address essential aspects of the nation's early history (for example, the Continental Congress, the Constitution, the Bill of Rights, and the role of the executive branch of American government), but they do so in a way that allows teachers to help students understand how to use certain structural features to navigate informational texts, specifically biographies. The questions reinforce the power of narrative history to convey essential information in a way that is engaging for students.

1. **What do you learn about Washington in the illustration on page 4? What part of the text does this illustration support?**
   - When Washington was a boy, he enjoyed being in the outdoors and catching fish. His outfit indicates that he lived a long time ago.
   - On page 5, the text describes Washington's birth and his having five younger brothers and sisters. In the description of his childhood, it says that he liked to fish, swim, and ride horses.

2. **After reading pages 6 through 13, describe Washington's education as both a boy and a young man.**
   - According to page 6, he had tutors at home because there were no schools nearby. He learned reading, writing, and arithmetic. He was very good at math but not very good at spelling.
   - According to page 7, his father died when he was eleven years old. Because of this, Washington was not able to go to school in England to finish his education. Later on, he successfully taught himself to be a surveyor using his talent in math.
   - According to page 9, Washington listened closely to his half-brother Lawrence's description of war. Washington learned about moving troops, supplying them with food and weapons, military strategy, and how to fight with a sword. The illustration and caption describe how Washington learned the art of fencing.
   - On page 11, the book says he also learned much from the Native Americans from his experiences as a surveyor. Washington learned native woodcraft and how to move silently through the woods.
3. **According to pages 14 and 15, why were the English and the French fighting against each other in America?**
   - Both the English and the French wanted more land in North America.
   - The French wanted to have the land to the west of what the English controlled and had claimed land from Canada to Louisiana.
   - The English wanted the French to leave the forts in the Ohio Valley.

   Note: *Students will want to note that Washington was living in a British colony and so was considered "English."*
4. **According to pages 14 through 16, what was Washington's first mission with the Virginia Army?**
   - The governor asked Washington to take a letter to a French fort in Ohio, demanding "that France leave its forts in the Ohio Valley." The English had been fighting the French for control of American land. Washington and his men had to "trek" through the wilderness, through Native American land, to get there. The French commander said no, and the French and Indian War began.
5. **How do the illustration and the informational inset on page 15 support the text about the difficulty of Washington's mission to the French fort in Ohio?**
   - The illustration shows Washington trying to get home from the mission in the snow; he is in a dangerous situation on a raft in a cold river.
   - The informational inset supports the account, adding an additional event. After Washington returned to the governor, he was asked to write a report of his experience. Instead of going to bed, he stayed up all night writing the report by candlelight.
6. **What did Washington learn from his experience with General Braddock?**
   - The text on page 17 says, "He learned that a truly great leader must always learn—or die."

     Note: *Students may also want to use evidence from the text on page 16 to explain what he means.*
   - According to page 17, General Braddock insisted on fighting "the English way" when he came to America. He wanted his soldiers to march "in neat lines" and "to loud fife music and drums." Washington and other officers tried to teach him that war in America was different, but "Braddock refused to change," so he died in battle. If he had listened to the Americans and learned a new way to fight, he might have survived the skirmish.

7. **According to this text (pages 20 and 21), what was the Continental Congress, why was it formed, and what did it do?**
   - To pay for the French and Indian War, England had been placing high taxes on goods sent to America.

     Note: *Teachers should pause and ensure that students know what* taxes *are.*
   - The Americans felt the taxes were unfair, and Washington "proposed that Americans refuse to buy things from England."

     Note: *Teachers might pause here to discuss the meaning of* protest, *a term also used here*: *"This protest sent a clear message to England that the colonies would not put up with unfair taxes."*
   - "Leaders and thinkers from each colony formed the Continental Congress" to decide what to do about the problems the American colonies were having with England.
   - The Continental Congress decided that America needed an army to fight the English and voted for Washington to be commander in chief of the new Continental Army.
8. **How do the illustration and inset on page 20 help you understand the colonists' problems with England?**
   - The illustration and inset on page 20 describe the Boston Tea Party, the colonists' protest over taxes on tea and other goods. We learn that "50 angry Americans . . . dumped 340 chests of English tea in the sea!"
9. **Why did Washington refuse to be paid as the commander in chief of the Continental Army? What character quality does this refusal show?**
   - According to page 21, he "wanted only to do his duty."
   - Washington was patriotic.
10. **According to the text on pages 22 and 23, what were Washington's problems with his army?**
    - They were not professional soldiers. "They were not used to marching or following orders."
    - They did not have enough supplies ("uniforms, guns, bullets, or food").
    - The "Minutemen" came from the countryside in a minute, but Washington said they also "disappeared in a minute when it was time to drill."

      Note: *Teachers might ask some students about the meaning of this sentence from the inset on page 23: "Minutemen were more independent than professional soldiers."*
11. **How do the text features on pages 24 and 25 support the main idea of those pages' text?**
    - The main idea of these two pages is that "the American colonies were slowly becoming a nation."
      - The flag, shown on page 24, has thirteen stars and stripes, one for each of the thirteen colonies. January 1776 was the month when America got its first flag.
      - On the bottom of page 24 is a drawing of the public reading of the Declaration of Independence. According to the text, the colonies became a country when this document was signed on July 4, 1776.
      - The informational inset and painting on page 25 describe the writing of the Declaration of Independence and illustrate its signing, respectively.
12. **According to pages 28 through 31, how did Washington put on a "surprise party" for the Hessians during the American Revolution?**
    - The "surprise party" was really a surprise attack on professional German soldiers who were fighting for England. On the night of December 26, 1776, the fishermen in Washington's army rowed quietly across the Delaware River to carry men and supplies for an attack on the Hessians camped in Trenton, New Jersey.

- The next morning, Washington's men surprised the soldiers and captured nine hundred of them.

  Note: Teachers might ask students about the significance of the following sentence from page 27: "Americans had little more than the will to win."

13. **How do the authors describe the appearance of the Continental Army on pages 32 and 33? How did Washington help them to appear able and ready to defeat the British?**
    - The army was described as "ragged," wearing a "shabby assortment of tattered uniforms, work clothes, Indian shirts, and even some enemy coats."
    - The army marched in a parade through Philadelphia. They marched in rows of four to make the parade longer. They put sprigs of green in their caps to look like they had something matching on their "uniforms." They "sang and drummed loudly to show their fighting spirit."
14. **On page 35, how do the authors use numbers to tell the story of the hard winter in Valley Forge?**
    - They use numbers to tell how many men died of cold, hunger, and disease: twenty-five hundred Americans.
    - They use numbers to tell how many men snuck out to go home: twenty-five hundred Americans.
    - They use numbers to tell how many men were as tough and stubborn as Washington, staying to fight: six thousand Americans.
15. **According to page 39, why was the Constitution important to the formation of the United States?**
    - The Constitution outlined "how the new American government should work."
    - After the Constitution was approved in June 1788, "America had a real government."
16. **The word *unanimously* means that everyone voted the same way. In this case, Americans voted unanimously for Washington (page 40), electing him as the first president. What does this tell us about Washington?**
    - It means that everyone who voted thought he should be the leader of the country.
    - Washington was "the most famous and beloved hero in the new nation" (page 38), so he was very popular among men who could vote for president.
17. **What do the authors mean when they say that Washington "tried to be a fair president" (page 42) and also "tried to balance the needs of all the states" (page 43)? Cite evidence from the text to support your assertions.**
    - He worked with both parties in the new country; each party had a different view of how the government should work.
    - He "toured the tiny nation, listening to people's problems. He welcomed all Americans to come and talk to him."
    - He "supported the Bill of Rights" because he had "fought hard for America's freedom." "The Bill of Rights makes sure that the government won't take away freedom."
18. **Why did people think Washington would be the president for the rest of his life? Cite evidence from the text to support your assertions.**
    - According to page 44, they expected him to be "like a king." Kings serve their whole lives. Washington "refused to run for a third term" because "he believed the American government would be better off with a new leader every four to eight years."

19. How do the authors compare the Washington Monument to Washington himself?

- They write, "The tall spike reached up toward heaven, like the ideals of the hero who loved America," thus comparing the straight, tall monument to the heroic first president.

PERFORMANCE ASSESSMENTS

1. Have students reread the summarizing paragraph on page 47 of the text. Using the five key terms therein (*surveyor, farmer, soldier, president*, and *legend*), they should create a multimedia, informative/explanatory presentation of the life of Washington. Students should include a sentence that introduces their topic, use facts and definitions to develop points, and provide a concluding statement or section. This task could also be modified to be a writing assignment only. At earlier levels, students may draw or dictate their informative/explanatory multimedia text and/or write a label, sentence, or series of related sentences. See standards for more details.

2. Have students write an opinion paragraph in which they say whether they think Washington was a great American. Students should write a sentence that states their opinion, provide two or three relevant reasons or details from the text that support their opinion, use linking words, and provide a concluding statement. At earlier levels, students may draw or dictate their opinion and/or write a label, sentence, or series of related sentences. See standards for more details.

CONNECTIONS TO COMMON CORE STATE STANDARDS FOR ENGLISH LANGUAGE ARTS

- Questions 1, 5, and 8 ask students to consider the role of illustration in supporting understanding of an informational text (RI.K.6,7; RI.1.6,7; RI.2.6,7).
- Questions 2, 3, 4, 10 through 14, and 17 give students a chance to reread text closely to identify key details and concepts within and/or across paragraphs (RI.K.1,2; RI.1.1,2; RI.2.1,2).
    - Question 12 also asks students to understand and explain a metaphor (RI.K.4; RI.1.4; RI.2.4; L.K.5; L.1.5; L.2.5).
- Question 6 requires students to infer information from details described in the text and to use evidence to support their assertions (RI.K.1,2,3,8; RI.1.1,2,3,8; RI.2.1,2,3,8).
- Questions 7, 16, 17, and 18 allow students to identify, connect, and extrapolate from key details and concepts presented in an informational text (RI.K.1,2,3; RI.1.1,2,3; RI.2.1,2,3).
    - Questions 17 and 18 also address the authors' purpose and require the use of evidence to support assertions (RI.K.6,8; RI.1.6,8; RI.2.6,8).
- Question 9 asks students to identify—and infer important information from—a key detail about the subject of this biography (RI.K.1,2,3; RI.1.1,2,3; RI.2.1,2,3).
- Question 11 allows students to analyze several kinds of informational text features to determine how they help support the main idea of a given section of text (RI.K.6,7; RI.1.6,7; RI.2.6,7).
- Question 15 asks students to identify a key detail from the text (RI.K.1; RI.1.1; RI.2.1).
- Question 16 focuses students' attention on the authors' diction and on the connotations of words (RI.K.4; RI.1.4; RI.2.4; L.K.4,5; L.1.4,5; L.2.4,5).

- Question 19 addresses the authors' choice of simile and its effect in terms of conveying content (RI.K.4,6; RI.1.4,6; RI.2.4,6; L.K.5; L.1.5; L.2.5).
- The first performance assessment gives students the chance to work with standard features of an informational text, focus on vocabulary, and develop an informative/explanatory presentation about an informational text, demonstrating comprehension of key details, main topics, and concepts in a historical biography. It also requires them to formulate a multimedia presentation of their assertions (RI.K.1,2,3,5,6,7,8; RI.1.1,2,3,5,6,7,8; RI.2.1,2,3,5,6,7,8; SL.K.2,5; SL.1.2,5; SL.2.2,5; W.K.8; W.1.8; W.2.8).
    - This task also prepares students for standard W.4.9, which begins in grade 4.
- The second performance assessment asks students to formulate an opinion piece and support assertions with evidence from the text (W.K.1; W.1.1; W.2.1).
    - This task also prepares students for standard W.4.9, which begins at grade 4.

MORE RESOURCES

HISTORICAL FICTION

Tricking the Tallyman: The Great Census Shenanigans of 1790 by Jacqueline Davies

PRIMARY SOURCES

George Washington's Rules of Civility (Library of Congress)

Washington's handwritten inaugural address, 1789 (Library of Congress)

Thomas Jefferson election campaign banner, 1800 (Smithsonian Institution)

POETRY AND MUSIC

"Washington" by Nancy Byrd Turner (All Poetry)

ART AND ARCHITECTURE

George Washington (Lansdowne portrait), painted by Gilbert Stuart (National Portrait Gallery)

Portrait of James Madison, ca. 1792 (National Portrait Gallery)

USEFUL WEBSITE

Information on George Washington's Rules of Civility (National Public Radio)

UNITED STATES HISTORY, ERA 8

Going West: Opportunity and Peril on America's Frontier

(1800 to 1830s)

GRADES: K, 1, 2

OVERVIEW

Although America was still mostly a nation of farmers in the early 1800s, the temptation to expand the western border was compelling. This period saw rapid growth in economic and industrial development as urban factories sprang up and delivered goods to markets both at home and abroad. At the same time, the first modern roads and canals allowed Americans to move easily between busy trading ports and once-isolated inland communities while continuing the drive westward into new territory. Younger students will take a journey in *How We Crossed the West: The Adventures of Lewis and Clark* and analyze the relationship between the explorers and the native people they encountered along the way. After reading the chapter on the Erie Canal in *A History of US: The New Nation: 1789–1850*, students in upper elementary grades will be prepared to analyze primary sources or to glean the insight of a civil engineer to construct their own multimedia presentations showing how new modes of transportation change life in a community.

○ ○ ○

Interested in learning more about this time period? Read a more complete history in the "Era Summaries."

LEARNING EXPECTATIONS

Lower elementary: Students should understand that the growing American nation quickly pushed westward in pursuit of opportunity and began to make itself felt in the world. Students should understand that Americans' way of life was quickly changing as commerce brought people closer together.

Upper elementary: Students should know that America began to expand dramatically, both commercially and physically (to the West, with new territory and settlement), and to take a more assertive place in the world. They should understand that commercial development moved with the expanding population, and they should grasp the importance of "internal improvements"—chiefly roads and canals—in allowing people and commerce to expand. They should also realize that commercial expansion created new dangers as well as new opportunities, and that people disagreed strongly about the federal government's involvement in promoting commercial development.

SUGGESTED ANCHOR TEXTS

How We Crossed the West: The Adventures of Lewis and Clark by Rosalyn Schanzer
Pioneer Days: Discover the Past with Fun Projects, Games, Activities, and Recipes by David C. King
Seaman's Journal: On the Trail with Lewis and Clark by Patricia Eubank

FEATURED ANCHOR TEXT

HOW WE CROSSED THE WEST: THE ADVENTURES OF LEWIS AND CLARK BY ROSALYN SCHANZER

This book was selected because it is based on the journals of Meriwether Lewis and William Clark, making the text authentic and exposing students at an early age to the power of primary sources. The information is presented in a lively way, with detailed illustrations consistent with the style of journals from the era. The text subtly introduces important and sometimes difficult issues pertaining to this defining period in American history at a level appropriate to students in the primary grades. It is worthy of reading again and again, seeing new layers of information each time.

TEXT STUDY

The text-dependent questions represent many opportunities to support instruction of the Common Core State Standards for English language arts while also introducing important, nuanced historical content about relations between Native Americans and American explorers as the explorers moved farther and farther west into Native American territories. The questions offer students opportunities to learn about the author's craft as they note arguably small but important details about life during this period of American westward expansion. These questions also address what students will have learned from reading primary source materials, an essential skill for student historians. Finally, this narrative history contains compelling characters, from whose stories students can learn much about this time in American history.

1. **According to the cover illustration and title, who are the historical "characters" in this text, and what is the historical setting?**
   - According to the cover illustration, the characters in the account are people from a variety of ethnic backgrounds: white explorers in coonskin hats and fringed jackets, an African American man, a Native American woman and baby, and a dog. Watching along the edge of the water are other Native Americans.
   - From the illustration we can also see that the setting is mountainous, with a river rushing through a gorge.
   - The title of the book tells us that the setting is the crossing of the West and the people leading the adventure are Lewis and Clark.
2. **View the map in the front pages of the book. What does the author, who is also the illustrator, want the reader to notice on this map?**
   - She wants the reader to see the area of the United States where Lewis and Clark explored and the route they took.

- She wants the reader to see the Native American nations and where they were along the journey.
- She wants the reader to see the rivers Lewis and Clark had to cross and the mountains they had to climb.

3. **According to page 1, why did President Thomas Jefferson want more exploration of the West?**
   - He knew there was a mysterious world beyond the Mississippi River. He wanted to know about the rivers, the people, the plants, and the animals. He especially wanted to find a water route leading to the western ocean.
4. **Who wrote the letter included on page 2 of the book, to whom was it written, and what did it say?**
   - Lewis, Jefferson's "private secretary" (we learn on page 1), wrote to a man called "Clark," asking him to go with him "to explore those western rivers which may run . . . to the western ocean."
   - Lewis said they would meet and begin to trade with Native American tribes, to discover new plants and animals, and to make new maps.
5. **In Clark's letter, included on page 3 of the book, what does he say? How would you describe Clark's response?**
   - The very day after he received the letter, Clark wrote back to say he would go with Lewis.
   - Clark says that he read Lewis's letter "with much pleasure."
   - "I will cheerfully join you," he says.
   - We know from his fast response for this era and his words that he was happy to join the exploration.
6. **Why is it helpful to read these "primary sources" (or "eyewitness accounts") from historical events?**
   - It is useful to examine primary sources because they help explain what really happened (that is, without someone else interpreting the facts for the reader).
   - We hear directly from people on the exploration about what happened.

   Note: *It might be appropriate to discuss the root word* prime *as well as other nouns and adjectives that use that root word to help students understand what a primary source is.*
7. **When reading each journal entry, how can you tell if Lewis wrote it, if Clark wrote it, or if another crew member wrote it?**
   - According to the author's note on the dedication page, there is a cursive L (Lewis), C (Clark), or O (other party members) at the end of each journal entry, showing which man wrote the entry.
8. **From whose journal are we reading on page 4? What do the section names on pages 4 and 5 help the reader understand about these two pages?**
   - We are reading Lewis's journal entry; he is describing the problems with building his boat for the journey.
   - The reader can understand from the section names ("Building the Keelboat," "Loading the Boat," "A Few Original Members," and "Selecting Recruits for the Journey") that these pages are about the various steps in preparing for the journey.

   Note: *Teachers could ask some detail questions about these pages; for example,* "What is listed on page 4?" "Who was the youngest recruit on the journey?" *and so on.*

9. **According to pages 6 and 7, what were some challenges faced during the beginning month of the journey?**
   - The mast of the boat broke.
   - The ticks and mosquitoes were troublesome.
10. **According to pages 8 and 9, what wildlife was seen on the plains? Why where the men so happy to see the wildlife?**
    - They saw catfish, turkeys, geese, beaver, deer, prairie dogs, buffalo, and antelope.
    - We can infer that the men were happy because of all of the animals that provided food. The author tells about how party members caught three large catfish that had a lot of fat in them. In a journal entry, Clark describes seeing "great numbers of deer" and adds "Men in high spirits."

    Note: *Teachers could point out that in their respective journals, Lewis and Clark do not always write in complete sentences; they are often "jotting down" their thoughts, as in the last phrase just given. Teachers might compare that to when students themselves sometimes write in their journal (to emphasize the difference between a journal and a completed and published work). Some students may be able to turn these phrases into complete sentences as a grammar exercise.*

    Note: *Teachers could also ask about how the animals are described (for example, "alarmed" prairie dogs, "shy and watchful" antelope) to reinforce grammar standards (here, 1e for kindergarten, grade 1, and grade 2).*
11. **Why do you think pages 10 through 13 have the section names "Among the Indians" and "Trouble"? Summarize what happens on these pages and cite details from the text to support your summary.**
    - These pages describe what happened as Lewis and Clark came into contact with the Native Americans. Some contact was friendly; some was not.

    Note: *If appropriate, teachers could introduce the concept of "cooperation and conflict," which is often used to summarize interactions between American settlers and Native Americans.*
      - As they traveled, Lewis and Clark learned about different Native American nations by trading with them, eating with them, and in some cases scuffling with them.
      - The Oto and Missouri nations traded watermelons for the roasted meat that Lewis and Clark gave them (page 10).
      - Lewis fired an air gun (page 10), which "astonished those natives."

    Note: *Teachers could ask students what they think the word* astonished *means and why the Native Americans might have been astonished by the shots. Native Americans had never seen guns before—an important historical detail that foreshadows the conflict on page 12.*
      - The Omaha nation hunted buffalo and had been "ravaged" by smallpox, having lost four hundred people (page 10).
      - The Sioux "lived by the bow and arrow, making a vow never to retreat" (page 11). *Again, this foreshadows the event on page 12.*
      - Lewis and Clark gave the Sioux a medal, a uniform coat, and a hat, among other gifts, but feeling that they hadn't been given enough gifts, the Sioux seized one of the expedition's boats. They drew their bows and arrows, but Lewis and Clark's men "instantly pointed the swivel guns" at the Sioux; this "impressed them and they withdrew." Later, they "made up" over a peace pipe and a meal of dog meat (page 13).
      - The Arikaras were great farmers and were determined to stay away from any kind of spirits (alcohol) that the white man might give them. They were "astonished" at Clark's

black servant. They had never seen a black man before (page 14). They were "not fond of spirits or liquor of any kind . . . no man could be their friend who tried to lead to such follies" (page 15).
  - Teachers might discuss the meaning of the word follies.

12. **What can we infer from the fact that the Native Americans and Lewis and Clark's men were able to raise the peace pipe and "dance the war dance with cheerfulness" after their disagreement (page 13)?**
    - It is possible that the Native Americans, never having seen guns before, were impressed by the expedition's force and warfare, as outlined on page 12.
13. **On page 13, why has the author drawn Seaman with a worried expression? Cite evidence from the text to explain.**
    - The Sioux had just served dog meat to Lewis and Clark. If Seaman had been capable of understanding that his owners were eating dog, he might have gotten worried that they would eat him. The author was having fun with the reader by imagining the dog's expression of concern and disgust.
14. **According to Clark, who were the "most friendly Indians" inhabiting the Missouri?**
    - These were the Mandans.
15. **According to page 17, Mr. Toussaint Charbonneau wanted to be hired as an interpreter. Why did he introduce his wife, Sacagawea, to Lewis and Clark?**
    - Sacagawea was from the Shoshoni nation, from near the Rocky Mountains where they had many horses. Her husband believed she would be able to explain to the "Indians" that the explorers needed horses for their journey over the mountains.
16. **What was the author's purpose in including the information on page 18? Support your idea with evidence from the text.**
    - She wants the reader to know how terribly cold and difficult the 1804–1805 winter was.
      - The section name is "A Winter of Excessive Cold."
      - The journal entries all include information about how cold it was. One talks about men being frostbitten, and two mention very low temperatures (one being forty-five degrees below zero). One journal entry includes information about the amazing ability of Native Americans to withstand the cold. Another tells how Native Americans were able to jump across small cakes of ice on a river to catch a buffalo.
17. **Why was Sacagawea so happy to see the Shoshoni?**
    - The chief was her brother, known as the "Great Chief Cameahwait."
    - Sacagawea was finally reunited with her family and her Native American nation.

    Note: *Teachers may want to remind students that page 17 indicated that Sacagawea had been taken away from her nation at the age of ten.*
18. **The word *fortitude* means "determination." Why is this word used to describe Sacagawea on page 23 of the text?**
    - The text says that Sacagawea's "fortitude was equal to any person on board" when they were in a dangerous situation in the boat, almost losing supplies that they needed to complete the trip. Proving this fortitude, she "caught and saved most of the light articles washed overboard."
    - This passage says that Sacagawea was determined to save the supplies that were in danger of being lost in the water. In contrast to her husband, described as "the most timid waterman in the world," she was brave and equal to the men in her effort.

19. **According to pages 28 and 29, what were the challenges the explorers faced as they crossed the mountains?**
    - The roads were steep, stony, and covered with snow.
    - Horses fell down the mountains.
    - The men were so hungry, they had to kill a colt to eat.
    - It was so cold, their moccasins and the ink in their pens froze.
20. **How did the Nez Perce nation help the explorers?**
    - According to page 30, the Nez Perce drew them a map to show where the rivers would be on their journey ahead.
21. **How did the "Indians" on the shore know that the exploration party was peaceful?**
    - In a journal entry on page 32, Clark reports that "as soon as they saw Sacagawea, they understood our friendly intentions, as no woman ever accompanies a war party."
22. **According to the text on pages 32 and 33, what did the explorers see and hear as they moved on to Oregon?**
    - They saw harbor seals, ate salmon, and spied mountain goats on high cliffs of rocks.
    - They heard swans, geese, and brants. In fact, the noises these birds made were so horrid that Lewis could not sleep.
    - One chief opened his medicine bag and showed Lewis the fingers he had taken from enemies during times of war.

    Note: *You may want to remind children that the Native Americans would fight for their territory and their people.*
23. **How do the illustration and text on pages 36 and 37 convey that Lewis and Clark had accomplished their goal?**
    - The scene is beautiful, with wild waves and birds, seeming to burst with joy, as the text says, "Our goal is reached at last!" They had reached the Pacific coast and could see the ocean.

PERFORMANCE ASSESSMENT

Read the text to the students one more time to notice the interaction between explorers and the Native Americans. Draw the students' attention to the illustrated maps showing where the Native American nations lived. Discuss how frightening it must have been for the Native Americans to see these people for the first time. Discuss also how frightening it must have been for the explorers to meet unknown nations of Native Americans.

Ask the students to discuss whether, based on what they have read, these explorers and the Native Americans seemed to respect each other. Challenge students to write an opinion paragraph that answers the question about respect and supports their opinion with two ideas from the text. The paragraph should introduce the topic; state an opinion; supply reasons that support the opinion; use linking words (such as *because, and,* and *also*) to connect the opinion and reasons; and provide a concluding statement or section. At earlier levels, students may draw or dictate their opinion and/or write a label, sentence, or series of related sentences. See standards for more details.

Note: *From the beginning, the explorers went prepared to trade and had a Native American as a member of their team. They told of a good meeting with the Oto and Missouri nations. The Sioux felt they had not had enough gifts and stole a boat; both sides drew weapons, but they seemed to make peace. Later, the explorers hired Charbonneau to be an interpreter and his wife Sacagawea to help with relations. In the winter, they hunted buffalo with Native Americans, respecting their ability to jump from one cake of ice to another. The explorers danced for some chiefs. Lewis and Clark changed the way they built canoes by learning from the Native Americans. Although there is evidence of mutual respect and cooperation, it would not always be that way as the white man moved west and claimed land.*

CONNECTIONS TO COMMON CORE STATE STANDARDS FOR ENGLISH LANGUAGE ARTS

- Question 1 asks students to note what they can learn about the setting in an informational text from the cover illustration and the title (RL.K.3; RL.1.3; RL.2.3; RI.K.5,6; RI.1.5,6; RI.2.5,6).
- Question 2 addresses the skill of gleaning information from maps in informational texts (RI.K.5,6; RI.1.5,6; RI.2.5,6).
- Question 3 addresses a character's motivations, as in a literary text, but it also simply ensures that students can understand key details and identify a main topic in an informational text (RI.K.1,2; RI.1.1,2; RI.2.1,2).
- Questions 4 and 5 offer students a chance to understand the emerging structure of the book, clarify points of view from which the story will be told, and analyze characters' motivations from what they say in the letters (RL.K.3,6; RL.1.3,6; RL.2.3,6; RI.K.1,2,5,6,7; RI.1.1,2,5,6,7; RI.2.1,2,5,6,7).
- Question 6 addresses the importance of primary sources in general and in this text specifically. It also affords teachers an opportunity to focus on a language standard for this grade by analyzing the word *primary* and its root word, *prime* (W.K.8; W.1.8; W.2.8; L.1.4(c); L.2.4(c)).
- Question 7 requires students to have done a close reading of not only the main text but also the author's note at the beginning. Drawing attention to the author's note helps students learn that notes in informational texts and historical fiction will often contain useful information for understanding key aspects of the text (RI.K.5,6; RI.1.5,6; RI.2.5,6).
- Question 8 focuses students' attention on who is "speaking" and on how to use section titles to help guide their reading (RI.K.5,6; RI.1.5,6; RI.2.5,6).
  - If teachers use additional questions here, they will be reiterating the importance of understanding key details (RI.K.1,2; RI.1.1,2; RI.2.1,2).
- Questions 9 and 10 address the identification of key details. They also ask students to link those details to important concepts in regard to the exploration, requiring them to infer why such details were important to the survival of the men (RI.K.1,2,3; RI.1.1,2,3; RI.2.1,2,3).
  - Posing the additional questions for question 10 will help teachers convey some important concepts pertaining to the writing process, writing genres, and the power of diction in general and adjectives in particular (preparation for W.4.9; L.K.1; L.1.1; L.2.1).
- Question 11 requires students to read closely and to think carefully about the relationship between section titles and the content described in those sections. It also asks them to summarize the content from several pages, citing details as evidence of understanding (RI.K.1,2,3,5,6,7,8; RI.1.1,2,3,5,6,7,8; RI.2.1,2,3,5,6,7,8).
  - If the additional questions are addressed, students will analyze an important historical concept, "cooperation and conflict," and wrestle with its implications (RI.K.4; RI.1.4; RI.2.4; L.K.4,5; L.1.4,5; L.2.4,5).

  - Students may also consider the effect of the word *astonished* as it relates to the Native Americans' exposure to firearms at this time, another important historical topic (RI.K.4; RI.1.4; RI.2.4; L.K.4,5; L.1.4,5; L.2.4,5).
  - Here is also an opportunity to discuss the use of foreshadowing in an informational text (RI.K.3; RI.1.3; RI.2.3).
  - Finally, teachers may examine the denotation and connation of the word *follies* (RI.K.4; RI.1.4; RI.2.4; L.K.4,5; L.1.4,5; L.2.4,5).
- Questions 12, 15, and 17 ask students to make inferences from key details in an informational text (RI.K.3; RI.1.3; RI.2.3).
- Questions 13 and 16 ask students to consider the author's purpose in including an unusual illustration and a series of entries from explorers' journals, respectively (RI.K.6,7; RI.1.6,7; RI.2.6,7).
  - Question 16 requires students to cite evidence from the text to support their claims.
- Question 14 asks students to identify a key detail from the text (RI.K.1; RI.1.1; RI.2.1).
- Question 18 focuses on a key vocabulary word that is relevant to the plot, characterization, and history (RI.K.1,2,3,4; RI.1.1,2,3,4; RI.2.1,2,3,4).
- Questions 19 through 22 ask students to identify some key details from the text that convey the course and difficulty of the explorers' passage through the mountains and beyond (RI.K.1; RI.1.1; RI.2.1).
- Question 23 addresses the way in which text and illustration work together to convey meaning–here, the key concept of a successful expedition (RI.K.5,6,7; RI.1.5,6,7; RI.2.5,6,7).
- The performance assessment gives students an opportunity to analyze an informational text; consider the points of view of two groups of people; and form and write an opinion about a key concept in American history, using evidence from the text to support their claim (RI.K.3; RI.1.3; RI.2.3; W.K.1; W.1.1; W.2.1).
  - This task also prepares students for standard W.4.9, which begins in grade 4.

MORE RESOURCES

PRIMARY SOURCES

"Westward Expansion: Encounters at a Cultural Crossroads" (Library of Congress)

Includes a teacher's guide with additional primary sources, lesson activities, and explanations of concepts

Images from 1801 to 1861 (National Archives)

The Star Spangled Banner, photograph (Smithsonian Institution)

"King Andrew the First" political cartoon, 1833 (Library of Congress)

POETRY AND MUSIC

Francis Scott Key's handwritten lyrics to "The Star Spangled Banner," 1840 (Library of Congress)

ART AND ARCHITECTURE

Wagon Train to the West (Library of Congress)

Relief of Meriwether Lewis, William Clark, and Sacajawea (Smithsonian Institution)

Model for Signing of the Louisiana Purchase Treaty (Smithsonian Institution)

Portrait of Francis Scott Key (Library of Congress)

UNITED STATES HISTORY, ERA 9

Freedom for All: American Democracy Begins to Transform

(1820s to 1840s)

GRADES: K, 1, 2

OVERVIEW

Economic changes had already swept the nation by the 1820s, and democracy had expanded as most white men gained the right to vote. Now a great social transformation began as new ideas about religion, women's rights, and abolition took root. More groups of people demanded rights equal to those of free men, laying the foundation for ideological battles that would forever alter the nation. Differences in the rural and urban economies are highlighted in *The Listeners* and *The Bobbin Girl* in a way that is relatable for lower elementary students. Examining the lives of the two protagonists leads younger students to develop an informed opinion about where they would rather live—a rural or urban setting—and why. *Elizabeth Leads the Way: Elizabeth Cady Stanton and the Right to Vote* and *I Could Do That! Esther Morris Gets Women the Vote* prepare upper elementary students to compare and contrast the accomplishments of two pivotal women's rights activists.

○ ○ ○

Interested in learning more about this time period? Read a more complete history in the "Era Summaries."

LEARNING EXPECTATIONS

Lower elementary: Students should understand that Americans remained divided over what kind of society the country should have—agricultural and rural versus commercial and urban—and that as more men were able to vote, these divisions led to new political parties. They should also understand that many people tried to reform the country to end various injustices, even as expansion to the West increasingly forced out Native Americans. Further, students should realize that slavery, getting stronger in the South, was the focus of new tensions between North and South.

Upper elementary: Students should understand that in the Jacksonian era, white, male Americans achieved a new level of democratic power rarely seen before in the world. But they should also know that the thriving American democracy created a push for westward expansion, with dark consequences for Native Americans. They should understand that reformers, often motivated by religious fervor, tried to improve society and morality (and to control new immigrants whom they feared); they should also realize that slavery became more and more powerful in the South, even as the North turned more heavily against it—setting up the conflict that would dominate the country in coming decades.

SUGGESTED ANCHOR TEXTS

The Listeners by Gloria Whelan
The Bobbin Girl by Emily Arnold McCully
Andrew Jackson: Seventh President by Mike Venezia
Dolley Madison Saves George Washington by Don Brown
Marching with Aunt Susan by Claire Rudolf Murphy
Susan B. Anthony by Alexandra Wallner
The Flag Maker: A Story of the Star-Spangled Banner by Susan Campbell Bartoletti
The Town That Fooled the British: A War of 1812 Story by Lisa Papp

FEATURED ANCHOR TEXTS

THE LISTENERS BY GLORIA WHELAN

THE BOBBIN GIRL BY EMILY ARNOLD MCCULLY

Each of these books depicts life in America in the early 1800s. One book tells of a slave girl living on a cotton plantation in the rural South. The other book tells of a ten-year-old girl who works in a factory in a northern city that processes cotton into a woven cloth. These two books provide a backdrop for comparing a rural, agricultural life with an urban, industrial life. The author's note in each book provides crucial information about the time period and a context for examining added informational text within a literary book, a common feature of historical fiction. Reading these two books together allows students to examine the same time period in history from two different perspectives.

TEXT STUDIES

Reading these two works of historical fiction allows students to compare and contrast the experiences of two arguably similar characters in two different settings. The juxtaposition means that teachers may emphasize important features of literary texts, especially characterization and setting, while conveying essential content about this time period in American history. It is particularly interesting that the success of the work in one place relies on the success of the work in the other. Answering the questions correctly requires close reading.

The Listeners by Gloria Whelan

Note: *Due to the absence of page numbers in this text, page 1 will be designated as that containing the first illustration in the actual text.*

The questions for this text are divided into two sets. The first set of questions (1 through 3) is designed to lead students to an understanding of the setting and of the expectations for the slaves on a plantation. The second set of questions (4 through 9), requiring students to go back to the beginning of the text and read for a different purpose, is focused on the "listening" that the children did and the reactions of the adults to the news.

1. **Look closely at the illustrations on the cover of the book and pages 1 and 2 of the text. Describe the setting of the story from the details in the illustrations.**
   - The cover illustration suggests that the setting of the story is a cotton plantation.
   - In the illustrations on pages 1 and 2, the characters live in a small house (slaves' quarters) on the plantation. Roosters and hens are in the farmyard. The clothes are old-fashioned, and a woman is carrying a basket on her head.
2. **How does the morning begin for Ella May (the narrator)?**
   - On pages 1 and 2, the boss blows a bugle while it is still dark, and Ella May gets out of bed quickly to go pick cotton.
3. **Using evidence from the text and from the illustrations, tell what slaves do while working on the cotton plantation–in the morning, at noon, after lunch, as the sun sets, and after supper.**
   - In the morning:
     - They start working early, as the sun rises (page 12).
     - The young girl picks cotton as the "little prickers on the cotton plants bite" at her fingers (page 12).
     - The hardest work is done in the cool part of the morning (page 12).
   - At noon:
     - They eat in the field at noon (page 14).
     - They eat out of a trough and use clamshells for spoons. They eat salt pork, corn dumplings, and black-eyed peas (page 14).
   - After lunch:
     - They keep picking cotton after lunch, but it is hard to pick in the heat of the day (page 14).
     - The cotton has to be picked quickly, or the boss flicks the worker with his cane (page 14).
   - As the sun sets:
     - They come back after dark, while the sun is setting, each one carrying the cotton on his or her head (illustrations on pages 3 and 4).
   - After supper:
     - The children listen below the windows of the plantation house (illustrations and text on pages 5 and 6).
4. **According to the author's note at the beginning of the book, how did the slaves learn about what was happening on plantations?**
   - They sent small children to hide near the windows of the masters' homes to listen.
5. **According to the author's note and the text on page 6, why was the listening by the children such an important task?**
   - The lives of the slaves depended on circumstances they could not control.
     - They had no voice in deciding for whom they would work or where they would live.
     - They never knew when they were going to be separated from their spouses or children.
     - According to page 6, the master and mistress didn't tell the slaves anything. Eavesdropping was the only way the slaves received important news from the great house.

6. **On page 7, the author describes the children as "small as cotton seeds" and "quiet as shadows." What does the author mean by these two similes?**
   - The author is telling how invisible the children needed to be and how they could not be caught listening below the window. They had to stay out of sight, and they had to be completely silent.

7. **Cite specific examples of information heard by the listening children in this story. Tell how the adults react to the news by looking closely at the illustrations and the text.**

   Note: *Use this question to guide the reading of the remainder of the text, giving students more responsibility for finding the examples as they read.*

   - On pages 7 through 10, they learn about a new boss coming. The children and "mammies" are happy, but the daddy says, "I'm not clapping my hands 'til I see the new man." The expressions on their faces also reflect the opinions of the children, mammies, and daddy.
   - On page 16, they learn that Master Thomas is considering selling Ella May's father. Ella May reacts with fear, described by the author with a memorable image of "a flock of scared birds." The text says, "My heart's a flock of scared birds flying every which way," but then the master says that Ella May's father is "one of the best pickers and handy with machines," so they will keep him. The illustration shows her sadness as she hugs Sue, a girl whose father had been sold the year before. The adults take the information as good news.
   - On page 22, they learn that the boss is considering buying horses to help with plowing, and that makes the children happy because hoeing is hard work. However, the master decides that slaves are cheaper than horses. No adult reaction is recorded.
   - On page 27, they learn that the mistress wants to educate the slave children, but the master says that it is against the law to educate slaves. No adult reaction is recorded.
   - On pages 33 through 35, they learn that Abraham Lincoln has become the president and that the master considers him "a madman" who says that "slavery is wrong" and "slavery must end!" The children run with the news. Daddy responds with, "Moses is come! We're going to be free like the children of Israel. It's the Jubilee for sure!" The illustration shows the sheer joy on the faces of children and adults alike.

   Note: *The students may remember the story shared by the slaves' preacher on pages 19 and 20 that describes how Moses "freed the people of Israel." Note the use of the word* listening *as related to how "the good Lord" heard their songs.*

8. **Why do the children in this story still need to listen after the election of Lincoln?**
   - On page 37, Daddy says, "We see the road, but we don't see all the way to where the ending is." He says that they must keep listening: "We got to know how long is that road and how we will get down it."

   Note: *The illustration on page 37 shows a literal road and reinforces this imagery. Students will need to be guided to understand the road as a symbol for the long journey to freedom and equal rights.*

9. **Go back to page 27 of the text to read closely. What does Ella May mean when she says, "I say the poem all the way home and now it's my poem too"? Why is this poem such an important part of her listening?**
   - The author is showing how Ella May learns everything she can and how no one can prevent her from learning poetry just like Mistress Grace. It also shows how children can make a poem of their own, by memorizing it and making it a part of themselves.
   - When Ella May says, "When I go to sleep I pretend my scratchy straw mattress is a bed of roses," she is telling how she can use her imagination to rise above the hardness of her circumstances. Listening doesn't simply help her find out information for her parents; on this evening, it feeds her spirit and makes her richer inside.

The Bobbin Girl by Emily Arnold McCully

1. **Look closely at the illustrations on the cover of the book, the title page, and the dedication page. Describe the setting of the story by gathering evidence from the details in the illustrations.**
   - In the cover illustration, the time looks like long ago, especially considering the characters' dress: bonnets, shawls, and long dresses.
   - In the cover illustration, the place is a huge building, possibly in a town or city.
   - On the title page, the buildings have many windows and have smoke rising from chimneys.
   - On the title page, animals are used for work, as seen beside one of the buildings.
   - On the title page, all of the women are entering one door of the building, possibly for school or work.
   - On the dedication page, a young girl is carrying a box on her shoulder as a woman behind her is working at a machine holding many spools of yarn.
   - All of this information suggests that the setting is long ago, in a factory that employs many women to manufacture something involving yarn.
2. **The title of the book is *The Bobbin Girl*. How do the illustrations inside the front and back covers and on the dedication page give clues to understanding the word *bobbin*?**
   - In the inside cover illustrations, there are thirty-two spools of yarn in many different colors.

     Note: *Teachers might need to explain to students what spools are.*
   - On the dedication page, the young girl is carrying a box, and behind her are many spools of yarn.
   - There are a number of spools of yarn, so perhaps the word *bobbin* has to do with yarn.

     Note: *These illustrations suggest that her job must involve the spools of yarn, or bobbins.*
3. **Who is the main character in this story, and what do you learn about her from the first few pages of illustration and text?**
   - From the illustrations on page 2, we see that she is small. She signs something with a quill pen.
   - In an illustration on page 2, the man hands her something wrapped in a white bag.
   - Page 1 says that she is a ten-year-old girl named Rebecca Putney who lives in Lowell, Massachusetts.
   - Page 1 says that she works in a mill as a "bobbin girl."
   - Page 1 says that she lives in a company boardinghouse, run by her mother.
4. **Using evidence from the text and from the illustrations, tell what Rebecca does while working in the cotton mill—in the morning, at noon, in the afternoon, and after work has ended.**
   - In the morning:
     - She carries a box of empty spools (illustration on page 3).
     - The day starts early with a wake-up bell rung from the mill's great bell tower at 4:30 a.m. (page 3).
     - She has to be at work by 5:30 a.m. (page 3).
     - She begins working in an "earsplitting racket" at the mill (page 3).
     - She spends fifteen minutes every hour removing full bobbins of yarn from the spinning frames and replacing them with empty ones (page 3).
     - During breaks in her work, she slips outside and reads books, such as *Gulliver's Travels* (page 5).

- At noon:
  - The dinner bell rings, and the machines stop (page 5).
  - She dashes to the boardinghouse.
  - She has thirty minutes to eat a huge meal that her mother has cooked.
- In the afternoon:
  - She continues to work until 7:00 p.m., completing a thirteen-and-a-half-hour day (pages 8 and 9).
- After work had ended:
  - She has supper (page 11).
  - She is free to do what she wants until her 10:00 p.m. curfew, so she studies geography (illustrated on page 11).

5. **What is "Lowell Fever"?**
   - On page 5, Lowell Fever is described as "the mill girls . . . all improving their minds." It is a hunger and thirst for education during a time when women are not educated.
6. **How does the author show evidence of this "fever"?**
   - In the text and illustration on page 5, the girls have books hidden in the wall of the courtyard.
   - Page 5 describes how "The girls taped printed sheets and even math to their looms and the windows to study while they worked."
   - The text and illustration on page 6 indicate that Judith is saving her money to enroll in a women's academy. She reads while she eats.
   - In the text and illustrations on pages 9 and 10, four of the women are reading books around the fire. Judith is taking a German class, is said to be a member of the Literary Society, and is going to lectures to learn.
7. **Using evidence from the story, what were the problems with working in a cotton mill?**
   - According to page 8, fear of the overseer prevented people from coming to each other's aid.
   - According to page 9, the days were thirteen and a half hours long.
   - According to page 9, a lung disease attacked many in the mills; it was believed to be caused by breathing the wet, lint-filled air.
   - According to pages 14 through 16, the machines never stopped working, even for injuries. Owners blamed workers for the accidents.
   - According to pages 17 through 19, owners reduced wages for workers.
8. **According to the author's note, what were other problems with working in a cotton mill?**
   - As years went on, workers had to tend more machines for lower pay.
   - Machines were sped up.
   - Owners secretly slowed down the clocks to extend the workday.

PERFORMANCE ASSESSMENTS

Note: Introduce the performance assessments by discussing the terms rural *and* urban *and* agricultural *and* industrial. *Have students discuss which book,* The Listeners *or* The Bobbin Girl, *would fit under each word. Using the questions and answers for each book, discuss the similarities between the situations faced by both sets of workers in the early part of the 1800s: the long hours of the workday, the backbreaking work, the lack of opportunities for education, low or nonexistent pay, and the workers' lack of voice in improving working conditions.*

1. Assign this informative/explanatory paragraph writing task:

- Choose either the rural and agricultural setting or the urban and industrial setting. Tell what it would have been like to live in one of those settings. Be sure to use examples from the relevant text in your writing.

Students should write a sentence that introduces their topic, use facts and definitions to develop points, and provide a concluding statement or section. At earlier levels, students may draw or dictate their opinion and/or write a label, sentence, or series of related sentences. See standards for more details.

2. Focus on the issue of education. Discuss what the texts have to say about the education of slaves and the education of girls. Have students write an opinion paragraph in response to the following prompt:

- If you were a child in the early to mid-1800s, do you think it would be harder to get an education if you were a factory girl or a child slave? Support your opinion with evidence from the texts we read.

Students should write a sentence that states their opinion, provide two or three relevant reasons or details that support their opinion, use linking words, and provide a concluding statement. At earlier levels, students may draw or dictate their opinion and/or write a label, sentence, or series of related sentences. See standards for more details.

3. Give students the following prompt:

- How is the term *slave* used in each book? Find two instances in which the term is used in each book and write an informative/explanatory paragraph that compares the four usages to one another.

Students should write a sentence that introduces their topic, use facts and definitions to develop points, and provide a concluding statement or section. At earlier levels, students may draw or dictate their explanation and/or write a label, sentence, or series of related sentences. See standards for more details.

Note: *In* The Listeners, *the term* slave *is used in the harshest sense—conveying ownership, being sold, having no property, and earning no pay, while being owned by masters. In* The Bobbin Girl, *the workers use the term* factory slave *to describe themselves (that is, to convey that they are treated poorly). They have to work long hours, but they are still paid something and are not technically owned by the factory bosses.*

4. Using the song lyrics for "The Farmer Is the Man" and "The Cotton Mill Girls," continue to compare these two texts in light of working in either agriculture or industry. Ask students to write an informative/explanatory paragraph in which they must answer this question:

- According to these song lyrics, what were the biggest challenges for farmers, and what were the biggest challenges for factory workers? Use evidence from the texts we read to support your claims.

Students should write a sentence that introduces their topic, use facts and definitions to develop points, and provide a concluding statement or section. At earlier levels, students may draw or dictate their opinion and/or write a label, sentence, or series of related sentences. See standards for more details.

CONNECTIONS TO COMMON CORE STATE STANDARDS FOR ENGLISH LANGUAGE ARTS

***The Listeners* by Gloria Whelan**

- Question 1 asks students to note what they can learn about the setting of the story from illustrations (RL.K.1,3,7; RL.1.1,3,7; RL.2.1,3,7).
- Question 2 addresses the identification of key details and events (RL.K.1,2,3; RL.1.1,2,3; RL.2.1,2,3).
- Question 3 requires students to glean key details and events in the story from text and illustrations (RL.K.1,2,3,7; RL.1.1,2,3,7; RL.2.1,2,3,7).
- Question 4 asks students to use a feature of historical fiction (here, the author's note, which serves as informational text) to enhance their understanding of the historical content (RI.K.1,2; RI.1.1,2; RI.2.1,2).
- Question 5 asks students to glean key details and events in history from the author's note. Students must also infer the author's purpose in emphasizing the importance of children's listening (RI.K.1,2,3,6; RI.1.1,2,3,6; RI.2.1,2,3,6).
- Question 6 allows teachers to discuss the use of figurative language in a way that is particularly relevant to the historical content (RL.K.4; RL.1.4; RL.2.4; L.K.5; L.1.5; L.2.5).
- Question 7 addresses key details and actions that affect readers' understanding of plot and characterization. This question also asks students to use illustrations to enhance their understanding of plot, characterization, and the main topics of the story (RL.K.1,2,3,7; RL.1.1,2,3,7; RL.2.1,2,3,7).
- Question 8 asks students to explain characters' words and actions that are crucial to advance the plot and connect events in the story to important historical information (RL.K.1,2,3; RL.1.1,2,3; RL.2.1,2,3).
- Question 9 not only addresses important aspects of plot and characterization but also reminds students about the power of poetry and its memorization. Finally, it helps students extrapolate the deeper significance of the book's title (RI.K.1,2,3,4; RI.1.1,2,3,4; RI.2.1,2,3,4).

***The Bobbin Girl* by Emily Arnold McCully**

- Questions 1, 3, 4, and 6 ask students to use specific evidence from the text (and other features, such as illustrations) to demonstrate comprehension (RL.K.1,2,3,7; RL.1.1,2,3,7; RL.2.1,2,3,7).
  - Question 6 also addresses the author's use of evidence to support assertions (RL.K.1,2; RL.1.1,2; RL.2.1,2).
- Question 2 addresses the illustrations on the inside covers and dedication page and their relationship to the title (RL.K.1,4,7; RL.1.1,4,7; RL.2.1,4,7).
- Question 5 allows teachers to discuss the use of figurative language in a way that is particularly relevant to the historical content (RL.K.4; RL.1.4; RL.2.4).
- Question 8 asks students to use a common feature of historical fiction (here, the author's note) to enhance their understanding of the historical content (RL.K.1,2,3; RL.1.1,2,3; RL.2.1,2,3).

Performance Assessments

- The performance assessments require students to read closely and participate in class discussions, using text evidence to support their claims (SL.K.1,2; SL.1.1,2; SL.2.1,2).
- The first performance assessment asks students to write an informative/explanatory paragraph that demonstrates their understanding of what they have read, requiring them to compare two settings in preparation for writing (RL.K.1,2,3,9; RL.1.1,2,3,9; RL.2.1,2,3,9; W.K.2; W.1.2; W.2.2).
- The second performance assessment asks students to write an opinion piece using evidence from the text (and possibly from research) to support their assertions. It allows students to compare the experiences of two characters.
- The third performance assessment gives students a chance to consider the nuances, connotations, and authors' careful use of a key word, *slave*. It requires students to examine diction carefully and to compare and contrast the ways in which a particular term is used in two different texts (W.K.1,2,3,4,9; W.1.1,2,3,4,9; W.2.1,2,3,4,9; W.K.8; W.1.8; W.2.8; L.K.5; L.1.5; L.2.5).
- The fourth performance assessment asks students to examine the historical content through another medium—song lyrics—and write an informative/explanatory paragraph. This performance assessment expands their understanding of the texts and of this important era of American history, while also exposing them to other art forms (RL.K.1,2,3,9; RL.1.1,2,3,9; RL.2.1,2,3,9; W.K.2; W.1.2; W.2.2).

MORE RESOURCES

PRIMARY SOURCES

Photograph of picking cotton in the 1800s (Library of Congress)

Photograph of Addie Card, a twelve-year-old spinner in a North Pownel, Vermont, cotton mill (Library of Congress)

Photograph of children picking cotton (Library of Congress)

POETRY AND MUSIC

Mill workers' song lyrics: "Hard Times Cotton Mills Girls" (New Hampshire Historical Society)

ART AND ARCHITECTURE

Illustration of a bobbin girl by Winslow Homer (Lowell National Historical Park)

A House Divided: North versus South

(1820 to 1859)

GRADES: K, 1, 2

OVERVIEW

The U.S. Constitution banned the importation of slaves after 1807, but it did not answer the challenge of the Declaration of Independence, which asserted that all men have a God-given right to life, liberty, and the pursuit of happiness. As the country rapidly grew, the unresolved controversy over slavery became a bitter and increasingly violent schism. Most northerners held that slavery belittled all those, regardless of race, who lived by their own labor. Joining their horror at the treatment of African American slaves with a desire to see all men free, abolitionists fueled the conversation by exposing the shocking inhumanity of slavery. Among the abolitionists was the eloquent Frederick Douglass, who himself escaped slavery to find refuge in the North. The southern states pushed back against what they felt was a northern attack on their way of life and a violation of states' right to their own self-government. As new western lands were acquired and settled, the sections split over the status of the new territories: Would they be slave states or free states? The government of the young nation found itself unable to handle the crisis, and the sections began to break apart. Lower elementary students who read "When I Reach the Promised Land . . ." and *Henry's Freedom Box: A True Story from the Underground Railroad* will compare and contrast the experiences of two famous slaves who escaped to freedom in an informative/explanatory paragraph. *Words Set Me Free: The Story of Young Frederick Douglass* and an excerpt from *Narrative of the Life of Frederick Douglass, an American Slave* will give upper elementary students the evidence needed to explore, in an informative/explanatory essay, how learning to read set the famous abolitionist free.

○ ○ ○

Interested in learning more about this time period? Read a more complete history in the "Era Summaries."

LEARNING EXPECTATIONS

Lower elementary: Students should understand that northerners were determined to keep slavery from expanding, both for moral reasons and to serve their own interests. In contrast, southerners were determined to maintain slavery's expansion and to protect it, because they saw it as the basis of their way of life. Students should understand that the democratic government could not handle the collision of these views and that the country began to break apart.

Upper elementary: Students should know that the feud over slavery's expansion dominated the 1850s. They should understand that the morally driven abolitionist movement was quite small, but that most northerners—though not abolitionists, not demanding immediate emancipation in the South, and not focusing on the sufferings of slaves themselves—feared slavery would make anyone who worked for a living inferior to slave-owning aristocrats. Students should realize that the issue was made urgent by the rapid addition of new western territories, which had to be made either slave states or free states, and they should know that the quarrel turned increasingly violent over the course of the decade. The country's elected institutions proved unable to solve the crisis, which increasingly threatened the survival of the country.

SUGGESTED ANCHOR TEXTS

"When I Reach the Promised Land . . ." by Susan Buckley, pages 11–13, *Appleseeds*, March 2004
Henry's Freedom Box: A True Story from the Underground Railroad by Ellen Levine
Friend on Freedom River by Gloria Whelan
Moses: When Harriet Tubman Led Her People to Freedom by Carole Boston Weatherford
The Patchwork Path: A Quilt Map to Freedom by Bettye Stroud
Unspoken: A Story from the Underground Railroad by Henry Cole

FEATURED ANCHOR TEXTS

"WHEN I REACH THE PROMISED LAND . . ." BY SUSAN BUCKLEY, PAGES 11–13, APPLESEEDS, MARCH 2004

HENRY'S FREEDOM BOX: A TRUE STORY FROM THE UNDERGROUND RAILROAD BY ELLEN LEVINE

The article "When I Reach the Promised Land . . ." was selected because it is the account of Harriet Tubman's own journey to freedom via the Underground Railroad. This beautifully written article describes the creative escapes of desperate people. It is well-paired with *Henry's Freedom Box*, which was selected because it is a beautifully illustrated Caldecott Honor Book telling a true and unique story from the Underground Railroad. The text grabs the imaginations of young children with its stories of creative escapes and proves that narrative history is an effective vehicle for developing students' interest in a period of history and the people who lived through it.

TEXT STUDIES

The following text-dependent questions present many opportunities for educators to support the teaching of the Common Core State Standards for English language arts. They all require close reading.

"When I Reach the Promised Land . . ." by Susan Buckley, pages 11–13, *Appleseeds*, March 2004

1. **Look closely at the illustrations on pages 11, 12, and 13. How do these watercolor sketches help to tell the story?**
   - On page 11, the barefooted African American woman is looking determined as she walks through bushes and trees.
   - On page 12, a light-skinned woman is kindly pointing her in a direction. The African American woman looks straight ahead with that same determination.
   - On page 13, the African American woman appears overcome with gratitude; her hands are raised, and her mouth has a joyful expression. The yellow background looks like glory.
2. **What is the repeated phrase in the opening song lyrics? Why is that phrase important in this account?**
   - The repeated phrase is "the promised land." In the second line, the speaker reaches the promised land, and in the fourth line, it tells that she is bound for the promised land.
   - The title of the account is "When I Reach the Promised Land . . ." The title is taken from the lyrics of this song.
   - This whole account is a journey toward a land of promised freedom.
3. **How is the phrase "stole away" used in the first paragraph of the account?**
   - It is used as a way of saying that Harriet Tubman secretly escaped from the Brodas Plantation in Maryland.
4. **Why does the first paragraph say that Tubman "turned north"?**
   - In the paragraph, it says that as she turned, she left slavery behind her, and that she was making her way to freedom. We can infer that north was the direction of freedom.
5. **What made Tubman want to flee the plantation right away?**
   - There was a new owner of her plantation, and he needed money. He was selling slaves to get money.
   - Two of Tubman's sisters had been sold and sent farther south in chains.
   - She then heard that she and her brothers had also been sold.
   - She knew she had to leave immediately or she would remain a slave.
   - We can infer that if she were sent farther south, it would be even harder to escape to the freedom in the North: the time was "now or never."
6. **According to this text, why was the journey to freedom called the "Underground Railroad"?**
   - The plan included having "stations," or places where brave people hid escaping slaves. When it was safe, these brave men and women would send them on to another safe place or station.
   - The person who led groups of people to freedom was called a "conductor."
   - We can infer that the railroad did not involve a literal train on tracks, but rather was a system of conductors and stations.

7. **In the text, the author gives several examples of stations. What are the examples of stations in general? What are the stations where Tubman stayed?**
   - The general examples are in the second paragraph on page 12 (between the em-dashes): "on someone's farm or in a house, a church, or a store."
   - On page 13, the first paragraph states that Tubman's stations were in a free black's cabin, in a Quaker attic, and on a German farm.
8. **How far did Tubman have to go to reach freedom, and where was her "promised land"?**
   - She walked or traveled in a wagon ninety miles to reach freedom.
   - Her promised land was in the free state of Pennsylvania.
9. **How does the quotation at the bottom of page 13 relate to the illustration on that same page?**
   - The quotation is from Tubman herself. She writes, "I looked at my hands to see if I was the same person now I was free." The illustrator shows her hands clearly to indicate how they were symbols of Tubman's idea of freedom.

     Note: *Students can infer from this that Tubman could now do what she wanted with her own hands; her actions were no longer controlled by somebody else.*
   - Tubman also writes, "There was such a glory over everything, the sun came like gold through the trees, and over the fields, and I felt like I was in heaven." The illustrator changes the background color from blue in the first illustration to bright gold in the last illustration.
10. **According to the text, what did Tubman do with her newfound freedom?**
    - The first paragraph on page 13 says that Tubman became the most famous conductor on the Underground Railroad. She "conducted hundreds to freedom."

      Note: *Students can infer from this that she didn't stay in "the land of freedom," but risked being caught over and over again by helping others escape from slavery.*

Henry's Freedom Box: A True Story from the Underground Railroad by Ellen Levine

1. **According to page 1, who was Henry Brown, and when was his birthday?**
   - He was a slave and was not allowed to know his birthday.
   - This fact is important to note because it shows how, from the beginning, he did not have the rights of a human being in America.
2. **According to page 3, what did Brown's mother try to teach him in this conversation: "Do you see those leaves blowing in the wind? They are torn from the trees like slave children are torn from their families."**
   - She was using a simile to describe what it was like for slave children to be taken from their parents. She was probably trying to warn him about what she feared was to come.

     Note: *Although this is a bit of a challenge for this age group, the teacher could point out the fact that the author is foreshadowing future events here. A few pages later (on page 8), as Brown says good-bye to his parents, he sees the leaves swirling in the wind again and probably remembers his mother's words.*
3. **Why was Brown so disappointed by the conversation with the master, according to pages 5 and 6?**
   - His master was dying, and sometimes masters gave their slaves freedom after they died. But instead of granting Brown his freedom, he gave him to his son and told Brown that he had to obey his new master.

4. **According to page 8, what did the bird symbolize to Brown on the day he left his family?**
   - He saw the bird soar high above the trees and thought about how the bird must be happy because it was free.
5. **According to pages 9 through 19 of this text, what was it like to be a slave?**
   - They worked hard, had no rights to make their own decisions, and were owned by someone.
   - They had children, but they didn't know when their children would be sold.
   - They had spouses, but they had no idea if they would be allowed to stay together.
   - They were beaten and treated unfairly.
   - Their quality of life depended on who was their owner.
6. **Look closely at the illustration on page 17. How does this illustration support the text?**
   - The illustration shows Brown's friend James whispering into his ear that his wife and children have just been sold in the slave market.
7. **Explain the author's use of the word *twisted* in the following sentences on page 16: "Henry twisted tobacco leaves. His heart twisted in his chest."**
   - She is using it literally in the first sentence.

     Note: *Teachers could have children actually twist a piece of paper.*
   - In the second sentence, she uses it to describe a feeling in Brown's heart, which was "broken," "in agony," or other language to this effect.
8. **According to the top of page 24, what prompted Brown to think about freedom?**
   - It was that same image of a bird flying out of a tree into the open sky.

     Note: *Students might want to see this repeated image by going back to page 8.*
9. **What was Brown's greatest challenge, and how did he overcome it?**
   - He lost everything when his wife and children were sold. He decided that he had to be free, so he found some help from people who were also against slavery—abolitionists—and mailed himself north to Pennsylvania and to freedom.

     Note: *Teachers could use this discussion to describe the extraordinary challenges Brown faced during the trip in the box.*
10. **How does the author begin and end this historical account?**
    - She begins by saying that Henry did not have a birthday, and she ends by saying that from now on, his birthday would be his first day of freedom. This detail gives the story a sense of coming full circle.
11. **According to the author's note on page 39, what was the Underground Railroad?**
    - The Underground Railroad was "all the secret ways slaves made their way from the South to the North." It was not a real railroad, but it represented any means of travel that slaves could manage. Some rode in carts or on horseback, walked through swamps, and crossed rivers. The people who helped were called "conductors" or "station masters."

PERFORMANCE ASSESSMENTS

1. After reading the accounts of Tubman's and Brown's journeys to freedom with students, ask them to compare and contrast Tubman's and Brown's experiences. Have students write an informative/explanatory paragraph (or group of sentences) that describes one or two ways in

which Tubman's experience was similar to Brown's and one or two ways in which Tubman's experience was different from Brown's. See standards for more details.

At the earlier levels, students may need to dictate or draw part of their response. For example, give students a sheet of paper with a dividing line and ask them to illustrate Tubman's experience on one side and Henry's on the other. Ask them to explain their drawing.

2. Read the chapter titled "A Shipment of Dry Goods" from the book *Escape from Slavery: Five Journeys to Freedom* by Doreen Rappaport. Discuss how the two stories are about Brown but differ in the telling. The Rappaport story is longer and includes many more details.

Note: *Teachers may want to preread the text to monitor the language they are comfortable reading aloud to students.*

3. Have advanced students view this illustration of Henry "Box" Brown from a Pennsylvania history website: http://explorepahistory.com/displayimage.php?imgId=1-2-1E65.

Read the caption below the image to introduce the word *abolition*. As a class, create a (digital) concept map for this word or for the word *abolitionist*, doing the research necessary to complete it. Print and allow students to use the concept map to illustrate the word *abolition* or *abolitionist* and/or to write an informative/explanatory paragraph (or group of sentences) using the word *abolition* or *abolitionist*. At the earlier levels, students may need to draw or dictate their response.

CONNECTIONS TO COMMON CORE STATE STANDARDS FOR ENGLISH LANGUAGE ARTS

"When I Reach the Promised Land . . ." by Susan Buckley, pages 11–13, *Appleseeds*, March 2004

- Question 1 addresses the use of illustrations and their relationship to the text (RI.K–2.5.7).
- Questions 2, 3, 4, and 6 focus on key ideas and details; they allow for a discussion of the author's craft—diction in particular—and of how narrative techniques (such as repeated phrases and figurative language) may be used to enliven an informational text and enrich understanding of historical content (RL.K.1,2,3,4; RL.1.1,2,3,4; RL.2.1,2,3,4; RI.K.1,2,3,4; RI.1.1,2,3,4; RI.2.1,2,3,4; L.K.5; L.1.5; L.2.5).
- Questions 5, 7, 8, and 10 ask students to glean key ideas and details from an informational text (RI.K.1,2,3; RI.1.1,2,3; RI.2.1,2,3).
- Question 9 focuses students' attention on the author's craft, in particular how and why the author chose to use quotations and an illustration for rhetorical effect and to convey essential content (RI.K.7,8; RI.1.7,8; RI.2.7,8).

***Henry's Freedom Box: A True Story from the Underground Railroad* by Ellen Levine**

- Questions 1, 3, 5, and 9 allow students to identify key details and ideas (RI.K.1,2,3; RI.1.1,2,3; RI.2.1,2,3).
- Question 2 gives students a chance to discuss how narrative techniques (here, simile and foreshadowing) may be used in an informational text to enhance comprehension of essential historical content (RL.K.4; RL.1.4; RL.2.4; RI.K.4; RI.1.4; RI.2.4; L.K.5; L.1.5; L.2.5).

- Questions 4 and 8 ask students to analyze the use of a symbol. By focusing on this aspect of the author's craft, students may recognize that rich informational texts often use strong narrative techniques and figurative language to enhance understanding of essential historical content (RL.K.4; RL.1.4; RL.2.4; RI.K.4; RI.1.4; RI.2.4; L.K.5; L.1.5; L.2.5).
- Question 6 addresses the use of an illustration and its relationship to the text (RI.K.5.7; RI.1.5.7; RI.2.5.7).
- Question 7 asks students to discuss how narrative techniques (here, connotations of words) may be used in an informational text to enhance comprehension of essential historical content (RL.K.4; RL.1.4; RL.2.4; RI.K.4; RI.1.4; RI.2.4; L.K.5; L.1.5; L.2.5).
- Question 10 gives students an opportunity to examine the author's craft (in this case, how and why the author chose to start and end the book in a particular way for rhetorical effect) (RI.K.3,6; RI.1.3,6; RI.2.3,6).
- Question 11 affords students an opportunity to read "another" text on this topic and garner more relevant historical information (RI.K.9; RI.1.9; RI.2.9).

Performance Assessments

- The first performance assessment offers students a chance to compare two texts written on related topics in an informative/explanatory paragraph (RI.K.1,2,3,9; RI.1.1,2,3,9; RI.2.1,2,3,9; W.K.2; W.1.2; W.2.2; and great scaffolding for W.4.9).
- The second performance assessment also offers students a chance to compare orally two texts written on the same topic (RI.K.1,2,3,9; RI.1.1,2,3,9; RI.2.1,2,3,9; SL.K.1; SL.1.1; SL.2.1).
- The third performance assessment asks students to interpret a political cartoon, conduct research on a related topic, and complete a concept map and/or render their understanding in an informative/explanatory paragraph (RI.K.1,2,3,7; RI.1.1,2,3,7; RI.2.1,2,3,7; W.K.2; W.1.2; W.2.2; and great scaffolding for W.4.9).

MORE RESOURCES

PRIMARY SOURCES

Antislavery meeting poster (Library of Congress)

Abraham Lincoln campaign poster (Library of Congress)

Inauguration of Mr. Lincoln, photograph, 1861 (Library of Congress)

"A Number of Valuable Slaves: Life as an Enslaved People" (Library of Virginia)

Contains many primary source documents within

"Voices from the Days of Slavery: Former Slaves Tell Their Stories" (Library of Congress)

POETRY AND MUSIC

Follow the Drinking Gourd: A Cultural History

USEFUL WEBSITE

"Harriet Tubman: Civil War Spy" (*National Geographic Kids*)

Blue versus Gray: Civil War and Reconstruction

(1860 to 1877)

GRADES: K, 1, 2

OVERVIEW

Whether the United States would survive as a nation was at times not altogether certain during the Civil War. The political parties had grown even further apart over the slavery issue. The Democrats' 1860 convention split, with the North and South each nominating its own presidential candidate. The Republicans coalesced behind Abraham Lincoln. Because of the strength of the Republicans in the North, Lincoln became the sixteenth president (without ever being listed on ballots in the South). Convinced that the antislavery radicals had seized control of Washington, South Carolina voted to secede from the Union, and other Southern states soon followed. They formed their own nation: the Confederate States of America. With no common ground to be found between the North and South on the issue of federal and state sovereignty or on the issue of the future of slavery, the nation plunged into outright civil war. What began as a fight to save the Union and uphold democracy would eventually grow, due to Lincoln's own resolution, into a larger battle over the final abolition of slavery. The end of the Civil War left many unsolved questions—how to rebuild the South, how to reincorporate it into the Union, and the rights and protection of freed former slaves. Lower elementary students will read *Abraham Lincoln: Lawyer, Leader, Legend* to uncover the sixteenth president's evolving views on slavery, and they will present his ideological development on an illustrated timeline. A *Civil War Scrapbook: I Was There Too!* gives upper elementary students opportunities to compare and contrast the actions of individuals who were seen as heroes by those on one side of the war and as villains by those on the other, and to then craft an opinion essay defending their conclusion on how one such individual should be remembered.

○ ○ ○

Interested in learning more about this time period? Read a more complete history in the "Era Summaries."

LEARNING EXPECTATIONS

Lower elementary: Students should understand that though the crisis was rooted in slavery, the Civil War began as a battle over the fate of the Union. Yet they should also understand that, as the events of the war spurred people to reconsider their views, it became a war to end slavery as well. Lincoln's role as the Union's leader and his iconic status in American memory should be emphasized. Students should also understand that the end of slavery was just the start of a long fight to establish full civil rights for African Americans.

Upper elementary: Students should understand how the division of the country and the fracturing of the political parties allowed states in the North to elect Lincoln, and how the South's rejection of his election sparked secession. They should know that the North believed the Union must be saved to save democracy, and also that Southerners—most of whom were not slave owners—were willing to fight to protect their states from what they saw as outside control. Students should understand Lincoln's role in deciding to expand the war against slavery; they should realize that hard fighting against the South by black troops and the impressive example they set helped convince most Northerners that slavery must be ended forever. Students should realize that those advocating for "radical" Reconstruction tried to keep ex-Confederates from controlling the South by empowering African Americans, but that northern reluctance to press so far helped southern resistance win in the end. The Reconstruction amendments to the Constitution should be remembered for their later importance as the fight for African American rights continued.

SUGGESTED ANCHOR TEXTS

Abraham Lincoln: Lawyer, Leader, Legend by Justine and Ron Fontes
A. Lincoln and Me by Louise Borden
Abe Lincoln's Hat by Martha Brenner
Ben and the Emancipation Proclamation by Pat Sherman
Mr. Lincoln's Whiskers by Karen B. Winnick
Thank You, Sarah: The Woman Who Saved Thanksgiving by Laurie Halse Anderson
The Last Brother: A Civil War Tale by Trinka Hakes Noble
The Silent Witness by Robin Friedman
When Abraham Talked to the Trees by Elizabeth Van Steenwyk

FEATURED ANCHOR TEXT

ABRAHAM LINCOLN: LAWYER, LEADER, LEGEND BY JUSTINE AND RON FONTES

This book was selected because it is an excellent, fact-filled biography of Lincoln. The writing is appropriate for young students, and the details of Lincoln's life are rendered through a variety of illustrations, maps, and rich text. The book also includes common structural elements of an informational text (for example, a table of contents, a glossary, and an index), which are useful for instructing students about how to navigate this type of historical text. As a narrative history, the text exhibits some of the traits of literary text (such as character development); it is useful for teachers to note that the inclusion of narrative writing techniques often enlivens the telling of history.

TEXT STUDY

The following text-dependent questions require close reading and enable teachers and students to focus on the structural features of an informational text, the authors' craft, inferring skills, the usefulness of illustrations, and the power of narrative history.

1. **Study the photograph on the bottom of page 4. What is pictured? What information does the caption provide?**
   - It is a small, log house without windows showing.
   - It has a split-log fence around it.
   - The caption says that it is a "replica" of Lincoln's cabin.

   Note: This replica is a model of Lincoln's real home. The teacher might pause to discuss the meaning of the word replica.

2. **What does the word *humble* mean? How were Lincoln's beginnings humble, as described on page 4? Why do you think the authors chose this word?**
   - The word *humble* can mean "not vain or boastful" when discussing a person. When it is used to describe a home, it means "simple" or "understated."
   - Lincoln lived in a log cabin with a packed-dirt floor and only one window.
   - Lincoln's bed was made of poles, cornhusks, and bearskins.
   - Thomas, Lincoln's father, could barely write his own name, and his mother, Nancy, couldn't read or write at all.
   - The authors probably chose the word *humble* to show that Lincoln was not born into a wealthy or educated family, which could have made his life easier. The authors are preparing the reader to see how Lincoln fought hard to educate himself and to succeed in life.

3. **Why are the illustration and paragraph dealing with slavery included on page 6 of the text?**
   - When Lincoln was living on a farm on the Cumberland Trail, he watched travelers heading west, but he also saw slaves being taken south to be sold.
   - The illustration and the text about slavery explain what Lincoln knew about slavery when he was a boy.

   Note: Teachers might pause at the inset box on page 6 and ensure that students know what slavery is. The inclusion of this information on slavery is important because it sets the stage for Lincoln's future work to free the slaves.

4. **On page 7, Lincoln is quoted as saying that he went to school "by littles"? What did he mean?**
   - He didn't go to school regularly. He went "a little now and a little then." His chores came first, and he had to walk a long way to get to school.

5. **According to page 9, why did Lincoln's father decide to move to Indiana? What effect do you think this had on Lincoln?**
   - Thomas wanted to live in a territory where there were no slaves because he hated slavery.
   - Lincoln may have learned from his father that slavery was wrong.

6. **Describe Lincoln's love of books and his learning from books. Why do you think the authors included these details?**
   - According to page 1, Lincoln would walk fifty miles to borrow a book.
   - He didn't just read the books; he used the books to copy down new ideas and to write about such issues as animal cruelty and "why American government was great."
   - According to the inset on page 10, he studied George Washington and Benjamin Franklin.
   - On page 12, it says that Lincoln also loved imaginative and adventure stories like "The Arabian Nights."
   - The authors probably want to show that Lincoln was very curious and clever.

7. **How did Lincoln learn to give speeches? Why do you think the authors included these details?**
    - According to page 12, he watched preachers and learned how to vary his voice and use his arms to keep the listener's attention.
    - According to page 13, he learned to stand on a stump and entertain audiences with his humor.
    - According to page 15, he went to see the traveling court of a judge and lawyers when it came to town.
    - According to page 17, he asked the town's schoolmaster to teach him the art of speaking clearly—"grammar and elocution."

      Note: *Teachers may want to pause to help students understand what grammar and elocution are—briefly and simply—to help reinforce these concepts and prepare students for their own study of those important skills.*
    - He also joined the New Salem Debating Society to learn to present his opinions.
    - The authors are probably trying to show us that Lincoln was interested in public speaking from a very early age.
8. **At the age of nineteen, what did Lincoln see that horrified him?**
    - According to page 16, while he was visiting New Orleans, he saw slave markets for the first time.

      Note: *The illustration and inset, also on page 16, describe a slave market, telling how people were sold like animals and separated forever from family.*
9. **What two "victories" are described on page 20? Why were they important?**
    - Abe won the state legislator election.
    - He had the capital of Illinois moved to his town, Springfield.
    - These victories showed Lincoln's determination and his ability to be successful.
10. **What can you learn from the map on the bottom of page 21?**
    - There were free states in the northern part of the United States.
    - There were slave states in the southern part of the United States.
    - The territories were neither slave nor free.
11. **According to the text on page 23, how were Mary Todd and Lincoln similar?**
    - They both cared about justice (being fair), politics (being involved in government), and poetry.
    - They each lost their mother when they were young.
12. **According to page 26, what did Lincoln see in Washington, DC, that was shocking to him? Why do you think the authors included this detail?**
    - He saw slave markets there, in the capital of the country.
    - Even though the Constitution said that all men were created equal, there were slaves being sold like animals.
    - The authors probably want the readers to know that Lincoln was becoming very angry about slavery.
13. **While Lincoln was a lawyer, how did he use his talent for reading books to show that a man named Duff did not kill someone? What does this tell us about Lincoln's ability as a lawyer?**
    - According to page 28, a witness said that he saw Duff kill the other man by the light of the full moon. Lincoln used an almanac to show that the moon was only a sliver on the night of the killing. It proved that the witness was lying, and Duff was freed.
    - Lincoln demonstrated that he was a wise and capable lawyer.

14. **In Lincoln's speech, what did he mean by "a house divided"?**
    - The text on page 29 says that he was talking about how America was half slave and half free. He said that it had to be all slave or all free.
15. **After viewing the illustration and reading the caption on page 31, explain how Stephen Douglas and Lincoln were compared to a purebred poodle and a farmyard hound, respectively.**
    - Douglas was like a poodle because he was well dressed and well fed, traveling to each debate in a private railroad car.
    - Lincoln was like a hound because he traveled on a public train and rode a hay wagon to his hotel.
16. **Why was Lincoln's debate with Douglas important?**
    - Slavery became an issue that people talked about.
    - Lincoln proved that he was great at using his words.
17. **When Lincoln ran for president, why did he lose in every southern state?**
    - On the bottom of page 33, it says that Lincoln was "anti-slavery," and on the map on page 21, we see that the South consisted entirely of slave states.
18. **What happened in the South as President Lincoln rode the presidential train to the White House?**
    - Seven states from the South left the United States. They formed their own country and elected their own president.
19. **What was the name of the war that began between the North and the South?**
    - According to page 37, it was called the Civil War.
20. **In the illustration on page 41, Lincoln is reading a famous document. What is it called, and what did it mean?**
    - It is the Emancipation Proclamation.
    - The text says that the word *emancipation* means "to set free" and that the word *proclamation* refers to a formal statement.
    - The text goes on to explain that this document freed slaves in the South and let Northern blacks join the Union army.

    Note: *Teachers might remind students that there had been slaves in the United States since the seventeenth century, underscoring the significance of this event.*
21. **What is the name of Lincoln's most famous speech? How long was it?**
    - Lincoln's most famous speech is known as the Gettysburg Address (page 43).
    - It lasted under three minutes.

    Note: *Teachers might discuss the stated topic of the speech, "the sacredness of American government."*
22. **According to page 45, how did Lincoln die?**
    - After the South surrendered, Lincoln and his wife went to the theater to enjoy a funny play. An actor named John Wilkes Booth snuck up behind him and killed him. The actor and his friends were angry because they felt that Lincoln had "ruined America, and only his death would save the South."

    Note: *Teachers could discuss why some people might think Lincoln had "ruined" the United States.*

23. According to the caption on page 47, what is in the Lincoln Memorial?

- It houses a twenty-foot-tall statue of Lincoln made from twenty-eight blocks of white marble, fitted together to look like one piece.

PERFORMANCE ASSESSMENTS

1. Go back through the text-dependent questions and review each question pertaining to Lincoln's attitudes about slavery and actions against slavery. Have students work together as a class to create an illustrated timeline showing how Lincoln's views on slavery developed over the years until he was able to do something about it as president of the United States. For younger students, this activity could be as simple as documenting three events.

2. Have students each write an expository/explanatory paragraph that shares one text-based truth about Lincoln. Students should state the fact and then support it with details from the text. See standards for more details.

For example, a student could write about how Lincoln worked hard to be a great speaker. Beginning with Lincoln's imitations of a preacher, his practice on a stump, and his viewing of the traveling court, a student could trace Lincoln's journey to becoming a confident debater and a well-known speech-giver as president of the United States.

CONNECTIONS TO COMMON CORE STATE STANDARDS FOR ENGLISH LANGUAGE ARTS

- Questions 1 and 15 each ask students to glean information from an illustration and caption as well as to extrapolate larger concepts from the details therein (RI.K.1,2,3,7; RI.1.1,2,3,7; RI.2.1,2,3,7).
- Question 2 requires students to focus on an important vocabulary word that is related to Lincoln's character. It also asks students to cite evidence from the book that supports the authors' use of the word. Finally, it addresses the authors' craft by asking students to think about why the authors chose a certain word (RI.K.1,2,3,4; RI.1.1,2,3,4; RI.2.1,2,3,4).
- Question 3 asks students to think about why certain information is included in an informational text (RI.K.1,2,3,8; RI.1.1,2,3,8; RI.2.1,2,3,8).
- Question 4 focuses students' attention on a figure of speech (used by Lincoln) that is relevant to understanding an important aspect of Lincoln's education and early life—and therefore his character. Students must describe key details that support their understanding of the use of that phrase (RI.K.1,4; RI.1.1,4; RI.2.1,4; L.K.5; L.1.5; L.2.5).
- Questions 5, 6, 7, 8, and 12 prompt students to recall important details of Lincoln's life and consider their possible effects on Lincoln. Many of them also ask students to consider why the authors chose to include these details (RI.K.1,3,8; RI.1.1,3,8; RI.2.1,3,8).
- Question 13 allows students to focus on the details of an important event in Lincoln's early legal career and explain its significance (RI.K.1,2; RI.1.1,2; RI.2.1,2).
- Question 14 addresses the meaning and significance of an important historical metaphor (RI.K.4; RI.1.4; RI.2.4; L.K.5; L.1.5; L.2.5).

- Question 9 and questions 16 through 23 ask students about key details, also prompting students to consider the significance of the events described in this informational text (RI.K.1,2,3; RI.1.1,2,3; RI.2.1,2,3).
- Question 10 asks students to consider what information they can glean from a map included in the text (RI.K.5; RI.1.5; RI.2.5).
- Question 11 allows students to compare the characteristics of the main "character" in this biography to those of another essential character in the "story." Teachers may want to compare this kind of "character development" to that which is discussed in the standards for literary texts (RI.K.1,2,3; RI.1.1,2,3; RI.2.1,2,3; RL.K.3; RL.1.3; RL.2.3).
- The first performance assessment prompts students to reread and then present key concepts from this informational text. It reinforces sequencing skills and the ability to put events into context (RI.K.1,2,3; RI.1.1,2,3; RI.2.1,2,3).
- The second performance assessment provides an opportunity to write an informative/explanatory paragraph that discusses a key concept and includes text evidence to support a claim (RI.K.1,2,3; RI.1.1,2,3; RI.2.1,2,3; W.K.2,3,7,8,9; W.1.2,3,7,8,9; W.2.2,3,7,8,9).

MORE RESOURCES

HISTORICAL FICTION

Civil War Drummer Boy by Verla Kay

PRIMARY SOURCES

Collection of Civil War images and primary sources (Library of Congress)

Primary sources and images from the Civil War and Reconstruction (National Archives)

Fort Sumter, December 9th 1863, View of South East Angle (Library of Congress)

White flag of truce, 1865 (Smithsonian Institution)

POETRY AND MUSIC

"The Flag of Fort Sumter," song lyrics (Library of Congress)

Songs of the Civil War (Library of Congress)

ART AND ARCHITECTURE

Surrender of General Lee, 1865 (Smithsonian Institution)

Resistance and Recovery: Rebuilding a War-Torn Nation

(1870s to 1890s)

GRADES: K, 1, 2

OVERVIEW

With casualties on both sides numbering in the hundreds of thousands, the North and the South moved at different paces in their respective recoveries from the nightmare of the American Civil War. At the same time, expansion to the West accelerated as new railroads provided a means to move people and goods into newly opened lands, with devastating consequences for the Native American nations that lived there. Advances in machinery and industry took hold, and cities prospered while, conversely, farming products sank in value. Industrialization, however, often brought even harsher conditions for the working poor. Eventually, new labor movements demanded safer working conditions and fairer wages. At the same time, Europe also was experiencing its own population boom, which led to overcrowded cities and towns and few opportunities for work. America shone as a beacon of opportunity to Europeans, but immigrants often encountered discrimination in America and struggled to make new lives in northern cities. African Americans, too, would face new barriers in their quest for freedom: segregation and sharecropping became the way of the "New South," and northern states were far from free of discriminatory practices. Lower elementary students will read *Journey of a Pioneer* and determine the most important character quality of a pioneer, using evidence from the text to defend their opinion. Chief Joseph's "Lincoln Hall Speech" from 1879 gives upper elementary students the context to articulate, in a well-supported informative/explanatory essay, how Joseph made the case for equality.

○ ○ ○

Interested in learning more about this time period? Read a more complete history in the "Era Summaries."

LEARNING EXPECTATIONS

Lower elementary: Students should understand that late-nineteenth-century America became more diverse, but also more divided. Immigrants began arriving in great numbers, but many already living in America did not want them there. Settlers moved west, but the prices of farm goods fell; work could be hard to find, and some industrialists became very rich while their workers stayed very poor. Students should know that discrimination and segregation became rampant in the South.

Upper elementary: Students should understand the enormous strains that the "Gilded Age" brought to America: industry leaders achieved enormous prosperity, but at the cost of poverty for their workers; opportunity brought masses of new immigrants, who then faced discrimination and exclusion; western settlement brought new hope for settlers, but falling farm prices meant deep debt for many of them; and the Plains Indians were nearly destroyed in the process of westward expansion. Students should realize that although the New South represented a modernization of the region, many remained mired in poverty, working for low wages or sharecropping—especially African Americans, who faced increasing discrimination and the rise of open Jim Crow segregation.

SUGGESTED ANCHOR TEXTS

Journey of a Pioneer by Patricia J. Murphy
Building Liberty: A Statue Is Born by Serge Hochain
Cheyenne Again by Eve Bunting
Dakota Dugout by Ann Turner
Dandelions by Eve Bunting
Naming Liberty by Jane Yolen
Prairie School by Avi
The Statue of Liberty by Lucille Recht Penner

FEATURED ANCHOR TEXT

JOURNEY OF A PIONEER BY PATRICIA J. MURPHY

This book, written as a diary, was selected because it is an inviting account of pioneer life. Although the book is historical fiction, the events and travel are based on the diary entries of real pioneers. The author uses a combination of drawings, maps, and informational insets of primary sources to supplement the composite telling of a covered-wagon trip headed west.

TEXT STUDY

These text-dependent questions allow students to read closely a fictional child's account of important historical events. The questions ask students to consider the structural features of an informational text, the author's craft, and several instances of figurative language. The performance assessments give students a chance to convey understanding of the text through opinion and narrative writing.

1. **In the illustrations on pages 4 and 5, who is writing, and what is she thinking about?**
   - A girl is writing with a pen and ink by candlelight. She is thinking about something her dad said to her mom and her while they were eating a meal.
2. **According to the text on pages 4 and 5, who is writing, and what is she writing about?**
   - Olivia Clark of Elk Grove, Missouri, is writing on March 23, 1845. She is describing how her life is going to change because her "Pa" has just announced that they are "moving west to Oregon Territory."

3. **According to page 5, what were the reasons that people were moving to the Oregon Territory?**
   - People were looking for free, open land because small plots of land do not produce many crops.
   - People were looking for a new start because "times are tough."
4. **What can be learned from the caption and the maps on the bottoms of pages 6 and 7? How do the caption and the maps support the text on those two pages?**
   - The map shows the Oregon Trail (from Independence, Missouri, to Oregon City in the Oregon Territory) in the nineteenth century. It shows the rivers and natural landmarks that people would have passed on the trail. It shows the general locations of the Oregon Territory and "Mexican Territory."
   - Although there is no key to explain distance, the caption says that the trail was a two-thousand-mile path and that it was used from 1843 to the 1870s.
   - The caption supports what the text says, that it would "take many months to get there" and that they would travel "long distances through the wilderness."
   - The maps also illustrate the long distance of the trail, especially when comparing the first (older) map of the trail to the "Modern United States" map, which helps confirm how much of the United States the trail covered.
5. **According to the text, what was probably the most important item to pack on the trip west? Use evidence from the text, the inset photograph and caption, and the illustration on pages 8 and 9 to support your assertion.**
   - The most important item to take was probably food.
     - The text says that the mother had filled large barrels with food, and that the family had sold furniture and "anything else that didn't fit."
     - The inset photograph shows how small the inside of the wagon was, the caption saying that food took up most of the room in the wagon and that "many personal items had to be left behind."
     - The illustration shows "Pa" lifting one of the barrels filled with food.
6. **Explain what a "wagon train" was, according to the text.**
   - According to page 13, a wagon train was a group of wagons. The trains were organized with people's skills in mind. You can infer from the listed skills (of doctors, blacksmiths, and builders) that the goal was to help each other as they traveled, constituting what seems to have been a traveling community.
7. **How does Olivia use the word *fall* in two different ways on the bottom of page 15?**
   - Olivia says, "We travel up to 15 miles until night falls—or we fall over."
     - Saying that night "falls" is another way of describing the time when it begins to get dark.
     - People "fall" over when they are so tired that they literally drop to the ground.
   - Olivia is comparing how long the days are to how tired the people are after walking most of the day.
8. **According to the text, why did the travelers put their wagons in a "corral" at night to set up their camp?**
   - According to page 16, the circle of wagons was formed for two reasons: first, to keep their animals *in* the camp, and second, to keep the wild animals *out* of the camp.
9. **From the evidence on pages 18 through 21, what reasons might there have been for traveling in a wagon train instead of making the trip as a one-family unit?**
   - On special nights, the families sang, danced, and made music together.
   - The men of the camp provided protection for the whole camp by taking turns sitting watch.

- People in the train helped others cross rivers.
- If families lost everything in an accident, other families were there to help them.

10. **According to pages 22 and 23, what did Olivia learn about Native Americans?**
    - She learned that Native Americans were not as scary as she thought they would be.

    Note: *In the inset, it is interesting to note that the buffalo stampedes were actually more of a danger to the pioneers than were the Native Americans they would meet.*

11. **What is the main idea of pages 24 and 25? How does Olivia support the main idea with details?**
    - The main idea is that food on the trail was different from food at home.
    - Olivia gives specific details in the text about the food pioneers ate on the trail.
        - Most days they ate cornmeal, beans, rice, and bacon or dried beef.
        - On days without fires, they ate cold meals.
        - If they hunted, they might eat an antelope, a rabbit, or a bird.
        - When they gathered, they ate berries.
    - There are actual photographs of some of the food they ate: dried beef, rice, cornmeal porridge, coarse cornmeal, elderberries, and blackberries.
    - The illustration on the top of page 25 shows pioneers cooking over a fire.

12. **What was hard about crossing the Rocky Mountains?**
    - According to page 26, climbing the steep sides was hard, and pioneers had to lighten their wagon loads by throwing things away—even important items, such as a stove or a trunk.
    - According to page 27, going down the mountain was also hard because they had to tie the wagon to a tree to keep it from heading down the mountain too quickly.

13. **What does Olivia mean by "the trail is filled with goodbyes"?**
    - On page 28, Olivia talks about such tragedies as illness and death.
    - She continues on page 29, talking about people who were struck by lightning, shot in hunting accidents, drowned while crossing rivers, or killed by wagons and buffalo.
    - She ends this section by explaining how families eventually parted ways to settle in different parts of the Oregon Territory.

14. **What did the pioneers do after they arrived in the West?**
    - According to page 30, they chose a plot of land to farm. Then they built a house and began a new life.

15. **According to the "Pioneer Facts" page at the end of the book, why were the pioneers called "emigrants"?**
    - Because the Oregon Territory wasn't actually part of the United States yet, they were thought of as leaving one country and settling in another. The word *emigrant* refers to someone who leaves one country and settles in another.

    Note: *Students may hear the similarity to the word* immigrant, *but this word refers to someone who enters a country from another place. The emigrant leaves, and the immigrant comes.*

PERFORMANCE ASSESSMENT

Give students the following prompt:

- In your opinion, what was the most important characteristic in a pioneer? After choosing the characteristic, write a paragraph citing evidence from this book to support your opinion.

Students should write a paragraph that states their opinion, include two or three relevant reasons or details that support their opinion, use linking words, and provide a concluding statement. At earlier levels, students may draw or dictate their opinion and/or write a label, sentence, or series of related sentences. See standards for more details.

EXTENSION

Ask students to write a journal entry between two journal entries in the book. Tell them to include imaginative details and sensory words, but also to base their writing on facts learned in the text. Ask students to "recount a well-elaborated event or short sequence of events, include details to describe actions, thoughts, and feelings, use temporal words to signal event order, and provide a sense of closure" (standard W.2.3). At earlier levels, students may draw or dictate their narrative piece and/or write a label, sentence, or series of related sentences.

CONNECTIONS TO COMMON CORE STATE STANDARDS FOR ENGLISH LANGUAGE ARTS

- Question 1 addresses the information readers can glean from illustrations (RI.K.7; RI.1.7; RI.2.7).
- Questions 2, 3, 8, 10, 11, 12, 14, and 15 ask students to recall details from the text (RI.K.1,2; RI.1.1,2; RI.2.1,2).
  - Question 11 also asks students to note how the author supports a main idea with evidence (RI.K.8; RI.1.8; RI.2.8).
  - Question 15 also emphasizes a domain-specific vocabulary word (RI.K.4; RI.1.4; RI.2.4; L.K.5,6; L.1.5,6; L.2.5,6).
- Question 4 prompts students to examine a caption and maps included with the text and compare the information in the caption and maps to the information provided in the text itself (RI.K.1,7,8; RI.1.1,7,8; RI.2.1,7,8).
- Question 5 requires that students read closely and draw inferences from the text, from an illustration, and from an inset photograph and caption to draw a conclusion and make a generalization about the historical content presented (RI.K.1,7,8; RI.1.1,7,8; RI.2.1,7,8).
- Question 6 not only emphasizes a key detail in this informational text structured like a diary but also invites students to consider the use of figurative language and the historical significance of a particular phrase (RI.K.1,4; RI.1.1,4; RI.2.1,4; RL.K.5; RL.1.5; RL.2.5).
- Question 7 also asks students to examine the use of figurative language—here, a homograph, *fall* (RI.K.1,4; RI.1.1,4; RI.2.1,4; L.K.1,5; L.1.1,5; L.2.1,5).
- Question 9 requires students to synthesize information in the text and draw a conclusion (RI.K.1,2,3; RI.1.1,2,3; RI.2.1,2,3).
- Question 13, like questions 6 and 7, gives students a chance to examine figurative language while also noting important content (RI.K.1,4; RI.1.1,4; RI.2.1,4; RL.K.5; RL.1.5; RL.2.5).

- The performance assessment and the extension allow students to convey their understanding of important historical content while also practicing the skills of opinion and narrative writing, respectively (W.K.1,3,9; W.1.1,3,9; W.2.1,3,9).
    - The extension also allows students to render their understanding of events in the text in a narrative piece requiring text evidence (RI.K.1,2,3; RI.1.1,2,3; RI.2.1,2,3; W.K.2; W.1.2; W.2.2; and preparation for W.4.9).

MORE RESOURCES

PRIMARY SOURCES

Inspection station at Ellis Island (Library of Congress)

Map of immigration routes (Library of Congress)

Young miners (Library of Congress)

Chief Powhatan talking to John Smith (American Rhetoric)

Photographs of architecture from the late nineteenth century (Library of Congress)

POETRY AND MUSIC

"Give Me Your Tired, Your Poor," Irving Berlin song, 1929 (American-Israeli Cooperative Enterprise)

Uses as its lyrics a poem written by Emma Lazarus in 1883, "The New Colossus," part of which is found on the Statue of Liberty. This song was written for a musical called Miss Liberty *and is one of Berlin's most famous compositions.*

The Next Benchmark: America Is a Global Leader

(1890s to 1920)

GRADES: K, 1, 2

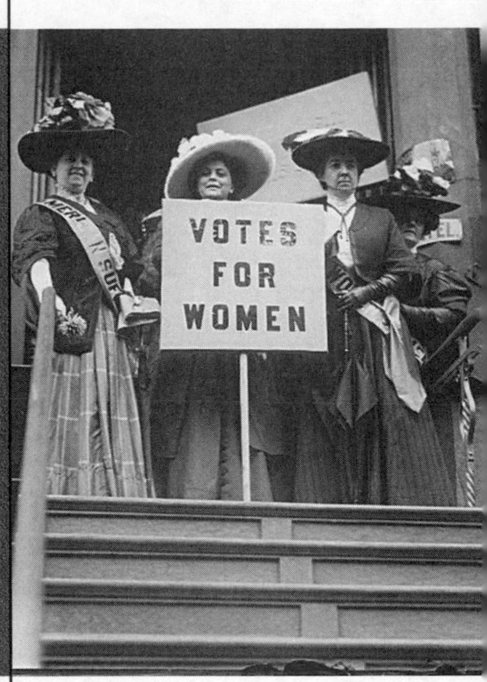

OVERVIEW

The United States grew stronger and more stable as it moved away from the chaos of the Civil War and built economic strength. The time soon came for the nation to take its rightful place as a leader on the world stage. The brief Spanish-American War, America's role in settling the Russo-Japanese War, and the nation's powerful position in world commerce made a forceful global impression. While America's global presence grew, however, there were complex problems that needed to be addressed at home. Progressives challenged the social and economic injustices that still lingered from the Industrial Revolution, and women's rights came to the forefront. But although progress was made on these fronts, racial discrimination continued—and unresolved issues would haunt the growing country for decades to come. Lower elementary students will read A *Weed Is a Flower: The Life of George Washington Carver* and then use evidence from George Washington Carver's biography to explain how Carver was a transformational historical figure. Upper elementary students will read two texts about Ellis Island. They will then explain its significance, drawing on evidence from first-person and historical accounts.

○ ○ ○

Interested in learning more about this time period? Read a more complete history in the "Era Summaries."

LEARNING EXPECTATIONS

Lower elementary: Students should understand that America became more and more powerful in the world as it became more economically important, leading to new engagement as a world power. They should also understand that Americans pressed for bold reforms to address growing social and economic inequality at home.

Upper elementary: Students should understand that American global influence grew steadily as the country became more economically powerful and more closely tied to the rest of the world. They should know that the Spanish-American War launched the United States as a true world power, and that it sparked debate at home over whether America should build an empire overseas. Students should know that Progressivism challenged the social and economic inequities that had dramatically worsened in the Gilded Age, but they should also see the contradictions that marked the Progressive Era: the racial doctrines behind America's foreign expansion also encouraged further discrimination against immigrants and African Americans, even as great Progressive reforms boosted the rights and welfare of ordinary citizens.

SUGGESTED ANCHOR TEXTS

A Weed Is a Flower: The Life of George Washington Carver by Aliki
All Aboard! Elijah McCoy's Steam Engine by Monica Kulling
In the Garden with Dr. Carver by Susan Grigsby
More Than Anything Else by Marie Bradby
The Camping Trip That Changed America: Theodore Roosevelt, John Muir, and Our National Parks by Barb Rosenstock

FEATURED ANCHOR TEXT

A WEED IS A FLOWER: THE LIFE OF GEORGE WASHINGTON CARVER BY ALIKI

This book was selected because it is a beautifully written biography of Carver. Beginning with his early childhood, it is a story of overcoming obstacles. Rich illustrations and highly interesting text combine to help students read about Carver's lifelong contributions in the fields of science and education. When this book is paired with a fictionalized biography of Booker T. Washington, students will be able to see the way two brilliant and courageous men's lives intertwined with purpose at the turn of the twentieth century, a time of great inventiveness and change in America.

TEXT STUDY

The following text-dependent questions require close reading. The performance assessment requires students to conduct research (and compare and/or contrast the lives of the men researched), write informative/explanatory paragraphs (or sentences), and make connections between quoted speech and the information they will have gleaned from the texts.

1. **Study the illustration on page 1. What details can you learn about George Washington Carver's family?**
    - They were African American.
    - The family probably lived long ago because the woman in the illustration is wearing a long dress and an apron.
    - The family included a mother with two children.
    - In the illustration, they look sad.
    - In the illustration, the young boy looks afraid.
2. **What was hard about Carver's early life?**
    - According to page 2, Carver was a sickly child born into slavery. His father died, and his mother was left alone with two children. The author says that because he was the son of slaves, he had no hope for the future.

3. **On page 2, how does the author prove that Carver grew up to be "no ordinary man," in spite of his difficult childhood? What do you notice about each pair of key words?**
   - He turned "evil into good."
   - He turned "despair into hope."
   - He turned "hatred into love."
   - The word pairs are antonyms. Evil and good, despair and hope, and hatred and love are paired as opposite ideas. We learn that Carver did not let the bad things that happened to him keep him from being positive.

     Note: *Even though the word* despair *may be new to young children, pairing it with hope gives it the definition of "hopelessness" or "no hope."*
4. **How did Carver end up motherless?**
   - According to pages 3 through 5, a band of slave kidnappers came to Carver's farm in the night and kidnapped the baby (Carver) and his mother. Although one of Moses Carver's men eventually found baby George Washington Carver and returned him to Moses Carver, his mother was never found.
5. **How does the author explain George Washington Carver's curiosity and how it helped him as a child? Give examples from both the text and the illustrations to support your answer.**
   - His curiosity led him to create things and to be helpful to others.
     - According to page 6, he wanted to know everything about nature. He always asked questions about the rain, the flowers, and the insects. His questions were so good that even the adults couldn't answer them.
     - The illustration on page 6 shows him pointing out a bug to Susan Carver.
     - The illustration on page 7 shows him planting a garden of flowers.
     - The text on page 8 says that he spent hours each day caring for the plants in his garden. It also says that if the plants weren't growing well, "he found out why."
     - He cared for each individual plant "as though it was the only one in his garden," covering the plants in the winter and planting new seeds in the summer.
     - Carver became known as the "Plant Doctor," and people came to ask his advice about their plant problems.
6. **Study the illustration on pages 9 and 10. How does the illustration help the reader understand what Carver desired to do and was not allowed to do? How does the text help the reader understand what Carver desired to do and was not allowed to do?**
   - The illustration communicates that Carver, a black boy, was not a student in the school.
     - A teacher is teaching students in a school building.
     - All of the students are white, and the teacher is white.
     - Although it looks like Carver is the same age as the students, he is standing outside with a flower from his garden. He is looking with curiosity into the window, as if he wants to be inside with the other students.
   - The text says that Carver "wanted to learn and yearned to go to school." It also says that even though slaves had been freed, "schools nearby were not open to blacks."
7. **Why did Carver move from family to family beginning when he was ten years old, and how did he survive?**
   - According to page 9, he left home at a very young age, when he was ten, because he wanted "to find answers to his questions."

- According to page 11, he stayed wherever he could find a school to attend. He found families to live with and worked very hard doing chores to earn his way; "even the smallest chore was important to him."
- The people who took him in "loved this quiet boy who was so willing to help" (page 11).

8. **According to page 13, why was it hard for Carver to get a college education?**
   - Many colleges did not accept black students.
   - He didn't have parents who could help him save for college, so he had to work and save the money for tuition.
   - Even after he got to college, he had to continue to work to stay there, so he opened a laundry and washed other students' clothes.
9. **Aside from his love of plants and gardening, what other talents did Carver possess?**
   - According to page 13, he played the piano.
   - He sang beautifully.
   - He was an outstanding painter and even considered becoming an artist.
10. **According to the text, what were Carver's main contributions in agriculture?**
    - According to page 16, he studied plants, flowers, and soil. He learned the names of the weeds. He experimented with his own plants to find out answers.
    - According to page 17, he taught poor, black farmers how to grow crops better.
    - According to pages 20 and 21, he taught them to grow other crops in addition to cotton, such as sweet potatoes and peanuts. He learned how to make one hundred products from a sweet potato and three hundred products from a peanut.
    - According to page 24, peanuts and sweet potatoes became the two most important crops in Alabama because of Carver's research and teaching.
11. **On page 16, we find the title of the book when the text says that Carver "often said 'A weed is a flower growing in the wrong place.'" What do you think Carver meant by that phrase, and why do you think the author chose to use this phrase in the title?**
    - The phrase means that Carver liked all plants.
    - The phrase means that he always saw the good in things.
    - The phrase is a good summary of Carver's attitude toward life and of how he lived his life.
12. **This book about Carver's life is a moving depiction of slavery and segregation in the American South during that time. Reread the book and explain how society in the American South affected African Americans, and how Carver's actions helped this community.**
    - Carver began his life in slavery in Missouri. After securing his freedom, he still could not study with white children because of segregation. He moved to Kansas and saved money for college, but he had to find one that would allow black students to attend. He moved to Iowa to attend a college that would admit him. He chose a profession to help free, poor, black farmers who were still raising cotton because growing cotton was all they knew how to do. He taught them how to plant other crops as well, and he helped them become more successful. He helped change the quality of life for blacks through his innovations with sweet potatoes and peanuts.

    Note: *You may want to note that when Carver died, segregation was still the norm.*

PERFORMANCE ASSESSMENT

On page 2 of the book, the author describes Carver's uniqueness by saying, "He was a man who turned evil into good, despair into hope and hatred into love." Have students write an expository/explanatory paragraph based on one of those parallel phrases. Give students the following instructions, after reminding them of the author's description:

- Choose one of the text's phrases to introduce your topic. For example, "George Washington Carver was a man who turned despair into hope." Then give two or three relevant supporting details from his story to demonstrate how he turned despair into hope. End your paragraph with a strong concluding sentence.

At earlier levels, students may draw or dictate their explanation and/or write a label, sentence, or series of related sentences.

EXTENSIONS

1. Introduce students to Booker T. Washington by reading the fictionalized biography *More Than Anything Else* by Marie Bradby. As a class, do some additional research to learn about Washington's life. Compare the lives of these two great men (Carver and Washington) who began in slavery and worked so hard in education and science. Look for the ways they were similar and the ways they were different, and discuss them together. Make a (class) list of their contributions and the similar and different ways in which they chose to work toward change. This activity could be turned into an informative/explanatory writing assignment in which students compare and/or contrast the two men. At earlier levels, students may draw or dictate their explanation and/or write a label, sentence, or series of related sentences.

2. Washington said, "There was never a time in my youth, no matter how dark and discouraging the days might be, when one resolve did not continually remain with me, and that was a determination to secure an education at any cost" (from Washington's autobiography, *Up from Slavery*). Discuss as a class how this statement relates to Carver's desire and determination to be educated. This activity could be turned into an informative/explanatory writing assignment. At earlier levels, students may draw or dictate their explanation and/or write a label, sentence, or series of related sentences.

CONNECTIONS TO COMMON CORE STATE STANDARDS FOR ENGLISH LANGUAGE ARTS

- Question 1 asks students to extract information from an illustration (RI.K.7; RI.1.7; RI.2.7).
- Questions 2, 3, 4, and 7 through 10 ask students to identify relevant details to form logical inferences (RI.K.1,2,3; RI.1.1,2,3; RI.2.1,2,3).
  - Question 3 also allows students to note nuances in word meanings and relationships (RI.K.4; RI.1.4; RI.2.4; L.K.5; L.1.5; L.2.5).
- Questions 2 through 10 require students to cite evidence to support their understanding of key details and concepts (RI.K.8; RI.1.8; RI.2.8).
- Question 11 allows students to consider the author's purpose by examining the title of the book and making connections between the title and concepts addressed in the book (RI.K.4,6; RI.1.4,6; RI.2.4,6).

- Questions 5 and 12 offer students opportunities to focus on rereading and retelling while also noting connections between events and larger concepts addressed in the book (RI.K.1,3,6; RI.1.1,3,6; RI.2.1,3,6).
- Question 6 asks students to synthesize information from both an illustration and the text and to explain the events described, citing evidence from both (RI.K.1,2,3,7; RI.1.1,2,3,7; RI.2.1,2,3,7).
- The performance assessment requires students to examine the use of an important phrase in the text as well as characterization techniques. It asks students to write an informative/explanatory paragraph (or sentences). Students must also cite evidence to support their assertions (RI.K.1,2,3,4,8; RI.1.1,2,3,4,8; RI.2.1,2,3,4,8; W.K.2; W.1.2; W.2.2).
- The first extension gives students a chance to compare two different texts and characters that address similar time periods and concepts. (RI.K.9; RI.1.9; RI.2.9; W.K.3; W.1.3; W.2.3; SL.K.1; SL.1.1; SL.2.1).
- The second extension gives students a chance to examine a quotation from one informational text and consider how it might apply to another informational text studied (SL.K.1; SL.1.1; SL.2.1; W.2.2).

MORE RESOURCES

PRIMARY SOURCES

Wreckage of the USS *Maine* at the second anniversary, 1900 (Smithsonian Institution)

Procession accompanying Theodore Roosevelt's campaign in Chicago, 1912 (Library of Congress)

Photographs of Hawaiian people and activities, 1880s–1890s (Smithsonian Institution)

National Association for the Advancement of Colored People (NAACP) advertisement, 1920 (Ohio Historical Center Archives Library)

"Jailed for Freedom" women's suffrage pin, 1917 (Smithsonian Institution)

Portrait of W.E.B. Du Bois, 1911 (Smithsonian Institution)

Portrait of Al Capone, 1925 (National Portrait Gallery)

POETRY AND MUSIC

"The More I See of Hawaii, the More I Like New York," 1917 (Duke University Library)

"Women's Political March," musical score, 1911 (Library of Congress)

"Jakerloo Jazz," sheet music, 1919 (Classic Ragtime Piano)

Early Tin Pan Alley music recordings (Library of Congress)

USEFUL WEBSITES

"Legends of Tuskegee" (National Park Service)

"Theodore Roosevelt the Young Naturalist," video (American Museum of Natural History)

The Great War: Rallying American Patriotism

(1914 to 1929)

GRADES: K, 1, 2

OVERVIEW

At first a reluctant participant, the United States entered Europe's Great War in 1917 when events forced President Woodrow Wilson's hand. In the decade following the war, prosperity and cultural expansion gave rise to the Roaring Twenties and the Jazz Age. But though post-war prosperity was good for some, the divide continued to widen between those who "had" and those who "had not"; immigrants flooded the country, and the ideas of many Americans of what their country should be were challenged. After reading *Bessie Smith and the Night Riders*, lower elementary students will be asked to determine whether or not the protagonist was a hero and to defend their opinion using evidence from the text. Upper elementary students will explore the accomplishments of the American automaker in *Henry Ford: Putting the World on Wheels* and use the evidence from his biography to articulate and defend their opinion on what character trait was most integral to Henry Ford's success.

○ ○ ○

Interested in learning more about this time period? Read a more complete history in the "Era Summaries."

LEARNING EXPECTATIONS

Lower elementary: Students should understand that the First World War—a devastating global conflict in which the United States became embroiled—ushered in a period of dramatic prosperity and wilder culture (the Roaring Twenties), but that prosperity left many people behind and threatened many Americans' ideas of what the country should be.

Upper elementary: Students should know that America was reluctant to be drawn into the First World War, but that Germany's provocations became more than most were willing to accept. They should understand that the war, once America finally entered it, helped propel the United States to greater global prominence—even though American hopes of a noble and lasting peace came to nothing. Students should be aware of the great prosperity of the post-war decade and of the less restrained society of the Jazz Age, but they should also know that runaway prosperity left many behind and that the Jazz Age sparked a backlash from more traditional forces.

SUGGESTED ANCHOR TEXTS

Bessie Smith and the Night Riders by Sue Stauffacher
Hanging off Jefferson's Nose: Growing Up on Mount Rushmore by Tina Nichols Coury
Knit Your Bit: A World War I Story by Deborah Hopkinson

FEATURED ANCHOR TEXT

BESSIE SMITH AND THE NIGHT RIDERS BY SUE STAUFFACHER

This book was selected because it shares both the historical account (in the author's note) and a fictionalized account of Bessie Smith, a blues singer in the early 1900s, who had an encounter with the Ku Klux Klan in July 1927. Young learners will see the differences between historical fiction and nonfiction, but they also will come to see how truth may be revealed in both genres.

TEXT STUDY

Close reading of both informational text and historical fiction here introduces the important concept that authors may write different kinds of historical accounts for different purposes. Close reading of historical fiction gives teachers a chance to emphasize important aspects of analyzing literary text that are delineated in the Common Core State Standards for English language arts, while at the same time conveying important historical content. It introduces the power of narrative history to students at an early age.

1. **According to the illustration on pages 1 and 2, what is happening at the beginning of this story?**
   - In the illustration, a group of people are eagerly going toward an arriving train. Many of them are waving, suggesting that they are greeting the train with enthusiasm. People's facial expressions are happy. A poster advertising a Bessie Smith performance is visible. It contains the words *world famous* and *live*. A little girl is running to join the crowd.

   Note: Students could use these clues to infer that Smith has just arrived on a train, and that the crowd is excited to see her. Students may also note that there are both African Americans and whites in the crowd, suggesting the singer's wide popularity at the time.

2. **Read the text on pages 1 and 3. Describe the setting where this story takes place. Why is it important to the characters in the story?**
   - From the text on page 1, we know that the place is Concord, and it is Smith who is arriving by train. She is the most famous blues singer in the South, and possibly the world.
   - According to page 3, the train in which Smith rode was "twice as big and three times as fine as the one the rich folks rode in from Atlanta." Smith must be important and famous.

   Note: Teachers might simply ask younger students, "Who is telling the story?" and expect students to say something like, "The little girl." Teachers might also ask, "How do we know it is she who is telling the story?"

3. **From pages 3 and 4, how does the reader know that Smith was a successful performer?**
   - The train car was made especially for her and had a big sign with her band's name on it: "Bessie Smith and her Harlem Frolics."
   - Smith carried herself with style, wearing a bright red dress and a feather boa.
4. **According to the clues on page 6, what are "the blues"?**

   Note: *Teachers might first ask students if they have ever heard of "the blues" to see if students know what it means or implies.*
   - Smith sang as if her heart were breaking, so the songs must have been sad.
   - The songs contain words like *lonely*, and have such lyrics as "I'll give the world if I could only/Make you understand."

   Note: *Teachers might help students understand that the second line of the song lyric conveys a sense of frustration, which often makes people sad or "blue."*
5. **Why was Emmarene Johnson, the narrator, unable to go to Bessie's show? How do the text and illustrations explain how she solved her problem?**
   - On page 7, the narrator says that she had no shoes or "Sunday dress" to wear, nor the money to buy a ticket.
   - On pages 7 and 9, the narrator explains that she hid in the woods close to the tent where Smith was performing, and then peeked into the tent after the last person had gone inside.
   - The illustration on pages 9 and 10 shows clearly the distinction between barefooted Emmarene outside the tent and the people with fine shoes inside the tent.
   - The illustration on pages 11 and 12 shows Emmarene looking in the tent while the concert is going on.
6. **According to the text and illustrations on pages 13 through 16, who were the people coming toward the tent, and what were they doing? How does the text help you identify the strange visitors?**
   - The illustrations show people dressed in white costumes who are riding horses. The costumes have holes for eyes and pointed hats. The people are carrying fire torches. Two of the people are pulling out the tent stakes that hold the tent to the ground.
   - On page 13, Emmarene identifies the men as "Night Riders" and says that they are coming for Bessie.
   - The text on page 15 says that the Night Riders are known only for causing trouble.
   - The illustration on pages 15 and 16 shows people who are bewildered.
7. **How did Smith respond to the Night Riders' coming to cause trouble? How was her response different from the others' responses? Was she scared?**
   - According to page 15, instead of running from trouble (the Night Riders), she headed right toward them.
   - According to pages 17 through 23, instead of being intimidated by their frightening threat of burning down the tent with "all those black folks" inside, she shouted at them to run; instead of hiding from them, she confronted them. Then she flapped her arms and let out a deep moan. The shimmery dress reflected the light from the fire, and she looked "like a pearly bright phoenix bird rising up to the Promised Land."

   Note: *Teachers might explain what the mythology of the phoenix is and what the "Promised Land" is, and discuss the significance of the simile in this context—especially the use of the adjective* pearly *to describe the phoenix bird.*

- Note: *Teachers can guide students to understand that Smith kept her composure even though she must have been scared, which shows Smith's strong character.*

8. **The word *Klansmen* is used for the first time on page 23. To whom is the author referring?**
   - The author is using another term for the same group of people, the Night Riders.

   Note: *This term will be revisited in questions 9 and 11 as well as when students study the author's note.*

9. **On page 23, how does the author use words and phrases to show the Klansmen's response to Smith? How do these words and phrases help the reader imagine the scene?**
   - The words and phrases the author uses create a sense of the complete panic and confusion felt by the Klansmen, which caused them to leave as quickly as possible.
     - The leader's horse "reared right up" at the sight of Bessie.
     - The leader's torch grazed the back of the horse and "set it off like a firecracker."
     - Other horses "bolted."
     - "Torches got dropped," and "a couple sheets caught fire."
     - Klansmen were "yelping up a storm" as they "took off" back into the woods.

10. **What lesson did Emmarene learn from Smith that night? What does she say that explains what she learned?**
    - She learned to confront trouble instead of running away from it.
    - According to page 27, she learned that "you can look the devil in the eye and spit on the ground."
    - She "decided that if Bessie Smith wasn't gonna take no mess, neither was Emmarene Johnson."

    Note: *Teachers might discuss with students what it means to "look the devil in the eye and spit on the ground" and to "take no mess," examining the power of figurative language.*

11. **Read the informational text in the author's note located at the back of the book on pages 29 and 30. What is the purpose of the author's note? What does it tell us that the story does not?**
    - The author's note explains the historical facts about the event described in the story.
    - It gives additional information about the event that the story does not provide.
    - It suggests more books to read for those interested in learning more about Smith.

    Note: *Teachers might explain that many works of historical fiction include an author's note to give readers more information about the historical facts.*

12. **According to the author's note, who were the Night Riders?**
    - They were the Ku Klux Klan (KKK), a group of people who terrorized southern blacks and whites who disagreed with them about the rights of African Americans and whites who sympathized with them.
    - They wore white sheets and came out at night to set fire to homes and lynch men, accusing them of crimes they did not commit. People were very afraid of them.

    Note: *Teachers might explain that the KKK terrorized other people too—people with whom they disagreed, such as those whose religion was different from theirs.*

13. **According to the author's note, how did traveling in a custom train car make life easier for Smith and her fellow performers?**
    - During this time in history, few hotels accepted black performers. Performers could use train cars to travel in, to carry their equipment and tents, and to sleep in at night while performing in different cities.

14. According to the true account of the story in the author's note, how might Smith's actions that July evening have saved lives?

- Six Klansmen had come to the tent and had begun pulling up the stakes holding down the tent. It is likely that the Klansmen intended to harm the people in the tent. She ran out and told the men, "You just pick up them sheets and run." They did. She showed she was not afraid of them and may have saved hundreds of innocent lives.

15. In her note on page 30, the author calls what Smith did "a selfless act of heroism." What is she saying about Smith?

- Smith's actions were selfless, according to the note, because the men were very frightening and most people were too afraid to stand up to them. She thought not of herself, but of others. She was a hero because she saved others, even when her prop boys ran off afraid. Her heroic actions inspired others, just as the narrator was inspired.

  Note: Teachers could do a "parts of speech" table or chart with students that shows the differences between (and relationships among) such words as hero, heroic, *and* heroism.

PERFORMANCE ASSESSMENT

After reading both accounts of this Smith story–the fictionalized account in the picture book and the account in the author's note that follows–ask students to write an opinion paragraph about Smith. Pose the following question:

- Would you call Bessie Smith a hero? Why or why not?

Students should write a sentence that introduces their opinion, provide two or three relevant supporting details to support their opinion, and close with a concluding sentence that restates their opinion. At earlier levels, students may draw or dictate their opinion and/or write a label, sentence, or series of related sentences. See standards for more details.

EXTENSION

Have students listen to the music of another blues musician of this time, such as Duke Ellington or Louis Armstrong. Then read aloud a biography or biographical story about the musician. As a class, record interesting information about the musician (if applicable, note how he or she was similar to and/or different from Smith). Have students write an informative/explanatory paragraph that summarizes the key details about the musician's life and music. Students should write a sentence that states who the musician is and why he or she is important, provide two or three relevant supporting details to support their assertion, and close with a concluding sentence that restates their introductory statement. At earlier levels, students may draw or dictate their opinion and/or write a label, sentence, or series of related sentences. See standards for more details.

CONNECTIONS TO COMMON CORE STATE STANDARDS FOR ENGLISH LANGUAGE ARTS

- Question 1 asks students to consider how text and illustrations work together to convey historical information as well as to establish the plot and point of view for this story (RL.K.1,2,3,6,7; RL.1.1,2,3,6,7; RL.2.1,2,3,6,7; RI.K.1,2,3,6,7; RI.1.1,2,3,6,7; RI.2.1,2,3,6,7).

- Question 2 asks students to infer key information from both the text and an illustration (RL.K.1,7; RL.1.1,7; RL.2.1,7).
- Question 3 requires students to infer information from song lyrics included in the text (RL.K.1,4; RL.1.1,4; RL.2.1,4; L.K.5; L.1.5; L.2.5).
- Questions 4 and 5 require students to identify key details and infer others from both the text and the illustrations (RL.K.1,2,3,7; RL.1.1,2,3,7; RL.2.1,2,3,7).
- Questions 6 and 7 give students a chance to learn how characterization and the use of figurative language may enhance the recounting of historical content. They also ask students to explain key details from the story (RL.K.1,2,3,4; RL.1.1,2,3,4; RL.2.1,2,3,4; L.K.5; L.1.5; L.2.5).
- Questions 8, 9, and 10 require students to use evidence from the text (what characters say) to demonstrate understanding of key details and concepts. They also direct students' attention to the author's use of strong figurative language (RL.K.1,2,3; RL.1.1,2,3; RL.2.1,2,3; RI.K.4; RI.1.4; RI.2.4; L.K.5; L.1.5; L.2.5).
    - Question 9 also allows students to compare and contrast informational text with literary text on the same topic, prompting them to note the purpose of an author's note in a work of historical fiction. It also directs students' attention to the author's use of figurative language (RL.K.2,4,5; RL.1.2,4,5; RL.2.2,4,5; RI.K.1,2,3,6,9; RI.1.1,2,3,6,9; RI.2.1,2,3,6,9; L.K.5; L.1.5; L.2.5).
- Questions 11 through 15 offer students a chance to note key details and concepts from informational text and offer teachers a chance to explicate the historical content (RI.K.1, 2,3,5,6; RI.1.1,2,3,5,6; RI.2.1,2,3,5,6).
- Question 14 asks students to consider a character's actions as well as the implications of a phrase that describes the character's actions (RL.K.3,4; RL.1.3,4; RL.2.3,4; L.K.5; L.1.5; L.2.5).
- Question 15 also invites students to extrapolate from what they have read to discuss the significance of the text and its historical content. It also gives students a chance to discuss various forms of words using the same root (such as *hero*, *heroic*, and *heroism*) (RL.K.2; RL.1.2; RL.2.2; L.K.1,4; L.1.1,4; L.2.1,4).
- The performance assessment asks students to write an opinion paragraph demonstrating their understanding of events in the story and their implications (W.K.1; W.1.1; W.2.1).
- The extension, which incorporates listening to music, asks students to read a related biography or biographical story and write an informative/explanatory paragraph about a musician (RI.K.1,2,3,6,8; RI.1.1,2,3,6,8; RI.2.1,2,3,6,8; SL.K.1; SL.1.1; SL.2.1; W.K.2,8; W.1.2,8; W.2.2,8).

MORE RESOURCES

PRIMARY SOURCES

Photograph of a 1920s car assembly line (Library of Congress)

Photo of the HMS *Lusitania*, taken between 1907 and 1915 (Library of Congress)

Zimmermann Telegram, 1917 (National Archives)

"Your Work Means Victory" poster, 1917 (Smithsonian Institution)

Photograph of Langston Hughes, 1925 (Smithsonian Institution)

POETRY AND MUSIC

"The Negro Speaks of Rivers," a Langston Hughes poem, set to music, 1949 (Library of Congress)

Warren Harding campaign song, 1920 (Library of Congress)

"Charleston Rag," ca. 1917 (Library of Congress)

"Playlist: Temperance & Prohibition" (Library of Congress)

ART AND ARCHITECTURE

Boston Avenue Methodist church–example of art deco architecture, 1928

Prosperity Has Its Price: Economic Collapse and World War II

(1929 to 1945)

GRADES: K, 1, 2

OVERVIEW

Much of the prosperity of the 1920s was built on a financial house of cards that collapsed in 1929 and plunged the nation into the worst economic situation in its history, the Great Depression. In those hard times, a new vision emerged for the role of government in American life. President Franklin D. Roosevelt aggressively promoted his New Deal legislation, and when it encountered opposition from the U.S. Supreme Court, he attempted–unsuccessfully–to increase the number of justices in an effort to maintain a majority favorable to his policies. The New Deal ultimately established greater federal control of the economy along with a series of basic economic protections for citizens. The collapse of the world's economies generated a widespread state of despair, leaving some nations vulnerable to rising Fascist extremism–which posed a deadly threat to the concept of democracy. The Fascist regimes drove Europe into renewed conflict, and expansionist Japan pulled America into the growing Second World War. This time, Americans would rally together and support their nation's entrance into what became a defense of human freedom across the globe–even as the home front still presented its own challenges. *Finding Daddy: A Story of the Great Depression* gives lower elementary students a glimpse into the hardships families faced during the Great Depression through the eyes of a young girl named Bonnie. Students will craft well-supported opinions on whether or not Bonnie was strong. The strength of the relationship between a British and an American leader is profiled in *Franklin and Winston: A Christmas That Changed the World*. Upper elementary students will read this narrative description along with an informational text about World War II, writing essays comparing and contrasting the ideological differences between the Axis and Allied forces.

○ ○ ○

Interested in learning more about this time period? Read a more complete history in the "Era Summaries."

LEARNING EXPECTATIONS

Lower elementary: Students should understand that the sudden collapse of the economy caused the new president, Roosevelt, to fundamentally change the role of the government in American life, using federal powers to protect citizens from disaster. They should know that World War II pitted the United States against dangerous enemies that threatened all human freedom, and that the war pulled most Americans together in what they saw as a great cause, even as some minorities were treated unfairly.

Upper elementary: Students should understand that the boom of the 1920s collapsed suddenly, dragging the country—and the world—into the Great Depression. They should realize that Roosevelt's New Deal changed the role of government in American life, authorizing the use of federal power to establish basic economic security and protections for citizens. Students should know that despair over the Depression helped create dangerous political movements in Europe; and they should also know that despite strong reluctance in the United States to become involved in Europe's war, Roosevelt's determination to stop Fascist Germany—and Japan's determination to drive the United States from the Pacific—helped pull the United States into the war anyway. Students should understand that the war united most Americans on the home front, but that some—particularly Japanese Americans and African Americans—suffered from the prejudices of the broader society.

SUGGESTED ANCHOR TEXTS

Finding Daddy: A Story of the Great Depression by Jo and Josephine Harper
Born and Bred in the Great Depression by Jonah Winter
Josephine's Dream by Joan Betty Stuchner
Lily's Victory Garden by Helen L. Wilbur
Seabiscuit: The Wonder Horse by Meghan McCarthy
Sky Boys: How They Built the Empire State Building by Deborah Hopkinson
The Unbreakable Code by Sara Hoagland Hunter
Wind Flyers by Angela Johnson

FEATURED ANCHOR TEXT

FINDING DADDY: A STORY OF THE GREAT DEPRESSION BY JO AND JOSEPHINE HARPER

This is a beautifully written and illustrated piece of historical fiction. It tells the story of a young girl who experiences the onset of the Great Depression. The story honestly confronts some of the struggles that families faced during that defining time in American history. The endpapers exhibit important and nicely crafted features of an informational text, such as a glossary, photographs of professional singers and actors, lyrics from songs of the era, and a timeline illustrated with photographs.

TEXT STUDY

These text-dependent questions ask students about such elements as character development; key details as they relate to main ideas; the power of illustrations and word choice; and even additional features, such as song lyrics. The questions are designed to help students glean information from various aspects of the text. One of the performance assessments gives students a chance to conduct further research using informational texts about the era addressed in the story and to write an opinion paragraph about the story with that context in mind.

1. **What evidence do the authors provide for the reader that Bonnie was not comfortable singing in front of other people?**
   - According to page 6, the teacher asked Bonnie to sing in front of her classmates.
     - The first sentence of the book is, "Bonnie couldn't do it."
     - The authors say that she "walked slowly to the front of the room."
     - The authors say, "Her hands trembled. Her breath was quick, and her throat closed tight. Not a single note would come out. Bonnie looked at the floor." She couldn't face the crowd, even though she knew them.
     - "She felt her face flush hot," the text says, and Bonnie "wanted to hide." Finally, "she shook her head, and ran back to her seat."
2. **What details do the authors provide that explain what family life was like for Bonnie and her parents?**
   - According to pages 8 and 9, Bonnie played after school, and her father would come home to join the game of hide-and-seek.
   - According to pages 10 and 11, Bonnie's mother made a nice meal for supper with hot biscuits, chicken, green beans, and apple pie.
   - According to pages 12 and 13, the family made music together with a fiddle and sang together after supper.
   - The last sentence on page 12 summarizes: "They had fun."
3. **What words, phrases, and sentences in the text on page 14 support the first sentence: "But things began to change at Bonnie's house"?**
   - "Daddy stayed home more."
   - "Something felt wrong."
   - "Daddy looked worried all the time, even when he smiled."
   - "They didn't have chicken or apple pie anymore."
   - They moved from their "pretty house" into a "sad little house with paint peeling."

   Note: *Teachers might ask students to restate the details about what life had been like before to underscore the contrasts.*
4. **How does the illustration on page 15 support the description of Bonnie's father on page 14?**
   - The reader can see that the father looks "worried" and "sad," as the text describes him.
   - The illustration is in sharp contrast to page 9's picture of pure joy, and the house depicted on page 15 looks darker than, and not as nice as, the one on page 11.
5. **According to the text, what is meant by the word *shanty* on page 16?**
   - The narrator uses the word to describe the house in which they now lived.
   - On page 15, the house is described as a "sad little house with paint peeling off the door."

- The glossary in the back of the book explains that a shanty was "a makeshift shelter without electricity or running water."

6. **Read the lyrics to "Happy Days Are Here Again," located on the inside back cover. What are some of the words and phrases in the song proving to Bonnie that the song wasn't true for them, as described on page 16?**
   - The song says the "sad times" and the "bad times" are gone. "We are rid of you at last."
   - The "cloudy gray times" are "a thing of the past."
   - "Happy days are here again."
   - "Your cares and troubles are gone."
   - The statements in the song weren't true for Bonnie's family at all during this part of the story because they did have "cares and troubles" and "cloudy gray times." They were not "rid of" sad and bad times.

   Note: *Teachers might discuss the figurative use of the words* cloudy *and* gray *to describe that time.*

7. **Why did Bonnie's father feel so sad?**
   - According to page 18, he was trying hard to find work but could only earn a few coins a day, if any.
   - The text on page 18 also says, "Times were tough and there wasn't much work now."
   - According to page 20, the neighbor woman insulted Bonnie's father by saying that a man without a job was useless and only pulled his family down.

8. **After Bonnie's father had been gone for a long time, Bonnie thought the following: "*I can always find Daddy, I will find him this time, too!*" (page 22). How do the authors use repetition to draw a parallel with an earlier section of the text?**
   - Earlier in the text, on page 8, the narrator tells the story of Bonnie and her dad playing hide-and-seek in the late afternoons as he came home from work. She says that Bonnie "could always find Daddy."

9. **How does the reader know that the people described on page 26 and pictured on page 27 are poor?**
   - The people are living in tents in the wintertime.
   - The people are huddled around campfires to stay warm.
   - The people are described as "hollow-cheeked," meaning they are thin and don't have enough to eat.

10. **What gave Bonnie the courage to sing her songs at the café?**
    - She wanted to find her father, and she knew she had to do something to get the people's attention at the café.
    - The text on page 32 says, "She needed to ask if they had seen Daddy. Bonnie knew how to do it."

11. **What clues did Bonnie have that it was her father in the back of the café?**
    - Her dog, Caesar, had run back to sit at her father's feet.
    - She saw her father's hat tipped down.

    Note: *According to page 8 in the text, Bonnie spotted her dad because of his hat. This foreshadows the recognition of the hat here in the story on page 36.*

12. **Why were the song lyrics of "Happy Days Are Here Again" now true for Bonnie's family?**
    - Bonnie and her father had come up with a way of making money through their musical talent.
    - "Happy days" were here again for them.
13. **According to the authors' note, what are the two truths about America's Great Depression on which this story is based? How do the photographs support one of the historical facts?**
    - Men abandoned their families because they were unable to provide for them.
    - People used their talent during the Depression to make money.
    - The photographs are of people who became famous actors or singers during the Depression.
        - The photographs include images of Ella Fitzgerald, Dickie Moore, Judy Garland, Shirley Temple, Mickey Rooney, and Woody Guthrie, all of whom became professional singers or actors during the Depression.
14. **How does the glossary in the back of the book help the reader understand the Great Depression timeline in the front of the book? Choose two examples to support your conclusion.**
    - The timeline depicts the ordered story of the Great Depression, with short captions to tell more about the photographs.
    - The glossary defines the words or phrases that are used in the timeline.
    - Some examples of the way the glossary supports the timeline are as follows:
        - In 1929, Black Tuesday happened. The glossary defines *Black Tuesday* as "October 29, 1929, the day the Wall Street stock market crashed."
        - The 1932 section of the timeline makes reference to Roosevelt's New Deal. The *New Deal* is defined in the glossary as "the economic recovery program of President Franklin Delano Roosevelt's administration."
        - 1932 also shows the Civilian Conservation Corps (CCC) at work. The glossary defines the CCC as "a federal government program that hired two million Americans to plant trees and to create campsites in the national parks and forests."

PERFORMANCE ASSESSMENTS

1. Ask students to write an opinion paragraph in which they state whether they think Bonnie was strong or not. Ask them to cite examples that support their assertions. Prior to this assignment, you could help students conduct simple research on the Great Depression by providing them with some simple texts that describe what happened. In this way, they might learn more facts about the causes and course of the Great Depression, developing a deeper appreciation for the context of Bonnie's plight. Students should write a sentence that states their opinion, provide two or three relevant reasons or details that support their opinion, use linking words, and provide a concluding statement. At earlier levels, students may draw or dictate their opinion and/or write a label, sentence, or series of related sentences. See standards for more details.

2. Give students the following task:

- Study the lyrics of a few of the songs mentioned in the final endpaper of the book. Choose one of the popular songs to listen to, and explain why that song may have been popular during times that were so hard for Americans.

CONNECTIONS TO COMMON CORE STATE STANDARDS FOR ENGLISH LANGUAGE ARTS

- Question 1 asks students to pay close attention to the details of the main character's behavior, from which they can infer her feelings (RL.K.1,2,3; RL.1.1,2,3; RL.2.1,2,3).
- Similar to question 1, question 2 asks students to pay close attention to details—this time about the setting and characters' actions—from which they can infer important information about the plot and characters (RL.K.1,2,3; RL.1.1,2,3; RL.2.1,2,3).
- Question 3 prompts students to locate evidence for the authors' own assertion in the text. Teachers may also take this opportunity to help students practice the skills of comparing and contrasting different aspects of a story (RL.K.1,3,5; RL.1.1,3,5; RL.2.1,3,5).
- Question 4 encourages students to look closely at an illustration and to compare the information in the illustration to what the text says. Students also compare illustration and text (RL.K.1,7; RL.1.1,7; RL.2.1,7).
- Question 5 focuses on a key word, asking students to use multiple aspects of the story (for example, the surrounding text and the glossary) to determine the meaning of that word (RL.K.4; RL.1.4; RL.2.4; L.K.5; L.1.5 L.2.5).
- Question 6 asks students to examine the lyrics of a song used in the text. This question helps deepen students' appreciation for the characters' plight by asking them to compare the experience of the characters to that which is described in the song (RL.K.1,3,4; RL.1.1,3,4; RL.2.1,3,4).
- Questions 7, 9, and 11 require students to make simple inferences from evidence in the text (RL.K.1,2,3; RL.1.1,2,3; RL.2.1,2,3).
    - Question 11 also provides teachers with a chance to introduce the technique of foreshadowing.
- Question 8 asks students to consider the authors' craft and to describe why a certain phrase is repeated (RL.K.3,4; RL.1.3,4; RL.2.3,4).
- Question 10 speaks to the main character's motivation and asks students to cite evidence for it (RL.K.1,2,3; RL.1.1,2,3; RL.2.1,2,3).
- In conjunction with question 6, question 12 offers students a chance to compare various plot incidents and note how the plot has developed. It also asks students to infer information from song lyrics and compare the lyrics to the details and events in the story (RL.K.1,2,3,4; RL.1.1,2,3,4; RL.2.1,2,3,4).
- Questions 13 and 14 give students a chance to examine and understand the relationship between two structural features of this informational text—the glossary and the timeline—and how the two components work together to provide important background information and context for the story (RI.K.2,5; RI.1.2,5; RI.2.2,5).
- The first performance assessment gives students a chance to conduct further research on the era addressed in the story using informational texts and to write an opinion paragraph about the story with that context in mind (RI.K.1; RI.1.1; RI.2.1; RL.K.3; RL.1.3; RL.2.3; W.K.1,7,9; W.1.1,7,9; W.2.1,7,9).
- The second performance assessment asks students to do some further research on the music of the era. Students must take into account what they learned from the text in explaining why a chosen song may have been popular (RI.K.1,2,3,9; RI.1.1,2,3,9; RI.2.1,2,3,9; SL.K.1; SL.1.1; SL.2.1).

MORE RESOURCES

HISTORICAL FICTION

Baseball Saved Us by Ken Mochizuki and Dom Lee

PRIMARY SOURCES

New Deal primary sources (Library of Congress)

Anti-Nazi propaganda (Library of Congress)

World War II enlistment poster (Library of Congress)

Photographs of New Deal policies in action (Library of Congress)

Photographs of women and the war effort (Library of Congress)

Enola Gay display (Smithsonian Institution)

Ansel Adams photographs of Japanese internment (Library of Congress)

Portraits of interned Japanese Americans (Library of Congress)

Manzanar Relocation Center from Tower, photograph, 1943 (Library of Congress)

Schoolchildren at Manzanar (Library of Congress)

Martha Graham, world-renowned dancer and choreographer, declining the Nazi invitation to perform at the Olympics, 1936 (Library of Congress)

Choreographers' protest of Nazism, 1937 (Library of Congress)

The New American Dream: Freedom from Tyranny

(1946 to Late 1950s)

GRADES: K, 1, 2

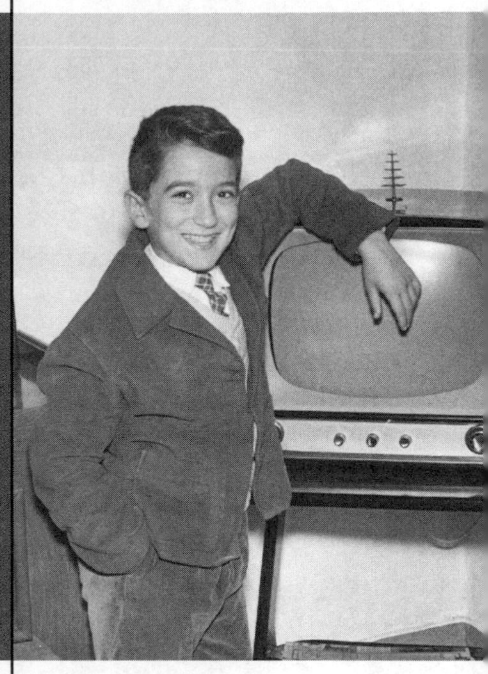

OVERVIEW

Energized by the tempo and technology that had characterized wartime production, and with the termination of the emergency supports of Franklin D. Roosevelt's New Deal, America experienced a new burst of post-war prosperity. As a result, the overall standard of living rose markedly for most Americans. Meanwhile, a new foreign enemy emerged: the Soviet Union (U.S.S.R.). Relations between the United States and the U.S.S.R. had been rocky at best both during and in the immediate aftermath of World War II. Their incompatible views of the world gave rise to the long conflict known as the Cold War. America and its allies faced a genuine threat from Soviet Communism, expansionism, and espionage—yet a Red Scare at home led to the violation of basic freedoms of expression and speech in the name of protecting democracy. But this period also saw a renewed, determined, and sustained push for civil rights and racial equality. Lower elementary students will explore what life was like for children in war-torn West Berlin after 1945 in *Mercedes and the Chocolate Pilot: A True Story of the Berlin Airlift and the Candy That Dropped from the Sky*, leading them to craft an evidence-based informative/explanatory paragraph discussing why the "Chocolate Pilot" was so important to the children he served. *The Wall: Growing Up behind the Iron Curtain* gives older students insight into why author Peter Sis so appreciated the freedom he encountered on the other side of the Iron Curtain.

○ ○ ○

Interested in learning more about this time period? Read a more complete history in the "Era Summaries."

LEARNING EXPECTATIONS

Lower elementary: Students should understand that Americans in the post–World War II world, even as they lived more comfortably at home, saw the new Cold War as a battle between democracy and tyranny and thought that whichever side came out on top would control the future of the world. Students should also know, however, that pursuit of Communists at home led to some people's rights being trampled. They should understand that the 1950s saw the start of a new and dramatic push for the rights of African Americans and other minorities.

Upper elementary: Students should understand that America changed dramatically after World War II. Even as standards of living improved at home, with people moving into suburbs and buying television sets, the United States found itself in a new standoff with a dangerous foreign enemy, the Communist bloc. Students should know that the fear of Communism at home, though not baseless, led to dangerous excesses that for a time threatened the rights of many Americans. But students should also be aware that the 1950s saw the rise of new and determined movements demanding full legal rights for minorities, and that the new civil rights push slowly made crucial gains—in the courts, through legislation, and through social pressure—in the face of harsh opposition.

SUGGESTED ANCHOR TEXTS

Mercedes and the Chocolate Pilot: A True Story of the Berlin Airlift and the Candy That Dropped from the Sky by Margot Theis Raven
Finding Lincoln by Ann Malaspina
Testing the Ice: A True Story about Jackie Robinson by Sharon Robinson

FEATURED ANCHOR TEXT

MERCEDES AND THE CHOCOLATE PILOT: A TRUE STORY OF THE BERLIN AIRLIFT AND THE CANDY THAT DROPPED FROM THE SKY BY MARGOT THEIS RAVEN

This book was selected because it tells the true story of an American pilot, Lieutenant Gail S. Halvorsen, and his "sweet intervention" for the children of West Berlin during the 1948 blockade controlled by Joseph Stalin. Set in the bombed remains of a war-torn city, the well-illustrated story describes the humanitarian aid provided by Americans by telling of such aid's impact on a young German girl named Mercedes. This book lays a simple foundation for later understanding of America's involvement in the Cold War.

TEXT STUDY

These text-dependent questions all require close reading if students are to respond with good answers. Teachers have a great opportunity in several places to emphasize the effect of the author's craft, especially the use of figurative language and other narrative techniques, in this informational text. The performance assessment and extension present opportunities for students to evince their understanding of the text as well as to conduct related research and present those findings orally or in writing.

1. **From the cover illustration and the title and subtitle of the book, explain why the young girl is looking up.**
   - Mercedes, the young girl pictured on the cover, is gazing up toward the sky to look for chocolate candy being dropped by a pilot in an airplane.
2. **Describe the "Berlin 1948" scene illustrated on pages 3 and 4.**
   - The buildings are destroyed, with walls broken down and windows blown out.
   - There are piles of rubble on the streets.

Note: Students may infer that this is a scene created by war, from bombs dropping on a city. (See question 4.) Although students would not be expected to make the connection, this is the scene in West Berlin following the destruction of World War II.

3. **The term *blockade* describes a barrier that is put up to keep supplies from getting into an area where people live. Although the war was over in Germany, the Russians had continued to capture territory and had put up a blockade in and out of West Berlin, Germany, to control it. What does it mean when the author writes, "Eggs were more precious than gold in West Berlin during the Russian Blockade"?**
   - Eggs were food and could be laid by the chickens in the family's backyard.
   - Food was the most valuable thing during the blockade, even more valuable than gold, because people needed food to survive.

   Note: An interesting discussion of just how much food was needed to keep the people of West Berlin alive is on page 2 of the text in the notes titled "The Berlin Airlift."
4. **According to page 7 of the text, what caused the damage to the front steps of Mercedes's apartment? How does this new information shed light on the cause of the damage to the city shown on pages 3 and 4?**
   - The text says the steps were "bomb-splintered."
   - As illustrated on pages 3 and 4, the damage to the city was caused by bombs.
5. **Why does the author call the planes "great soaring grocery stores"? Why did the people of West Berlin call them "Raisinbombers"?**
   - They are called "great soaring grocery stores" because they brought food supplies by air for the people of West Berlin. *Soaring* is a word used to describe the way birds fly, and the author also calls the planes "huge silver birds."
   - The people called them "Raisinbombers" because the groceries they carried included raisins, something the people loved to eat.

   Note: They may have called them bombers because of the recent use of planes in the war, carrying bombs to drop on the enemy cities.
6. **According to pages 11 through 13, how did the candy begin dropping over West Berlin?**
   - An American pilot, Lieutenant Halvorson, was delivering supplies to the Tempelhof airport in West Berlin.
   - One day he began to talk with some children at the end of the runway, and he wanted to give them something.
   - He had only two pieces of gum, so he tore each piece in half to share with four children.
   - He promised he would "drop gum and candy to them from his plane the next day!"
   - This American pilot used handkerchiefs to make "small candy-filled parachutes" to drop from his plane for the children at the airfield.
7. **How did the pilot come to be called "Uncle Wiggly Wings"?**
   - According to page 11, he had told the children to watch for "the wiggle of his plane's wings."

   Note: This name is also alluded to on page 20, where the author writes, "They spotted the wiggle of the Chocolate Pilot's wings!"
8. **How did the people of America help with the Chocolate Pilot's project?**
   - When American people heard about his gifts to the children of West Berlin, they began sending the pilot handkerchiefs for the parachutes.
   - They also sent enough candy to fill two large railroad boxcars.

9. **According to the text on page 17, what had happened to Mercedes's father in the war?**
   - Her father never came back from the war. This probably means he died fighting in the war.
10. **Why is "marshmallow clouds" a wonderful way to describe the candy parachutes dropping from the sky?**
    - Clouds are in the sky, and marshmallows are sweet, so the white handkerchief parachutes carrying the sweet candy were like marshmallow clouds falling out of the sky.
11. **According to pages 22 through 24, why did Mercedes write a letter to the Chocolate Pilot?**
    - Mercedes was very disappointed to miss catching a chocolate bar at the airstrip.
    - She remembered from the newspaper article how children wrote letters to the pilot from America.
    - She wanted the chocolate pilot to drop candy in the garden near the chickens.
12. **On page 25, what does the author mean when she writes that Mercedes's mother was "quietly keeping the thought behind her lips"?**
    - Frau Simon (her mother) was not saying anything out loud, but she was thinking it. She kept the thought inside her head instead of allowing it to become words that her daughter would hear.
    - Even though she mailed the letter for her daughter, Frau Simon did not believe the "busy pilot" had the "time to make every child's dream come true."
13. **How does the story change for the reader on pages 27 through 29?**
    - The reader is invited into a new setting: Halvorsen's world, Rhein-Main Air Force Base in Frankfurt, Germany.
    - The reader sees how the German letters had to be translated for the pilot to read.
    - The reader sees how the pilot read all of the letters and how some of the letters were answered.
    - The reader sees how the pilot was touched by the letters, both laughing and crying at the children's words.
    - The reader also sees how the pilot reacted to Mercedes's letter.
14. **How does the author show Mercedes's excitement at the arrival of her package?**
    - On page 33, it says she "quickly . . . tore into the package."
    - On page 36, the author uses exclamation points to show Mercedes's excitement when she saw the candy. "Chocolate bars! Packs of white and green mint gum! . . . Her Chocolate Pilot had found her at last!"
15. **According to the story, why did the Chocolate Pilot take the time to send the package to Mercedes?**
    - On page 37, it says he wanted to give her "a little joy."
16. **According to the epilogue, how did this story with Mercedes continue?**
    - In 1970, the Chocolate Pilot was invited to the home of a young couple for dinner.
    - When he arrived, he found out that the young wife was Mercedes and that she had kept his letter.
    - He continued to visit her through the years, always adding a little note to the bottom of the original letter.
17. **How did an American community help in the candy drops over West Berlin?**
    - According to page 43, the people of Chicopee, Massachusetts, organized local businesses and schools to collect handkerchiefs, candy, and gum for the people of Germany.

- They collected "11,000 yards of ribbons; 2,000 sheets for chutes; 3,000 handkerchiefs; and 18 tons of candy and gum" (page 43).
- The American airmen dropped two hundred fifty thousand candy parachutes by the time the effort was over.

PERFORMANCE ASSESSMENT

Give students the following task:

- Why was the American "Chocolate Pilot" so important to the children of West Berlin? Draw a picture and write a paragraph to answer this question, citing evidence from the text.

For their paragraph, students should write a sentence that introduces their topic, use facts and definitions to develop points, and provide a concluding statement or section. At earlier levels, students may draw or dictate their explanation and/or write a label, sentence, or series of related sentences. See standards for more details.

EXTENSION

Give students the following task:

- Using the last paragraph of page 43 as a beginning, research the other humanitarian candy drops by American pilots in our more recent history. This book discusses drops "to refugee camps in Bosnia in 1994 and in 1999 to Camp Hope, the U.S.-built shelter for Albanians fleeing from Kosovo." Convey research findings in a formal oral presentation or an informative/explanatory paragraph.

CONNECTIONS TO COMMON CORE STATE STANDARDS FOR ENGLISH LANGUAGE ARTS

- Question 1 asks students to examine the title, subtitle, and cover illustration of an informational text, helping them understand the function of each element and how they work together to convey the main idea of the story (RI.K.5,7; RI.1.5,7; RI.2.5,7).
- Question 2 focuses students' attention on what they can glean about the historical content of the book from illustrations (RI.K.7; RI.1.7; RI.2.7).
- Questions 3 and 5 ask students to interpret an idiom or other kinds of figurative language relevant to the historical content in the text (RI.K.1,2,4; RI.1.1,2,4; RI.2.1,2,4; L.K.5; L.1.5; L.2.5).
- Question 4 prompts students to identify and explain details in the text; it also asks them to relate the details to earlier illustrations in the text (RI.K.1,2,7; RI.1.1,2,7; RI.2.1,2,7).
- Questions 6, 7, 8, 9, 11, 15, and 17 require students to identify and explain details in the text (RI.K.1,2; RI.1.1,2; RI.2.1,2).
- Question 10 explores the effectiveness of a metaphor used in the text (RI.K.1,2,4; RI.1.1,2,4; RI.2.1,2,4).
- Question 12 allows students to consider the author's craft—in particular, the decision to use figurative language to convey a character's reluctance to speak. It also addresses the

author's use of characterization techniques, including in an informational text (RL.K.3; RL.1.3; RL.2.3; RI.K.1,2,4; RI.1.1,2,4; RI.2.1,2,4).

- Question 13 invites students to examine a shift in setting and point of view, including in an informational text (RL.K.3; RL.1.3; RL.2.3; RI.K.1,2,3; RI.1.1,2,3; RI.2.1,2,3).
- Question 14 also asks students about the author's craft, requiring them to explain the language the author uses to convey excitement (RL.K.3; RL.1.3; RL.2.3; RI.K.1,2; RI.1.1,2; RI.2.1,2).
- Question 16 encourages students to recognize the purpose and usefulness of epilogues as they note new information related to the content of the text (RI.K.1,2,3,6,9; RI.1.1,2,3,6,9; RI.2.1,2,3,6,9).
- The performance assessment gives students a chance to summarize the informational text in an informative/explanatory paragraph (RI.K.1,2,3; RI.1.1,2,3; RI.2.1,2,3; W.K.2,9; W.1.2,9; W.2.2,9).
- The extension allows students to conduct further research related to the topic of the text and to convey their research findings orally or in an informative/explanatory paragraph (RI.K.1,2,3; RI.1.1,2,3; RI.2.1,2,3; W.K.2,7,9; W.1.2,7,9; W.2.2,7,9; and, if an oral presentation is included, SL.K.4; SL.1.4; SL.2.4).

MORE RESOURCES

PRIMARY SOURCES

Newspaper article on Joseph McCarthy, 1953 (University of Iowa Libraries)

Julius and Ethel Rosenberg, 1951 (Smithsonian Institution)

Gary Cooper testifying before the House Un-American Activities Committee, 1947 (Library of Congress)

Dwight D. Eisenhower addressing the North Atlantic Treaty Organization, 1963 (Library of Congress)

Political cartoon depicting Mao Zedong and Nikita Khrushchev, 1960 (Library of Congress)

American Ballet Theatre performing in the Soviet Union, 1960 (Library of Congress)

USEFUL WEBSITES

Biography of Gail S. Halvorsen (PBS: *American Experience*)

"The Chocolate Flyer" (Harry S. Truman Library & Museum)

UNITED STATES HISTORY, ERA 17

Communism and Counterculture: The Challenges of the '50s and '60s

(1950s to Late 1960s)

GRADES: K, 1, 2

OVERVIEW

With the United States and the Soviet Union jockeying for position and fighting to gain allies across the globe, the stakes of the conflict between the superpowers were constantly being raised. As more catastrophic weapons were created, the dance between these two nations became ever more complex, their interaction spilling over into developing nations and fueling the race to space. Though war between the superpowers was narrowly averted in the brinksmanship of the Cuban Missile Crisis, a long and draining war by proxy would fester in Vietnam. While this international theater played out, the home front was seeing dramatic political and social change. From the Civil Rights Act of 1964 to President Lyndon B. Johnson's Great Society, this era would deeply change America's social and economic outlook and practices. *Martin Luther King, Jr. and the March on Washington* gives lower elementary students the context to explore the significance of Martin Luther King Jr.'s leadership by listening carefully to his "I Have a Dream" speech and creating a "found poem" featuring the masterful phrases and words spoken by King. Upper elementary students will explore the historical importance of America's first trip to the moon by reading *Moonshot: The Flight of* Apollo 11 and crafting research essays detailing a topic of interest to them or why the trip was historically important.

○ ○ ○

Interested in learning more about this time period? Read a more complete history in the "Era Summaries."

LEARNING EXPECTATIONS

Lower elementary: Students should understand that the Cold War pitted the democratic West against the Communist East, each attempting to dominate the rest of the world; both sides tried to avoid dangerous confrontations that could end up blowing up the world, but there were still close calls. Students should realize that the 1960s brought dramatic social and political change. The fight for civil rights began to change the country's laws, and the federal government increased its support for the poor and the elderly, but many Americans still fought over what kind of country the United States should be.

Upper elementary: Students should understand that with the invention of the hydrogen bomb in the early 1950s, the Cold War became too dangerous for direct fighting between the superpowers, even though tensions sometimes rose out of control—as in the Cuban Missile Crisis. Students should understand that the United States and the Soviet Union instead struggled to win the support of Third World countries and extend their global influence, as each tried to project the more impressive image, including in the space race. Students should realize that America's determination to block Communist expansion led to a difficult and controversial war in Vietnam, which helped spark a youth revolt against the traditional powers in society. At the same time, the federal government increased its support for social justice causes as civil rights activists won new legal victories and as President Johnson pressed for his Great Society programs. Students should understand, however, that such developments sparked backlash from the white South, and from a growing conservative movement opposed to "big government" programs.

SUGGESTED ANCHOR TEXTS

Martin Luther King, Jr. and the March on Washington by Frances E. Ruffin
Freedom on the Menu: The Greensboro Sit-Ins by Carole Boston Weatherford
Martin's Big Words by Doreen Rappaport
My Brother Martin: A Sister Remembers by Christine King Farris
Riding to Washington by Gwenyth Swain
Ruby Bridges Goes to School: My True Story by Ruby Bridges
The Beatitudes: From Slavery to Civil Rights by Carole Boston Weatherford
The Story of Ruby Bridges by Robert Coles

FEATURED ANCHOR TEXT

MARTIN LUTHER KING, JR. AND THE MARCH ON WASHINGTON BY FRANCES E. RUFFIN

This book was selected because it is a compelling account of an important day in history, August 28, 1963, and the one hundred years of racial strife in America that led to the March on Washington and King's famous speech that day. Full-color drawings and photographs are used to give the history continuity and to give the sense of an eyewitness account. The text also proceeds in a clever way, first by placing readers at the march on August 28, 1963, and then recounting important American history that led to that event, touching on the significance of King's giving his speech on the steps of the Lincoln Memorial.

TEXT STUDY

Answering the following questions about this rich and unusually structured text will require close reading from students. The questions help focus students' attention on the structure and power of this well-crafted informational text—a narrative history that addresses a significant event in American memory.

1. **What details can you see in the illustration on pages 4 and 5?**
   - There is a long line of buses heading in the same direction.
   - It looks like some of the people in the back of the line are carrying signs.
   - The setting is Washington, DC, because the Washington Monument is in the background.
   - People are in short sleeves, so it must be warm weather.
2. **How does the author show that people made great efforts to be in Washington, DC, that day?**
   - On page 4, the author says that more than two hundred fifty thousand were "pouring into the city."
   - She tells how they came by many forms of transportation—by plane, train, car, and bus.
   - On pages 6 and 7, she says that some walked from New York City (230 miles), and some came from Chicago by roller-skating for eleven days.
3. **What does the author mean by the expression "pouring into the city" on page 4? Why do you think the author chose the word *pouring*?**
   - People were rushing into the city forcefully, like fluid pouring out of a pitcher or over a waterfall.
   - This word is powerful, making a picture in the reader's mind of a forceful movement.

   Note: *Teachers may introduce here the idea of figurative language—and why authors sometimes use it for effect. Doing so will help scaffold students' understanding of metaphors and other figurative language, introduced formally in subsequent grades.*
4. **What is the setting of this historic event?**
   - The setting of this event is Washington, DC, on August 28, 1963.
   - According to the text and illustration on pages 8 and 9, the crowd is gathering at the Lincoln Memorial and all along the reflecting pool down toward the Washington Monument.

   Note: *If there is time, teachers might pause to teach a bit about the symbolic design of the National Mall.*
5. **Why do you think the author asks a question on page 9? Why doesn't she just tell the reader why the people were there?**
   - Asking a question forces the reader to think more about the significance of the event.
   - It makes the reader more actively involved in the account of events.
6. **How does the author use the setting to tell the story of Abraham Lincoln? What does the author want the reader to learn about Lincoln?**
   - After the author explains the setting of the event (the Lincoln Memorial), on page 10, she shows a close-up illustration of the statue of Lincoln in the memorial. She then takes the opportunity to tell the readers about the Civil War and how Lincoln helped end slavery.
   - The reader learns that although slavery ended one hundred years before, there was still no equality for black people at the time of the march.
7. **According to the text and illustration on pages 12 and 13, why did people come to Washington on this day?**
   - They came to protest against inequality (page 13) and to speak out against something they thought was wrong.

   Note: *Teachers might pause to ensure that students understand the words* protest *and* inequality.
   - The protest signs in the illustrations discuss specific issues of inequality. We see signs about voting, segregation in public schools, civil rights laws, and jobs.

Note: *Teachers might pause to ensure that students have at least a basic understanding of the words* segregation *and* civil rights, *depending on the grade level.*

8. **What is the main idea of pages 14 through 19? How do the key details, photographs, and illustrations support the main idea?**
   - The main idea is that for decades, laws in America dictated inequality for black people.

   Note: *This would be a good place to review the term* Jim Crow, *even though it is not included in this text.*

   - The author gives examples of the inequality through text, drawings, and illustrations.
     - Pages 14 and 15 include information about the laws that kept blacks and whites apart, showing a "whites only" self-service laundry. Segregation in hotels and restaurants is also mentioned.
     - On pages 16 and 17, the illustrator shows how blacks had to sit in the back of a bus, and a photograph depicts "colored" entrances for public places, such as theaters. The text adds that they also had to sit in the balcony at the movies.

   Note: *Teachers might pause to ensure that students understand the word* separate *and perhaps its various uses (that is, as an adjective and as a verb).*

     - On pages 18 and 19, the photographs show different water fountains for "whites" and "colored" people.
9. **Why was it important for the author to put a combination of full-color drawings and old photographs in the text?**
   - The example on pages 16 and 17 shows an old photograph of a movie theater with the "colored entrance" sign, making it a primary source for the time period. The drawing of the bus scene may remind readers of the Rosa Parks story, perhaps inviting them to imagine themselves on the bus.
10. **What evidence does the text provide that people began to demand change?**
    - According to pages 20 through 24, they began to march in protest of the inequality. They had sit-ins in restaurants and theaters where the rule was "whites only." They held signs and sang songs. Some people were put in jail.
    - According to pages 24 and 25, they finally decided to protest all in the same place, in Washington, DC. They chose Washington because it is where the laws are made.

    Note: *Teachers might note the significance of some protesters' being grandchildren and great-grandchildren of slaves, perhaps making them even more devoted to the cause.*
11. **How does the author bring the reader back to August 28, 1963?**
    - On page 26, she uses the word *so*. She is saying that it was because of all of the problems with slavery and segregation as well as the protests in various parts of the United States that everyone needed to come together to protest inequality.
12. **What is the effect of the story's being told in the present tense?**
    - It makes readers feel as if they are there, attending the march in real time.
13. **According to page 26, what was the name of this historic event?**
    - The name of the event on August 28, 1963, was the March on Washington.
14. **Using words and phrases from pages 32 through 36 of the text, describe Martin Luther King Jr.**
    - He was "a preacher, a son of a preacher," a Georgian, and a black person who grew up in the South. He was a protest leader, threatened and jailed for the stand he took.

15. **The text says King is "a man of peace," but he "is also a fighter." The text says he "doesn't use his fists or weapons. He uses words." What do you think the author means? What are some examples from the text that illustrate how he "fights with words"?**
    - The author means that King's words were powerful enough—like punches—to make people change the way they acted.
    - Speech excerpts on pages 36 and 37 show that his peaceful words were powerful weapons.

    Note: *When finished with the text, teachers might pause on page 47 to revisit the concepts discussed here.*

16. **Why was King's speech called the "I Have a Dream" speech? What was his dream?**
    - He repeated the phrase "I have a dream" nine times in his speech.
    - What he was describing was a "dream" because it wasn't happening at the time; he wanted to describe a vision for the future.
    - He dreamed that "[his] four little children will one day live in a nation where they will not be judged by the color of their skin."

      Note: *Teachers might pause to ensure that students understand this phrase and its implications.*
    - He dreamed that one day "little black boys and black girls will be able to join hands with little white boys and girls."

      Note: *Teachers might also introduce the concept of repetition as a rhetorical device in speeches.*

17. **Why do you think the author says, on page 40, that King's voice "rises and falls"?**
    - In a speech, it is a good technique to change the tone and pitch of your voice, depending on what you are saying.

      Note: *Teachers might read the speech for students, modeling where and how King's voice rose and fell. They might also play excerpts from a video of the event. Doing so might help students become aware of rhetorical skills.*

18. **How does the author begin and end the telling of this event?**
    - The story begins with people arriving by bus, car, train, and plane. On page 43, the account of the day ends with people starting back to their cars, buses, trains, and planes.

19. **Why was the protesters' trip home *not* the end of this story?**
    - According to page 44, a law was passed a year later, the Civil Rights Act of 1964, saying that people could not be separated based on the color of their skin.

20. **Reread the book. What did you notice about the structure of the text—that is, the way the story is organized? Why do you think the author tells the story in this way?**
    - The story begins in chronological order and then pauses, going back in time. It is interesting how the author moves the reader through history—back one hundred years; then through the years of segregation; through the times of protest; up to the day of the March on Washington, August 28, 1963; and finally to the Civil Rights Act of 1964.
    - The author wants to give the background of the story to explain why all of the people were coming and why they were willing to be outside in the heat to hear a speech.

PERFORMANCE ASSESSMENT

As a class, reread pages 36 through 41. Discuss the content of King's speech; the dream he had; and the repetition of "I have a dream." Listen to some or all of the actual words of King's "I Have a Dream" speech using the audio on the following site: http://www.americanrhetoric.com/speeches/mlkihaveadream.htm.

Also as a class, create a found poem by extracting favorite words, lines, and phrases from King's speech.

EXTENSION

Beginning with the first mention of "I have a dream" in the speech's transcript, assign the lines to children to practice reading with King's eloquence and delivery. Some students may be able to practice and perform the end section of the speech independently.

CONNECTIONS TO COMMON CORE STATE STANDARDS FOR ENGLISH LANGUAGE ARTS

- Question 1 asks students to consider how illustrations can provide key details and support for the main idea discussed in a text. It also helps students envision the setting (RI.K.1,2,6; RI.1.1,2,6; RI.2.1,2,6).
- Questions 2, 7, 10, 14, and 19 address key details, topics, concepts, and/or events both within and across paragraphs. They ask students to cite evidence from the text to support their answers (RI.K.1,2,3,8; RI.1.1,2,3,8; RI.2.1,2,3,8).
- Question 3 addresses the author's use of a particular expression, why she chose it, and what its effect is on the reader (RI.K.4,8; RI.1.4,8; RI.2.4,8; L.K.5; L.1.5; L.2.5).
- Question 4 asks students to identify the setting of the text (RI.K.1; RI.1.1; RI.2.1).
- Question 5 asks students to consider why the author uses a particular type of sentence for rhetorical effect (RI.K.6; RI.1.6; RI.2.6).
- Question 6 requires that students identify not only key details about the setting of the text but also what the author's purpose was in choosing to tell the story in this way (RI.K.1,2,3,6,8; RI.1.1,2,3,6,8; RI.2.1,2,3,6,8).
- Question 8 addresses a number of connected key ideas and details, as well as the power of the author's craft in structuring and illustrating the text (RI.K.1,2,3,4,6,7,8; RI.1.1,2,3,4,6,7,8; RI.2.1,2,3,4,6,7,8).
- Question 9 focuses more deeply on the author's choice to combine illustrations and photographs. This question helps students think about the relationships among text structure, details, and the historical content and ideas in the text (RI.K.6,7,8; RI.1.6,7,8; RI.2.6,7,8).
- Question 11 asks students to think carefully about the author's craft, especially her choices about structure and diction as they reinforce key details and concepts (RI.K.1,2,3,4; RI.1.1,2,3,4; RI.2.1,2,3,4; L.K.5; L.1.5; L.2.5).
- Question 13 helps students retain knowledge of the name of the important event discussed in this text (RI.K.1; RI.1.1; RI.2.1).

- Questions 15 and 17 challenge students to analyze the author's use of particular phrasing and figurative language both for their rhetorical impact and for their ability to help convey either important aspects of King's character (question 15) or the effect of his well-delivered speech (question 17) (RI.K.4,8; RI.1.4,8; RI.2.4,8; SL.K.3; SL.1.3; SL.2.3; L.K.5; L.1.5; L.2.5).
- Similar to question 13, question 16 emphasizes the importance of an iconic speech in American history by focusing on its name. This question asks students to cite evidence for why the speech is titled as it is, which reinforces its essential historical content and rhetorical power (RI.K.1,2,3,4,8; RI.1.1,2,3,4,8; RI.2.1,2,3,4,8; SL.K.3; SL.1.3; SL.2.3; L.K.5; L.1.5; L.2.5).
- Questions 18 and 19 focus on the structure of the text and the author's choices in organizing it this way (RI.K.5,6,7,8; RI.1.5,6,7,8; RI.2.5,6,7,8).
- The performance assessment asks students to reread, focusing on rhetorical devices in King's speech; it also asks them to write a found poem, giving them a creative way to focus on the most essential content (RI.K.1,2,3,4,6; RI.1.1,2,3,4,6; RI.2.1,2,3,4,6; W.K.3; W.1.3; W.2.3).
- The extension gives students practice with recitation (SL.K.1,6; SL.1.1,6; SL.2.1,6).

MORE RESOURCES

PRIMARY SOURCES

Vietnam War service medal (Smithsonian Institution)

"Nine Rules for Personnel of US Military Assistance Command, Vietnam," 1967 (Smithsonian Institution)

Black Panther Convention, Lincoln Memorial, 1970 (Library of Congress)

Photograph of the *Apollo* 11 launch, 1969 (Smithsonian Institution)

Draft resistance protest sign, 1967 (University of Washington)

Remains of Bikini Island after nuclear testing, 1968 (Smithsonian Institution)

Space race resources (History Channel)

"Soviet Fires Satellite into Space," October 1962 (*New York Times*)

Neil Armstrong's landing on the moon (National Aeronautics and Space Administration [NASA])

John F. Kennedy and Nikita Khrushchev in Vienna (Library of Congress)

Onlookers watching army missiles in Florida (Library of Congress)

United Nations Security Council: meeting on the Cuban Missile Crisis, October 1962 (Library of Congress)

ART AND ARCHITECTURE

Hair: The American Tribal Love Rock Musical, 1967 (Official Website)

> *Written during the time period. The official website features photos of the original cast and really showcases the world of the counterculture.*

Watercolor painting of *Apollo* 11 by Dale Meyers (Smithsonian Institution)

USEFUL WEBSITES

"I Have a Dream" speech recording (American Rhetoric)

History of the *Apollo 11* mission (NASA)

"October 4, 1957: Soviet Union Launches Sputnik Satellite," article (*New York Times*: *The Learning Network*)

"The History of Rocketry and Space Travel" (NASA)

The National Security Archive: "The Cuban Missile Crisis, 1962" (George Washington University)

UNITED STATES HISTORY, ERA 18

Modern Times: Presidential Scandals, Conservatism, and Unrest

(1968 to Present)

GRADES: K, 1, 2

OVERVIEW

Winning by a narrow margin, President Richard Nixon, a Cold War conservative, would nonetheless take up the mantle of Lyndon B. Johnson's Great Society, working with a Democratic Congress to push forward even further social reforms. But despite Nixon's successful efforts to reduce Cold War tensions, his inability to end the Vietnam War plagued his time as president—and his paranoid use of power against his political enemies brought about the Watergate scandal that destroyed his presidency. The aftermath found Americans sharply divided about the country's policies; and the nation's politics would follow suit. Conservatism became reinvigorated and found a leader in Ronald Reagan. Reagan worked to shrink the federal government, bolster military spending, and end the Cold War once and for all. But the end of the Cold War did not signal the end of unrest. America itself would sustain a major terrorist assault on its own soil in the September 11, 2001, attacks and a severe economic recession in 2008. Challenges and perils continue to be a part of the American experience. *America's White Table* deepens younger students' understanding of the sacrifices of men and women in uniform. Older students will gain an understanding of a pivotal event in U.S. history that still affects Americans to this day after a close reading of *September 11*.

○ ○ ○

Interested in learning more about this time period? Read a more complete history in the "Era Summaries."

LEARNING EXPECTATIONS

Lower elementary: Students should understand that Americans, in recent decades, have had many different views on how the country should respond to new directions and new challenges. In the 1970s, the war in Vietnam and President Nixon's abuse of his powers divided the country. A new conservative movement pushed to scale back government, wanting to reduce the expensive social role government had taken on in the 1960s, while pushing for a stronger stance against the Soviet Union (U.S.S.R.). The Cold War ended as the Communist world broke up under pressure, but the battle over American domestic policy would continue.

Upper elementary: Students should understand that the United States was badly divided in the 1970s and afterward. The war in Vietnam dragged on, even as Nixon worked to lower Cold War tensions; Nixon angered conservatives by continuing many 1960s government programs; and, finally, he destroyed his presidency in the Watergate scandal, abusing his powers and covering up crimes. Students should understand that a "New Right" movement, led by Ronald Reagan, came to challenge the rapid growth of government social programs and regulations, which they saw as expensive burdens on business that encouraged dependency on welfare benefits. As president, Reagan worked to cut taxes and shrink government, while increasing military spending to pressure Cold War adversaries. Students should realize that the need to match U.S. spending helped force the U.S.S.R. into reform, undermine the Communist bloc, and–boosted by Reagan's swing to diplomacy in his second term–end the Cold War. But that spending also drove up huge U.S. deficits. President George H. W. Bush helped build new alliances as the world changed.

SUGGESTED ANCHOR TEXTS

America's White Table by Margot Theis Raven
Fireboat: The Heroic Adventures of the John J. Harvey by Maira Kalman
The Brothers Kennedy: John, Robert, Edward by Kathleen Krull
The Wall by Eve Bunting

FEATURED ANCHOR TEXT

AMERICA'S WHITE TABLE BY MARGOT THEIS RAVEN

This book was selected because it tells of the sacrifice made by prisoners of war and service personnel who were missing in action during and after the Vietnam War. The unique approach to this topic, centering the story on the "white table" tradition among the armed services, conveys historical information about the war and helps students learn to analyze symbolism in historical fiction.

TEXT STUDY

The following text-dependent questions demand close reading of the text and help teachers highlight important aspects of storytelling, such as the use of repetition and symbolism, in historical fiction.

1. **Look closely at the illustration on the cover of the book. What do you see?**
   - There is a white tablecloth, a white plate with a slice of lemon on it, and a rose lying beside it. There is also a drawing of a table displaying similar objects.
2. **What clues about the meaning of the "little white table" are given on pages 1 and 2 of the text?**
   - The "little white table" brought tears to the eyes of the narrator's Uncle John.
   - It was Veterans Day.
   - It was set for one person, but no one would be eating there on that day.
   - Across the bottom of page 2 is written the first line of "My Country, 'Tis of Thee."
   - Dining halls of the Army, Navy, Marine Corps, and Air Force would also have a little table in them on that day.
   - The "little white table" tradition had started at the end of the Vietnam War.

3. **Acronyms are words made from the initial letters of a connected series of words. What do the acronyms MIA and POW stand for, and how are they used in this text? How are they related to the white table?**
   - The text explains that MIA refers to men and women in America's armed forces who are "missing in action."
   - The text explains that POW refers to men and women in America's armed forces who are "prisoners of war."
   - According to page 5, the white tables are set to honor especially those men and women in the armed forces who are either missing in action or prisoners of war.
4. **Describe how the table is set and what each of the objects on the table signifies, citing evidence from pages 7 and 10.**
   - The chosen table is small, "to show one soldier's lonely battle against many."
   - The white cloth covering the table honors "a soldier's pure heart when he answers his country's call to duty."
   - A lemon slice on the plate signifies "a captive soldier's bitter fate."
   - The salt on the plate represents "the tears of families waiting for loved ones to return."
   - A propped, empty chair is at the table "for the missing soldiers who are not here."
   - A black napkin symbolizes "the sorrow of captivity."
   - A glass is turned over "for the meal that won't be eaten."
   - A white candle is placed on the table "for peace," and a red rose placed in a vase with a red ribbon stands "for the hope that all our missing will return someday."
5. **According to the text, why would the white table be important to the narrator's Uncle John?**
   - Uncle John had been a prisoner of war, a POW, in the Vietnam War.
6. **On page 18 of the text, the mother is telling the story of Uncle John and ends with this: "A soldier risks his life for a fellow soldier, because the best of your country lives in every man and woman who would lay down their life for you." How does the story of Uncle John support that statement?**
   - When Uncle John was a soldier in Vietnam, he and three crew members were shot down behind enemy lines and became prisoners of war.
   - When given an opportunity to escape with two of the able men, Uncle John stayed behind with his wounded friend, Mike.
   - Later, seeing another opportunity, Uncle John escaped, carrying his friend on his back.
   - Uncle John had given up one opportunity to escape to stay with his wounded fellow soldier, and then he risked his life for his friend by bringing his friend with him on the second attempt.
   - This story illustrates Uncle John's love for his country by his going to Vietnam to serve, as well as his love for a friend and fellow soldier by his staying behind with Mike. In both parts of the story, Uncle John was laying down his life for his country, his family, and his friend.
7. **How was this Veterans Day compared to Thanksgiving, and how did the narrator, the ten-year-old niece of Uncle John, react to the comparison?**
   - According to page 20, the white table "needed words of gratitude, like Mama's Thanksgiving meal."
   - The narrator struggled to respond to this comparison, saying, "But I didn't know what I—a ten year old girl—could *ever* put on the table that was as important as each veteran's gift of freedom to me."

8. **How did Katie choose to show her gratitude to her Uncle John and other brave Americans who had given their lives for their country?**
   - She made a promise to write a book in which she would include her sister's song lyrics to "My Country 'Tis of Thee," her sister's hand-drawn picture, and her own retelling of Uncle John's story.
   - She kept her promise and wrote a book about America's white table tradition.
9. **What was Katie's hope for the celebration of Veterans Day in America?**
   - She hoped that the reading of her book would inspire people to set a white table on Veterans Day in their home.
10. **According to the final illustration and written page of the story, how did Katie honor her uncle, and how does he react? What can we understand about her uncle from the illustrations and his actions, both here and earlier on page 23?**
    - She etched "Hero" in the salt on the plate.
    - She saw "the tears of pride fill my Uncle John's eyes."
    - Uncle John's tears suggest that he is very proud of his niece and that he sincerely appreciated her honoring him.
    - According to page 23, when Samantha hugged her uncle, he hugged her back "even harder" than she hugged him, indicating, perhaps, that he was extremely grateful for her love and respect; that he was very grateful to have returned home safely; and that he was thinking of all soldiers who sacrificed in many ways to serve their country.

    Note: *These answers could vary; we have tried to note several possible interpretations.*

PERFORMANCE ASSESSMENTS

1. Talk to the students about symbols. Ask them to do some word work with the word *symbol*, perhaps in regard to the etymology of the word; other forms of the word (*symbolize*, *symbolism*); and/or other symbols with which they might be familiar, such as a cross, a peace sign, the Star of David, the dollar sign, and so forth. Ask them to make sentences that help them relate the ideas, such as "The dollar sign symbolizes money" or "The dollar sign is a symbol for money." Ask them to think about each of the symbols they can find in the story of the little white table as they reread it. Ask them to complete a chart as they write (or speak) about what each object symbolizes (the teacher might fill in the first row). The first two rows might look like this:

American flag (page 4)	The American flag is a symbol of America.
Small table (pages 7 and 8)	The small table is a symbol of the lonely soldier.

2. As a class, note the repetition of "It was just a little white table," each time followed by a powerful idea beginning with the word *but*. Together, make a chart that shows each of the ideas presented. The first three rows might look like this:

Page 2	". . . but it brought tears of pride to my Uncle John's eyes."
Page 3	". . . but earlier that day . . . since the Vietnam War ended."
Page 5	". . . but it felt as big as America."

After completing the chart, ask students each to choose just one of the big ideas. Have them write a paragraph about the idea. This informative/explanatory paragraph should focus on the contrast between the *little* white table and the *big* idea it symbolizes. Students should write a sentence that introduces their topic, use facts and definitions to develop points, and provide a concluding statement or section. At earlier levels, students may draw or dictate their explanation and/or write a label, sentence, or series of related sentences. See standards for more details.

CONNECTIONS TO COMMON CORE STATE STANDARDS FOR ENGLISH LANGUAGE ARTS

- Question 1 focuses students' attention on the cover illustration, inviting them to consider its potential symbolism (RL.K.1,7; RL.1.1,7; RL.2.1,7).
- Questions 2, 4, 5, and 9 ask students to identify and consider important details in the text that will help them determine the importance of bigger ideas in the text (RL.K.1; RL.1.1; RL.2.1).
- Question 3 requires students to cite details in the text, but also to recognize what acronyms are and what words they represent (RL.K.1,4; RL.1.1,4; RL.2.1,4; L.K.5; L.1.5; L.2.5).
- Question 6 prompts students to recall important details that support a statement made by one of the characters (RL.K.1,2,3; RL.1.1,2,3; RL.2.1,2,3).
- Question 7 examines the author's craft by asking students to note a particular comparison in the text and recognize the narrator's reaction to the comparison (RL.K.1,2,3; RL.1.1,2,3; RL.2.1,2,3).
- Question 8 not only requires students to cite key details but also helps develop their understanding of characterization techniques (RL.K.1,2,3; RL.1.1,2,3; RL.2.1,2,3).
- Question 10 allows students to analyze illustrations and characters' actions—and to consider them together to interpret the characterization technique used by the author (RL.K.1,2,3,7; RL.1.1,2,3,7; RL.2.1,2,3,7).
- The first performance assessment gives students a chance to develop their understanding of symbolism by rereading the text closely and focusing on important words (RL.K.1,2,3,4; RL.1.1,2,3,4; RL.2.1,2,3,4; SL.K.1; SL.1.1; SL.2.1; L.K.4; L.1.4; L.2.4).
- The second performance assessment helps students recognize the effect of repetition and symbolism in a narrative text. It also requires that students explain their understanding of the author's craft in an informative/explanatory paragraph (RI.K.1,2,9; RI.1.1,2,9; RI.2.1,2,9; W.K.2; W.1.2; W.2.2; SL.K.1; SL.1.1; SL.2.1).

MORE RESOURCES

HISTORICAL FICTION

It's Still a Dog's New York: A Book of Healing by Susan Roth

PRIMARY SOURCES

Antiwar demonstration advertisement in the *Washington Post*, 1970 (Library of Congress)

Washington Post article covering Richard Nixon's resignation, 1974 (*Washington Post*)

Berlin Wall resources (History Channel)

Ronald Reagan ending the Cold War, video (PBS: *American Experience*)

Camp David Accords, 1978 (Israeli Ministry of Foreign Affairs)

POETRY AND MUSIC

"Hello Ronnie, Good-Bye Jimmy," sheet music, 1980 (Smithsonian Institution)

Era Summaries

ERA 1: ACROSS BERINGIA: ORIGINAL PEOPLE OF NORTH AMERICA *(CA. 20,000 BCE TO CA. 1600 CE)*

INDIGENOUS PEOPLES ARRIVE

Although scholars disagree on when the first humans set foot in the Americas, recent archaeological work suggests that the first settlers crossed from eastern Asia to the Americas by at least 13,000 BCE—and probably earlier—during the last global Ice Age. The massive amount of water locked up in glaciers lowered worldwide sea levels and created a land bridge called Beringia between Siberia and Alaska (where the Bering Strait now lies).

Until recently, many archeologists had embraced the Clovis model, which stated that the Clovis people—known for their intricate stone tools and spear points—were the first to cross into the Americas from Asia via Beringia. But more recent findings suggest that humans were in the Americas before the Clovis culture, when the land bridge was still blocked by glaciers. One theory posits that early hunter-gatherers came down the Pacific coast, by sea and land that was then exposed by low sea levels, while the land bridge was still ice-locked. Later glacial melt would have submerged their settlements, leaving little evidence of their culture behind.

Around 12,000 BCE, the Ice Age ended, and glacial melt created an ice-free corridor across Beringia. Now larger groups came from eastern Siberia. It is most likely that these groups were the ancestors of the Native American populations that would settle most of North and South America.

DISTRIBUTION, DIVERSITY, AND CULTURAL REGIONS

Across the American continents, climates ranged from subarctic to tropical. These dramatically different environments led to diverse living conditions, animal populations, and natural resources. Settlement patterns and regional cultures were heavily influenced by distinctive opportunities for hunting, gathering, and settlement in each region.

Over thousands of years, the post–Ice Age climate shifted, altering plant and animal life forever. Climate change, possibly coupled with hunting by humans, led to the extinction of the wooly mammoth and other large animals. As resources changed, human communities were forced to change, too; some migrated to other regions, whereas others adapted to new conditions and took advantage of new resources.

Many people in North America lived as hunter-gatherers, divided into diverse language groups and spread across the continent. Peoples settled in distinct climatic zones, such as the Eastern Woodlands, Great Plains, Southwest, and Northwest Coast. Some groups lived in settlements for at least certain parts of the year, farming local plants and exchanging local resources with other groups through broad trading networks.

Farming communities were well established in Central America (also known as Mesoamerica) and South America by 1500 BCE, forming complex societies with social classes, political organization, and ritual practices.

NATIVE AMERICAN CIVILIZATION IN NORTH AMERICA AND BEYOND

In North America from circa 1000 BCE to 500 CE, the Adena and the Hopewell cultures built large ceremonial mounds, first along the Ohio River and later throughout the Mississippi Valley. Many of these mounds, and those of later cultures, can still be seen. The ruins puzzled early European settlers, who refused to believe that supposedly primitive Native Americans could have built them.

After 200 CE, settled farming communities appeared in North America's Southwest, cultivating crops (for example, beans and squash) introduced from Mesoamerica. The climate gradually became very dry, and groups fought over scarce food and water. They developed irrigation systems and, with warfare erupting over limited resources, started building defensible cliffside settlements.

Cultivated maize from Mesoamerica reached the Mississippi Valley after 700 CE. This allowed the extensive Mississippian mound-building cultures to develop and thrive over the coming centuries, with large ceremonial centers surrounded by agricultural communities in the fertile river floodplains.

In Central America, the militant Aztec Empire—centered on the enormous and advanced city of Tenochtitlan, present-day Mexico City—arose in the 1400s and dominated Mexico at the time of Spanish contact. A sophisticated warrior culture, the Aztecs aggressively exploited those whom they conquered for labor, resources, and human sacrifice.

The other major Native American empire that met the Spanish was the Inca Empire, which had come to dominate South America's Andes Mountains—in present-day Peru—by 1500. The Inca built spectacular urban structures and a sophisticated road system, but like the Aztecs, they also extracted labor, resources, and sacrifices from the local peoples they conquered.

THE EFFECTS OF EUROPEAN CONTACT IN THE AMERICAS

North America's southwestern cultures were already under siege by Mexican peoples and Navaho and Apache tribes before Europeans arrived in the sixteenth century. The Mississippian cultures, overcrowded and afflicted by disease, were also in decline before European contact. In Central and South America, the great Maya civilization had long since fallen by the time Europeans arrived, but the powerful Aztec and Inca Empires were both at their height when the Spanish first came.

The Europeans' contact with what they called the New World began when Christopher Columbus's Spanish-financed expedition landed in the Caribbean in 1492 (see era 2). For the native cultures, the consequences of this contact were immediate and dire. The Caribbean islanders were essentially reduced to slaves as the Spanish sought to extract mineral wealth and tighten their hold on their newly conquered territories. Within a few decades, the native island people virtually vanished.

Spanish expeditions soon moved to the mainland, challenging the Aztec and Inca Empires. Spanish forces succeeded by pitting groups of native peoples—whom the Aztecs and Incas had dominated and used for their human sacrifices—against the empires. Although the natives were willing to help Spain, they were soon subjected to the country's harsh rule and forced to convert to Christianity (see era 2).

Europeans' heaviest impact on the Americas was unintentional. The explorers carried pathogens that were common in Europe, Asia, and Africa, but to which the biologically isolated peoples of the Americas had no resistance. Measles, smallpox, and other diseases quickly spread throughout the Americas. Scholars disagree over the death toll, but these so-called virgin soil epidemics may have killed as much as 90 percent of the Native American population within a few generations of contact. Meanwhile, Europeans carried syphilis back to Europe, where it would become a major health scourge.

North America, settled by Europeans well after they conquered Central and South America, had already been devastated by disease before European settlers arrived there—in North America, cultural contact was therefore made with already weakened populations.

Disease, however, was only one part of the vast transfer of plants, animals, peoples, and cultures that began as contact opened between Europe, Asia, Africa, and the Americas—a process that has been called the Columbian Exchange.

Europeans also brought their livestock and crops. The horse, previously unknown in America, would have a profound influence on native ways of life. Many crops cultivated by Native Americans and some animals they had domesticated or consumed were quickly introduced to Europe, Asia, and Africa. These included maize, chilies (called "peppers" by the Spanish to spur competition with prized black pepper from Asia—a trade then dominated by Portugal), chocolate, turkeys, potatoes, and tobacco. The results of this exchange and diffusion would dramatically transform the economies, environments, and cultures of both hemispheres.

ERA 2: DRIVEN TO DISCOVER: EUROPEANS ESTABLISH THE NEW WORLD *(LATE 1400S TO LATE 1600S)*

EUROPE DISCOVERS THE AMERICAS

Europeans had long prized Asian silk and spices. But Central Asia's Silk Road—the ancient trade thoroughfare—was long and dangerous, and made Asian goods scarce and expensive. Europe also lusted after the East's legendary wealth, which was evoked in Marco Polo's hugely popular thirteenth-century account of his travels to China. By the fifteenth century, the Renaissance and its probing intellectual culture had inspired Europeans to look beyond their continent. New shipbuilding technology made long ocean voyages possible, while expanding commerce encouraged bold gambles for new sources of profit. At the same time, Europeans believed deeply in bringing the Christian gospel to new lands. Their quest for new routes to Asia thus began in earnest.

During the fifteenth century, the Portuguese pioneered ocean routes along the African coast and opened access to India. Spain's King Ferdinand and Queen Isabella feared that Portugal, their neighbor and rival, would monopolize trade with Asia. They sponsored Genoese navigator Christopher Columbus, who thought he could reach Asia by sailing west across the Atlantic. Though Viking colonists from Greenland had found Newfoundland around 1000 CE and briefly settled in a colony there, called Vinland, knowledge of their discovery had been long forgotten: Columbus had no inkling that unknown continents lay just where he thought Asia would be.

Columbus's three ships, the *Nina*, the *Pinta*, and the *Santa Maria*, landed in the Caribbean in 1492. In four voyages that spanned a decade, he explored the area's islands and reached South America. He remained convinced that he had found China and Japan (these were then considered part of the "Indies"—hence the name "Indians" for Native Americans). But other explorers like the Florentine Amerigo Vespucci, sailing in the service of Portugal, realized that Columbus had stumbled on a new world. A mapmaker soon honored Vespucci—who claimed to have discovered South America—by calling the new land America.

A 1493 papal decree and the 1494 Treaty of Tordesillas divided the entire non-Christian world between Portugal and Spain. A line down the Atlantic ceded Asia to Spain, and Portugal acquired India and Africa. The nations later learned that the treaty's dividing line actually ran through the newly discovered Americas. Portugal gained Brazil, which was east of the line. Spain gained everything else.

Spanish settlement quickly took hold in the Caribbean, where the native islanders were virtually enslaved. But disease and exploitation soon decimated the native communities, and the Spanish lost their labor supply. Despite early European hopes, the islands also failed to yield much gold or silver. But the Spanish heard rumors of wealthy empires on the mainland (Columbus thought these tales referred to China, which he still believed was just over the horizon).

In 1519, Hernán Cortés led an expedition from Cuba to Mexico. Though his army numbered only five hundred, he found allies in local peoples who had been subjugated by the militant Aztecs. Cortés took the Aztec emperor Moctezuma (or Montezuma) hostage, trying to rule through him; when this failed and Moctezuma was killed, the Spanish rallied their local allies to besiege and conquer the vast Aztec capital city of Tenochtitlan. By 1521, the Spanish had taken control of Mexico, imposing their own strong and often brutal rule in place of that of the defeated Aztecs.

From their Central American base, Spaniards then moved against the other great Native American power, the Inca Empire of the Andes. In 1531, brothers Francisco and Gonzalo Pizarro led an invasion of Inca Peru, again recruiting local allies against the Inca overlords. They defeated the emperor Atahualpa and held him for a massive ransom, before finally murdering him and installing a puppet leader in his place. The region descended into chaos during the ensuing decades of Inca revolts and Spanish infighting (during which both Pizarro brothers were killed by rivals). Spain managed to impose control, but only very slowly.

EUROPEAN RIVALS IN THE AMERICAS

As Spain tightened its grip on Central and South America, its American empire, called New Spain, melted down the gold and silver treasures of the conquered peoples and forced natives to dig for more. Gold and silver from the mines of New Spain filled regular treasure fleets, on which Spain's vast and growing global power soon came to depend. The Spanish state and the Catholic Church worked together to control the conquered peoples. They often imposed harsh government on them and stamped out native religious beliefs, which they viewed as idolatrous superstitions.

Other European powers did not accept Spain's exclusive claim to the New World. In 1497, Italy's John Cabot (who had been commissioned by England) discovered the North American mainland. Spain also claimed ownership of that continent and tried to keep others out, but North America was too large and too far from Spain's Mexican center of power. The Spanish were unable to block others who were also interested in controlling the newly found lands. England and France explored the coasts, and adventurers and entrepreneurs created new settlements. Rival empires emerged and expanded, fighting for ownership whenever they met.

An English group led by Sir Walter Raleigh tried to gain a British foothold on Roanoke Island (in present-day North Carolina) in 1587. A resupply mission, delayed by the Spanish Armada's attempt to invade England in 1588, finally arrived in 1590 and found the colony abandoned. The Virginia Company of London tried establishing the Jamestown settlement as a commercial venture in 1607. This British group hoped to match the Spaniards' success in finding precious metals, but found very little.

Led by John Smith, Jamestown survived disastrous early famine (the "starving time") to become the first permanent British settlement in America. When the settlers' attempts at Spanish-style mining failed, they turned to agriculture. Long-term settlers achieved wealth from commercial crops and valuable land, gradually replacing early gold-seeking adventurers. Over the coming decades, British settlement along the Atlantic coast would focus on farming and fisheries.

France also had its eye on North America and began expanding into Canada in the early seventeenth century. France's aim was always to make money, particularly through its fur trade with Native Americans. Although the French controlled much of Canada and the Mississippi Valley by 1700, they settled the land only lightly, viewing it mainly as a commercial base. France, in any case, quickly shifted its emphasis from North America to the more profitable sugar islands in the Caribbean.

Other European states also tried staking claims in North America, but few succeeded. The most profitable was a Dutch commercial enterprise, which mainly engaged in the fur trade.

But the New Netherland colony, established in the 1620s with New Amsterdam as its capital, came under British control in the 1660s and was renamed New York.

AIMS OF BRITISH SETTLEMENT DIFFER BY REGION

After the first settlers in Virginia failed to gain wealth through mining, new communities switched to farming such valuable cash crops as indigo, rice, and tobacco (a North American crop already cultivated by Native Americans but previously unknown to Europeans). Successful planters imported indentured servants, who were bound to serve their masters for a specific term of years. In turn, servants could attain their own wealth after they fulfilled their terms. For a brief period, Chesapeake society was unstructured enough to promote real social mobility, and indentured servants were able to work toward their own economic success.

In contrast, New England was settled by religiously motivated families who abandoned what they saw as a corrupt English church and fled the persecution they faced in England due to their outspoken nonconformity. The Pilgrims arrived first: they were strict Separatists who wanted to sever ties completely with the Church of England. After having tried to settle in Holland, they chartered the *Mayflower* to take them to America, hoping to build a godly community in the "wilderness." Landing at Plymouth in 1620, they rejected the English commercial investors who had backed their venture and created the Mayflower Compact. The document mirrored those compacts on which Separatist churches were founded, in that it created a government based on majority vote.

The number of Plymouth Pilgrims was soon dwarfed by a far larger migration of Puritans to New England. Though less radical than the Separatists, Puritans were strict Protestants who wanted to purify Christianity by restoring its earlier practices. After facing persecution under the strongly anti-Puritan King Charles I, their hopes of reforming the Church of England waned. Thus, some of them aimed to establish a godly society in the New World. The Puritans won a royally approved charter to establish a commercial colony, but they tricked the king and used the charter to establish their own government in Massachusetts: their faith, rather than potential profit for Britain, was what motivated them.

After the Puritans settled Boston in 1630 and began to expand, the Massachusetts Bay Colony became a magnet for further settlement. The Puritans centered their towns on independent church congregations. Their brand of Puritanism thus came to be known as Congregationalism. These colonies spread throughout New England, and each pursued its own form of Puritanism. Whereas the Virginia settlers focused on cash crops and dramatic profits, the Puritans supported their communities through farming and fishing.

As mid-Atlantic settlement grew around the newly won colony of New York, the region shifted its focus to seaborne trade and commerce. The Hudson River Valley was filled with large cash-crop farms, which were often controlled by powerful Dutch families from the earlier New Netherland colony. New York City, formerly New Amsterdam, became a prominent port for trade with Europe and other colonies. These global contacts, in addition to the earlier Dutch settlement in the area, created a dynamic religious and ethnic diversity in New York that was unique among the British colonies.

Most of the early colonies were established by companies that were created with royal consent to run profit-seeking ventures in America. But Britain soon pushed aside this corporate model, the king taking direct charge of many of the colonies. He appointed their governors, and Virginia was given a royal governor in 1624. Britain repeatedly sought to annul New England's almost completely independent charters, but Britain's civil war and the temporary overthrow of its monarchy delayed its efforts to assume control of the New England colonies for decades.

Another model for colony creation soon arose: individual proprietors began to found colonies as their personal ventures. As early as the 1630s, proprietary governments allowed powerful men to create colonies based on their personal beliefs and in the interest of personal profit. For example, Lord Baltimore established the proprietary colony of Maryland partly to create a haven for his fellow Roman Catholics.

THE COLONISTS ENCOUNTER THE NATIVE NORTH AMERICANS

By the time European settlers arrived in North America, the virgin soil epidemics unwittingly unleashed by the Spanish had already spread from the Caribbean and Mexico throughout the Americas. Though the exact death toll is unknown, 90 percent of the native population may have died in some regions. The groups and regional alliances that the Europeans encountered varied greatly, in regard to both their remaining strength and their attitudes toward the newcomers.

The French lightly settled a central region in Canada, using it as a base for trade *with* Native Americans. Though French Jesuits actively tried to convert the Native Americans to Catholicism and were sometimes attacked and killed, the French were more likely to clash with the enemies of their own Native American trading partners and religious converts: France fought with the Great Lakes region's powerful Iroquois Confederacy, an enemy of many French-allied peoples.

British regions were different because their communities often relied on farming instead of trade. Unlike the French colonies, British settlements thus needed land to expand. Although the British settlement pattern offered unique opportunities and personal freedoms to the British settlers, conflict with the native peoples already living on that land was inevitable.

In Virginia, the Jamestown settlers encountered a confederacy led by the powerful Chief Powhatan. Early relations between settlers and the native people were tense, as each tried to gain advantages from the other. Mutual mistrust and strained diplomatic efforts (including the kidnapping of Powhatan's daughter and emissary, Pocahontas, and her diplomatic marriage to settlement leader John Rolfe) escalated into fighting. By the 1620s, Powhatan's successor tried unsuccessfully to wipe out the growing colony. Thus began the long demise of the native peoples there.

In contrast, initial relations between local tribes and the New England settlers were often friendly. The Indians helped settlers survive by teaching them to farm local crops and take advantage of natural resources. The peaceful relations are famously commemorated in depictions of Plymouth's "first Thanksgiving." But New England's farm towns needed space, and settlers came to view the native people as obstacles to their success. Active efforts to convert and "civilize" the Native Americans—that is, to shift their mobile, hunter-gatherer lifestyle to a settled, Christian model—resulted in some groups of "praying Indians'" settling their own towns. Yet expanding colonies ultimately turned against even these groups.

To be sure, New England's early settlers and some tribes formed alliances that lasted for decades. But the settlers found themselves at odds with other groups, including their local allies' own traditional enemies. As early as 1636, tensions erupted into the brutally violent Pequot War between a tribal group and an alliance of New England colonies—with the colonists aided by native allies traditionally hostile to the settlers' Native American adversaries.

Rapidly expanding settlement worsened tensions throughout the colonies. Both sides increasingly abandoned all restraint, killing civilians wholesale in wars and raids. As the frontier moved steadily westward in the following decades, settlers' rapid encroachment threatened to extinguish Native American cultures. Ever-increasing bitterness drove many native groups to ally with Britain's imperial rivals, particularly the less land-hungry French with whom they could much more easily coexist.

ERA 3: UNIQUELY AMERICAN: THE BEGINNINGS OF A NEW NATIONALITY *(1607 TO LATE 1600S)*

THE EARLY COLONIES: REGIONAL DIFFERENCES ABOUND

Early southern colonists were mainly adventurers pursuing quick wealth through mineral exploration. When their hopes of easy fortunes faded, settlers turned to cash crops. Still, their singular aim was money—not the establishment of permanent settlements. Many came to America as indentured servants, serving the master who paid their passage for a fixed term: once free, a former servant could pursue his own fortune. Men far outnumbered women, making conventional married life impossible for most. The low birth rate, coupled with disease and civil unrest, created tremendous social instability in the southern colonies' earliest days.

Over time, the most successful planters gained land and wealth. As a result, opportunities for rapid advancement faded as southern society became more settled and more stratified. Below the great planters were yeoman farmers working small holdings as well as a large laboring underclass. Early on, women had achieved some independence and opportunity as looser rules weakened traditional barriers: there were, for instance, successful female landowners in the early period. But as permanent communities formed, women's opportunities vanished as they were pushed back into traditional domestic roles.

In Massachusetts, Governor John Winthrop invoked the Biblical image of a "city on a hill" (a virtuous beacon for the world) to describe the Puritan mission, a metaphor that would resonate powerfully for later generations of Americans. But the Puritans' true aim was to create a godly community for themselves—as opposed to a model for others. Whereas men led the southern migration, many Puritans arrived as members of nuclear families. The presence of women, a healthy population increase, and long life spans helped ensure social stability. The migration largely ended after 1642, however, when England's civil war offered Puritans an alluring opportunity to create a Puritan Britain. Some settlers returned to England, and the number of new colonial arrivals plummeted.

Compared with Britain, the New England settlements offered people relative equality in wealth, status, and education. Although women did not have official church leadership roles or a voice in government, their opinions often drove community attitudes and directions. And although religion remained central, larger towns that focused on fishing, shipbuilding, and overseas commerce emerged along the coast. Non-Puritans who arrived pursued economic opportunity, as opposed to religious community, and thus created additional tensions. Many Puritans were drawn into wider commercial networks that threatened the religious isolation the founders had envisioned, and children began to drift from their parents' Puritan zeal.

The middle colonies on the mid-Atlantic coast were mainly driven by profit. The Dutch created the most prominent settlement, New Netherland (which would ultimately become New York) as a commercial venture. The British who later took over the colony, and the many Dutch settlers who remained (including such families as the Roosevelts), also embraced a commercial focus as large towns like New York City emerged as powerful centers of overseas trade.

Uneven success led to great wealth and class division in these trading centers, and communities with both great affluence and dire poverty soon mirrored Europe's old and crowded cities. Inland, the great plantations in the Hudson River Valley further promoted stratification, with dominant Dutch families controlling vast stretches of land. At the same time, widespread commerce brought merchants and settlers from many countries and created a mid-Atlantic society with unusual ethnic diversity. In parts of the mid-Atlantic and South, poorer immigrants (including Scots, Irish, and Germans) were often drawn to the backcountry frontier, where they could take land (frequently from the Native Americans, toward whom they were often very violent) and build communities.

The colonies' rapid expansion worsened tensions with Native Americans, whose way of life was under siege. Early settler wars against the native groups had broken most of the rules that maintained any level of civility between settlers and Native Americans. Now each side was prepared to attack the other with almost unlimited fury. In New England, strain between settlers and several tribes erupted into King Philip's War in 1675. Native American forces were eventually defeated, but only after heavy fatalities and the total destruction of many colonial towns. In 1676, Virginia's governor tried to curb conflict between settlers and Native Americans that had driven frontier settlers from their homes. A frontier uprising against the governor, called Bacon's Rebellion, resulted in further warfare. Native Americans everywhere were losing ground.

RELIGIOUS TENSION AND TOLERANCE

Religion was pivotal in the lives of many Americans—both in New England, where settlements were established for chiefly religious reasons, and throughout the colonies. But colonists' attitude toward those with *different* beliefs and practices was a complex issue—and one that shifted dramatically over time.

Since the English Reformation under King Henry VIII, the Church of England (also known as the Anglican Church) had been an independent national institution led by the king. Some colonies, such as Virginia, the largest and most heavily populated of the southern provinces, simply followed England's model and officially established the Anglican Church. The church was supported by taxes imposed on the colonists. Unlike England, however, America had no Anglican bishops.

The New England colonies were created to provide freedom of worship for Puritans. Prominent Puritan ministers were among the first settlers, and the towns were designed around Congregationalist churches. Puritans had little tolerance for people of other faiths and actively sought to keep them out. Indeed, Massachusetts even executed several Quaker missionaries who dared to return after their banishment from the colony.

In the first few years of Puritan settlement, dissenters fled the New England colonies to establish the settlement that would become Rhode Island. Separatist minister Roger Williams had been cast out of Massachusetts after quarrelling with other preachers and challenging the government's power over religion. Anne Hutchinson and her followers had challenged the authority of the most prominent ministers in Boston, and sparked a major crisis that nearly tore Massachusetts apart. Insisting that government could not favor one faith over another, Rhode Island allowed full religious tolerance and separated church from state. This concept of religious freedom would gain ground through American history to come.

Proprietors of other colonies also pursued their own religious aims. The Catholic Lord Baltimore insisted on religious freedom for Catholics in his province of Maryland, whereas English Quaker leader William Penn established Pennsylvania as a Quaker haven and a proprietary commercial venture. This caused friction with the non-Quaker settlers who resented his political control despite the colony's full tolerance for other faiths.

THE RISE, ENTRENCHMENT, AND REGIONAL PATTERNS OF SLAVERY

Slavery had existed in most human societies from the earliest days. In Africa, forms of slavery had existed for millennia as debtors, criminals, and captives in war were all made slaves. Slave trades from Africa to the Muslim world, across North Africa and the Sahara, had also operated for centuries. As Europe's contact with Africa increased after the fifteenth century, its efforts to conquer African territory largely failed. However, a slave trade with coastal African kingdoms soon emerged.

A small number of African laborers were first brought to Virginia in 1619. At first, they were viewed as indentured servants: that is, potentially free after a fixed term of service. Some Africans achieved freedom and even became wealthy in the economically mobile society of the early South. But a far more rigid system of slavery quickly developed.

As large cash-crop plantations gained a foothold in the southern colonies, the need for labor skyrocketed. Yet as opportunities for rapid advancement diminished in the increasingly stratified colonies, the flow of white indentured workers steadily declined. Planters became highly dependent on African slaves, who were immune to many illnesses that afflicted settlers working in disease-ridden rice and indigo farms. Common racial beliefs of the time encouraged many planters to see black Africans as naturally inferior.

The Western Hemisphere's rapidly expanding labor demand led slave traders from various European nations to buy ever larger numbers of slaves from Africa's coastal states. Slave exports became a major source of those nations' wealth. Wars and raids ravaged the African interior, as people were captured by other Africans and forcibly marched to the coasts. As many as half died along the journey. Powerful African kings rented coastal land to Europeans for slave-trading fortresses, where slaves were sold to European merchants and packed onto ships for the dreadful Middle Passage to the Americas.

The vast majority of slaves went to the sugar plantations of the Caribbean and Portuguese Brazil, where dismal conditions and high mortality required a constant supply of fresh laborers. But slavery took hold throughout British North America, too. The institution was especially important in the South, with its large-scale system of cash-crop plantations. Slavery was not limited to the South, however: it also developed on the large plantations of New York's Hudson River Valley and in parts of southern New England. It also spread beyond plantations to cities, where slaves were trained as artisans or urban laborers, and to towns, where they were held as domestic servants and farm workers.

At first, the legal status of slaves raised hard questions. Would slaves be freed after a certain term of service? If they were indeed "servants for life," what would be their children's status? In the early years, answers varied by place and circumstance. In time, however, the legal status of slaves became more clearly defined. By the end of the seventeenth century, it was firmly established that slaves were permanently unable to be free, and that children would inherit their mother's bondage. Slavery was now an established part of early American society.

THE RISE OF REPRESENTATIVE GOVERNMENT AND POPULAR POWER IN THE COLONIES

One of the crucial developments in the colonies–one that would affect the colonists, the future United States, and ultimately the world–was the rise of local self-government. Because it could take months for a letter to cross the Atlantic, many government decisions had to be made in the colonies themselves. More important, by electing representatives who in turn held strong influence in their respective local governments, American settlers assumed more power than most people throughout the world enjoyed.

In Virginia, a representative body was introduced under the original corporate charter. Reforms introduced to satisfy the growing population created the Virginia House of Burgesses in 1619, elected by white, male, Protestant, landowning adults, which granted a very wide franchise by the standards of the day. This was the first elected legislature in British America, and it was retained when Virginia received a new charter as a royal colony in 1624. By the late 1630s, the burgesses were ordered to meet at least once per year.

The New England Puritans had planned to govern themselves all along. Though the British government had assumed that Massachusetts would be run from London as an overseas investment enterprise, the settlers brought the charter to America in 1629 and created a local government in Boston. A company head served as the colony's governor, the corporate board its legislature, and the shareholders its voters. The legislature, or the voters themselves, elected all officers. Although the colony accepted the king as head of the British Empire and flew the royal flag over Boston's fort (an important concession because the flag bore a cross, which Puritans considered idolatrous), the king had no role in their internal government.

There were other New England innovations. The town meeting served as the colonies' main means of local government. Local affairs were decided there by majority vote, and town representatives for the colonial legislature were chosen there as well. All adult, male, property-owning church members could vote; in New England's relatively egalitarian society, that included most men (and the property requirement was not always enforced). Tensions rose, however, as the region's commerce expanded and more non-Puritans arrived. Those who were not church members had no voting rights.

As other colonies were founded, colonial legislatures became the universal standard. Outside New England, property requirements excluded many men from voting, and power was confined more tightly to the wealthy elite. Nonetheless, the right to vote was far more widespread in the colonies than virtually anywhere else in the world, even in comparison to the election of Britain's Parliament. In the colonies, the powerful had to win the support of ordinary farmers—a reality that, in those times, was nothing short of revolutionary.

The circumstances of the seventeenth century helped strengthen local governments. Aside from its distance from the colonies, Britain had little time to focus on happenings amid its own more pressing political concerns: a bloody Civil War (1642 to 1649), the overthrow and execution of King Charles I (1649), a Puritan-led commonwealth in Britain (1649 to 1660), and the restoration of King Charles II (1660). Thus, the British government had to divert its attention from the colonies to largely manage its own affairs. After Charles II reclaimed the throne, Britain finally stabilized and turned its attention to the colonies. But Americans would not readily give up the self-governance on which they had come to rely.

ERA 4: TAXATION WITHOUT REPRESENTATION: TENSION MOUNTS *(CA. 1660 TO 1763)*

BRITAIN EXPANDS ITS RULE OVER AMERICA

After the fall of the Puritan commonwealth, which had ruled England after the 1649 execution of Charles I, and the restoration of King Charles II in 1660, the British government began to stabilize and turn its attention to America. During Britain's decades of crisis, its North American colonies had grown from a few scattered and tentative outposts to a rapidly expanding, lucrative network of plantations, towns, and trading ports. Now Britain had to determine how it could reap the highest profit.

In the seventeenth century, European powers increasingly saw colonies as producers of valuable raw materials (for example, food, cash crops, and mineral resources) and consumers of the mother country's own exported goods. Colonies existed to benefit the mother country—a premise that had led Britain to challenge Spain's claim to North America in the first place. This system of economic "mercantilism" viewed colonies as necessary in a nation's struggle for self-sufficiency, wealth, and dominance over its rivals.

Even under the Puritan commonwealth, Britain had tried to block the colonies from trading with anyone else. After the Restoration, Parliament passed a series of Navigation Acts, which mandated that colonial imports from Europe had to be carried on British ships. Meanwhile, America's main cash crops (namely, sugar, tobacco, and indigo) could only be exported to British territories. By the century's end, Britain had even tried to stop the colonies from exporting manufactured goods that might compete with its own products. Enforcement was difficult and erratic, and Britain's customs service steadily increased in power and size (and in the resentment it provoked) as it tried to maintain its authority.

Britain also sought tighter control in the political realm, especially over New England's nearly independent governments. Just after the Restoration, Charles II had in fact confirmed Connecticut's elected government with a new charter. But his brother James, Duke of York, believed in absolute royal authority. Before England's civil war, Charles I had tried to revoke the Massachusetts charter, and now James renewed the attack. In 1684, Charles II finally annulled the charter. A year later, James—now King James II—created the Dominion of New England. This single province included New York and all of the New England colonies. Under direct royal rule, the colonists' freedoms were sharply reduced: the dominion allowed neither elected officers nor assemblies.

Colonists chafed under the dictatorial dominion, but the Catholic James II was tolerated in England so long as his Protestant daughters remained his heirs. When James fathered a male, Catholic heir, the English were unwilling to accept a Catholic successor and deposed him in 1688's bloodless Glorious Revolution. When word of James's overthrow reached America the following year, colonists rebelled in Boston and New York, toppling the dominion. Colonists in Maryland also rose against the Catholic Lord Baltimore, Maryland's proprietor. Although it took twenty-five years, the Baltimore family—whose members were, by that time, Anglican converts—eventually regained power.

After James II was deposed and exiled, Britain's newly installed monarchs, King William III and his wife, Queen Mary II, installed a new government in New York, complete with a royally appointed governor and an elected assembly. Massachusetts failed to win back its old charter but was granted a new one. Although its governor was now royally appointed, the elected legislature held considerable power. The old requirement stating that only church members could vote was abolished, thus giving the vote to virtually all of the province's adult men.

THE COLONIES BECOME MORE MODERN, BRITISH, AND LIKE ONE ANOTHER

In the wake of the Glorious Revolution, the colonies became much more politically uniform as Britain pulled them more tightly into a British Atlantic world. Most colonies now had royally appointed governors. Connecticut and Rhode Island managed to keep their elected executives; Pennsylvania, Delaware, and Maryland remained under proprietors who could appoint royally approved governors. A powerful faction in Pennsylvania pushed hard against the Penn family proprietors: Benjamin Franklin spent years in London pressing for a royally appointed Pennsylvania governor, despite his later stance in the American Revolution.

The colonies' modernization was rapid. They developed complex commercial ties with Britain and with other British colonies. At the same time, many traded illegally with other European nations and their colonies, smuggling goods in defiance of the Navigation Acts. Expanding outside ties upset more isolated and conservative forces, especially in New England. Rifts formed in churches and communities, fueling suspicion and dangerous outbursts. In 1692, tensions between traditionalist Puritans in Massachusetts's Salem Village and their more commercially focused neighbors helped spark the Salem witch panic. Puritans worried that their religious mission was failing, and their suspicion of those with outside commercial ties helped bolster fears of a satanic plot against the godly.

Yet trade's transformative influence on society proved unstoppable: it was impossible to preserve the old Puritan ideal of godly communities isolated from worldly corruption in the American wilderness. In the first half of the eighteenth century, traditional religious authorities throughout the colonies were further threatened by the eruption of a populist evangelical Protestantism known as the Great Awakening. Led by such dynamic preachers as George Whitfield and Jonathan Edwards, the Great Awakening's fiery revivalist meetings challenged the more traditional churches and ministers. For many colonists, the split encouraged a broader sense of popular power against established authority.

At the same time, the colonies' cultural world expanded as they gained access to imported books and as their own literary production grew. American printing, rare until this point, became more widely established. Franklin's Philadelphia press is an important example from the early eighteenth century. Newspapers began circulating and soon became established throughout the colonies. News traveled from London and between colonies, helping create a common culture.

In short, the British colonies were developing into more diverse, modern societies. Trade across the Atlantic and between the colonies linked the colonies together while also increasing their contact with Britain. Books, printing, and the exchange of ideas helped the colonies build a shared popular culture. The colonies began to merge from a set of individual outposts, separate from the mother country and from one other, into a single British America with a more British identity—one that included the expectation that colonists would enjoy the traditional rights of Britons.

THE COLONIES' ROLE IN THE EMPIRE GROWS AND BECOMES MORE COMPLEX

As royally appointed governors gained power in the colonies, they established local networks of officeholders and supporters. This created discord between, on the one hand, the governors' followers and, on the other hand, elected politicians who were often hostile, especially because the elected assemblies retained sole power to introduce tax bills—and thus to control the purse strings. Because the governors represented Britain, such quarrels had the potential to create tension between the colonies and Britain itself. Such outcomes were actually rare, however. Most colonists were strongly loyal to Britain as a whole, and they tended to blame the governors themselves rather than their British superiors for any bad blood.

British control of American trade was also problematic. Although colonists generally acknowledged Britain's right to regulate colonial trade for the empire's benefit, many still resented the customs rules and their enforcement officials. Smuggling was rampant, and British attention to the colonies was still uneven. Trade regulations were often poorly and erratically enforced, and corrupt customs officers turned a blind eye to smuggling in exchange for a share of the profits. Any serious British attempt to crack down on smuggling would inevitably cause resentment in the colonies.

Meanwhile, the colonies were often drawn into the empire's frequent conflicts with its imperial adversaries. Beginning in the 1690s, Britain fought a string of wars in and around the Americas—sometimes against the Spanish, but more often against the French. Many Native American groups, who feared further encroachment on their lands by land-hungry British colonists, became French allies and fought against the British American colonies in wars, raids, and border skirmishes.

The last and largest of these wars—known in America as the French and Indian War (1754 to 1763) and in Europe as the Seven Years' War (1756 to 1763)—began because of British-French quarrels over the land west of the Appalachian Mountains known as the Ohio Country. Virginia sent an army under Colonel George Washington to secure the territory; his clashes with French forces led Britain to dispatch troops, and war rapidly escalated. By coincidence, at the very same time, a congress had been called to consider Native American relations and joint colonial defense. Delegates from seven colonies met in Albany, New York, just as the war was starting, and accepted a plan of colonial union proposed by Franklin. This was the first serious attempt at a colonial confederation, but Britain and the colonial governments promptly rejected it.

Britain lost its initial battles with the French and their Native American allies. But after the war spread to Europe in 1756 and ultimately escalated around the globe, Britain won allies and gained military might. By 1759, Britain had invaded Canada and taken Quebec. In 1763, the combatants signed a peace treaty in Paris; the French surrendered Canada and all lands east of the Mississippi. Britain had won an enormous victory, but with much difficulty and at great expense. British attempts to recoup some of those expenses from its American subjects would spark some of the most important events in modern history.

ERA 5: INDEPENDENCE: AMERICA GAINS ITS FREEDOM *(1763 TO 1783)*

THE FRENCH AND INDIAN WAR PRODS BRITAIN TO SEEK REVENUE FROM THE COLONIES

The French and Indian War and the global Seven Years' War that it sparked were long and costly. Although Britain successfully drove the French from Canada, the empire now had to defend the newly conquered Canadian territory—an expensive challenge made more difficult by the territory's hostile French population. Britain had begun the war to defend its North American colonies from the French, and King George III's ministers decided that the colonies should pay taxes to help cover the cost of the war.

To draw more revenue from the colonies, Parliament passed the Sugar Act in 1764. The customs duties on molasses and other imports that smugglers had so often avoided paying (partly because of ineffective or corrupt British customs officials) were now to be strictly enforced. Britain also greatly expanded officials' and courts' powers to enforce the customs regulations.

These changes outraged many colonists. Although they accepted Britain's right to regulate colonial trade for the empire's well-being, they considered the new rules overreaching, burdensome, and unfair. New rumors swirled, including one implying that Britain might begin taxing the colonies directly. Many Americans considered direct Parliament-imposed taxes unnecessary, unjust, and in violation of their rights.

But Parliament ignored the colonists' loud objections and passed another measure, the Stamp Act, in 1765. The act demanded that virtually all printed materials—from legal documents and newspapers to playing cards—be printed on stamped, taxed paper. Stamp taxes were common in England, so the king's ministers expected the colonies to accept the measure without complaint. The ministers even promised that all revenues raised would go toward America's defense, and they appointed colonists as stamp masters to distribute the stamped paper.

Parliament went still further when it passed the 1765 and 1766 Quartering Acts, which required local colonial governments to provide supplies and barracks, or quarters, for British soldiers stationed in their respective colonies. Americans viewed the measures as another tax—and thus as one more violation of their rights.

The ministers, Parliament, and King George III had made a terrible miscalculation. They saw the sums raised through the stamp taxes as fair contributions to the colonists' own defense. But for most Americans, the *amount* of money was never the issue. The colonies already paid heavy taxes to support their local governments and to pay down the colonies' own debts incurred in fighting the French and Indian War. Many paid these local taxes proudly, even boasting of the patriotic burden they were willing to shoulder in support of government and defense. The issue at hand was *how*, and by whom, taxes were imposed.

THE COLONIES REJECT BRITISH TAXATION AND RESPOND TO THE STAMP ACT

According to British legal tradition, taxes represented the people's free monetary gift to the king for the support of his government. Therefore, taxes could only be granted with the people's consent, in person or through their representatives. Although few men in Britain could vote, members of Parliament were seen as representatives of the whole nation. But no colonist could vote in any parliamentary election; Americans had no voice there, nor any control over Parliament's actions. Therefore, Americans had not consented to the new taxes, and Parliament's members were making a "free gift" of money that was not theirs to give.

Americans famously rejected taxation without representation. But the issue went far beyond money. If Parliament could take Americans' money without their consent, what could it *not* do? If the colonists paid the tax, they would be accepting Parliament's right to govern them however it pleased—without an American say in its actions. For most colonists, subjection to such rule—power without check—amounted to despotism and slavery, depriving them of basic British liberties. Although they still accepted the idea that Parliament should have some role in governing America, they argued emphatically that such a role must not include taxation.

The colonists erupted in fury over the stamp tax. Because almost all documents now required stamps, the tax was impossible to avoid, so Americans decided to prevent Britain from collecting it. Angry crowds destroyed stamped paper and forced stamp masters to resign, while local courts allowed business to continue without the purchasing of stamped sheets. Such popular leaders as Patrick Henry in Virginia and Samuel Adams in Massachusetts helped rally "Sons of Liberty" against Britain's new policies—though not against British rule itself. Meanwhile, Benjamin Franklin and other prominent Americans in London pressed the British government to repeal the Stamp Act.

Colonists also organized boycott movements against British manufactured goods, which were crucial to Britain's wealth. Some threatened Stamp Act supporters and destroyed their property. Nine colonies united to protest the act by sending delegates to a Stamp Act Congress in October 1765.

British policymakers were alarmed by colonial agitation, and came under pressure from British merchants fearful of America's nonimportation agreements. The British government was eager to find a way out of the crisis, but it refused to recognize any American claim that would limit Parliament's powers over the colonies. In March 1766, the ministry and Parliament repealed the Stamp Act—but on the premise that the law was unwise and inconvenient as opposed to unjust. To ensure that the colonists understood this distinction, Parliament passed the Declaratory Act, a measure that asserted Britain's *right* to control America "in all cases whatsoever."

Americans were jubilant over the repeal of the Stamp Act. They saw the Declaratory Act as a face-saving gesture only, and believed that Parliament had recognized its errors and was trying to correct its missteps. However, Britain was still determined to draw money from the colonies. A new minister thought an external tax on imports would bypass American objections. Yet although colonists would accept import duties meant to regulate trade, they were *not* willing to pay duties contrived to raise revenue without their consent.

CRISIS BUILDS TOWARD REVOLUTION

A year after repealing the Stamp Act, Parliament passed the Townshend Acts. Americans were now forced to pay taxes on tea, glass, paper, and other imports. The colonists, who had thought the taxation issue settled by the Stamp Act's repeal, were stunned by what they saw as a fresh attack on their liberties. Determined to avoid taxed goods and to pressure Britain, they formed associations to block British imports and produce their own clothing and other goods. John Dickinson's *Letters from a Farmer in Pennsylvania*, reprinted in newspapers and pamphlets throughout the colonies, helped focus and articulate opposition to Britain's policies.

Bursts of violent protest and attempts (led by Massachusetts) to coordinate the colonies' petitions against the acts were seen by nervous royal officials as acts of rebellion and were met with punitive British crackdowns. In October 1768, royal troops occupied Boston—a key center of protest—to enforce obedience. But nonimportation only took firmer hold and spread throughout the colonies.

As petitions and protests brought greater hostility from London, many Americans grew more disillusioned with and dubious about distant powers entirely beyond their control. Gradually, they began to reconsider the very nature of free government. They shaped their views with help from the writings of such political thinkers as the seventeenth-century's John Locke, who argued that God granted basic rights to people through nature and that all government power—even that of kings—was granted to rulers by the people through binding compacts. When founding colonies, Americans had believed they had formed contracts with the king, thus making the king the head of Americans' own local governments. But now they began to reject any automatic subordination to Britain and any role whatsoever for Parliament in governing America.

Faith had always played a central role in American life, and religious beliefs strengthened the growing liberty movement. Most believed they were defending rights that God had granted to the people, and thus their political cause was also a sacred one. Preachers stressed that God alone could rule absolutely, and many worried that coarse soldiers and corrupt British officials would undermine public morality. Yet there was also a long-established colonial belief that America was specially favored, and that divine providence would help America prevail as a seat of liberty so long as the people upheld their faith and their morals.

Bostonians, still garrisoned with troops, chafed under military occupation. On March 5, 1770, after days of clashes, panicked soldiers fired into an angry crowd and killed five colonists. This Boston Massacre—its image quickly immortalized in a defiant engraving by Paul Revere—struck many as the inevitable fruit of oppressive British policies. Though Americans did not yet know it, Britain's ministers had already moved to repeal most of the Townshend duties (except the tax on tea, which was left to uphold Parliament's power to tax). The key issues remained unresolved, and the partial repeal satisfied few Americans. Although their boycott of British imports mostly collapsed later in 1770, they continued the embargo on still-taxed tea.

The Tea Act of 1773 allowed Britain's East India Company to ship tea directly to America, thus lowering its price and undercutting smugglers. But Americans saw the lower price as a ploy to trick them into paying the Townshend tea tax. Committees of Correspondence, which had been formed as suspicions about British plans increased, allowed the opposition to coordinate throughout the colonies. The new tea consignees were threatened, and tea was destroyed. Crisis culminated that December in Boston. Tea ship captains feared public fury and tried to turn back to sea, but the governor refused to let them leave. Townsmen disguised as Native Americans dumped hundreds of chests into the harbor, an act that future generations (though not the participants) would dub the Boston Tea Party.

At the king's urging, Parliament responded with the 1774 Coercive Acts. Boston's port was to be closed until the tea was paid for; if crown officers were to kill rioters, they would be shielded from American courts; Massachusetts's government was drastically altered to curb the people's power; and troops reoccupied Boston. Far from cowing Massachusetts, the "Intolerable Acts" (as colonists called them) enraged nearly all Americans. As calls sounded for a congress to coordinate resistance, further laws only widened the breach. The Quebec Act not only set up a wholly undemocratic government in Canada but also gave full toleration to Canada's French Catholic majority, and American Protestants feared what they saw as the tyrannical influence of the pope. And a new Quartering Act allowed troops to be housed on private property without owners' consent.

THE REVOLUTIONARY WAR: AMERICA STANDS UP FOR FREEDOM, BRITAIN FOR ITS EMPIRE

The First Continental Congress met in Philadelphia in September 1774. Some delegates urged caution, but the majority warned the people to arm and pressed a new nonimportation agreement. Britain responded with Lord North's February 1775 conciliation plan, which only offered that if America submitted to Parliament's revenue demands, North would let the colonies raise the funds themselves. In April, British troops marched from Boston to seize weapons and powder at Lexington and Concord. Alerted by Paul Revere and others in a prearranged warning network, local militia Minutemen met the troops, pushed them back to Boston, and laid siege to the British-occupied town.

In June 1775, the Second Continental Congress asked Virginia's George Washington—prominent landowner, politician, militia commander, and veteran of the French and Indian War—to lead American forces around Boston. These forces would constitute the core of a new Continental Army. Even as Congress issued a statement that justified taking up arms, moderates drafted the Olive Branch Petition, which pleaded for a peaceful alternative solution. George III refused even to receive it. Trying to head off a British invasion from Canada, American forces launched a dismally unsuccessful strike on Quebec. But in March 1776, after months of siege, Washington forced the British to evacuate Boston. He expected the next British blow at New York.

Many Americans remained strongly loyal to Britain—their mother country—despite its attacks on their liberties. They had been reluctant to turn on the king or to consider independence. But the escalating war pushed a number of them to reconsider. *Common Sense*, a January 1776 pamphlet by English émigré Thomas Paine, impressed many with its direct attack on George III and on monarchy itself. Although some colonists still resisted, Congress took up the subject of independence in June 1776. With help from Franklin and John Adams, Thomas Jefferson drafted a declaration. On July 2, Congress voted for independence. And on July 4, the Declaration of Independence was adopted by "the United States in Congress assembled." In laying out the God-given rights of all men and the right of all societies to create their own governments, the declaration would help form a cornerstone of American beliefs and influence throughout the world.

As America formally claimed independence, Britain stepped up its effort to bring the rebellious colonies to heel. The American Revolution began in earnest, and it proved difficult for the new United States. Britain could rely on hired German mercenaries and Native American allies who feared American expansion into their lands. And although most Americans backed independence, there were still many Loyalists (insultingly called *Tories*—an old word for the supporters of absolutist kings) who wanted to defend British power. By late 1776, the British had driven Washington's forces from New York. Washington struck back at Trenton and Princeton, and salvaged his men's morale. But the British took Philadelphia the next summer, and Washington withdrew to hard winter quarters at Valley Forge.

Meanwhile, a large British army tried to cut off New York as it moved from Canada into rural New York. American forces there did far better, and they decisively defeated the British at Saratoga in October 1777. This victory was crucial because it convinced France to join the war on America's side. Whereas some French officers (like the Marquis de Lafayette) admired America's cause, its absolutist king despised the revolutionaries and joined the cause only to undermine Britain. Suddenly, the colonists had a strong ally with a powerful army and navy. The British feared French attack and left Philadelphia in summer 1778, as Washington's army pursued them into New York.

Britain shifted its efforts to the South, expecting Loyalist support and help from slaves. In exchange for loyalty, the slaves were offered freedom (although many would ultimately be abandoned by the British). In 1780, while Washington's men suffered in winter quarters near New York, fighting flared in the South. Loyalist and Native American forces led frequent raids. There were British victories, but the overextended British were forced to retreat to the coast. In spring 1781, Lord Cornwallis's main British force entered Virginia. The French fleet headed for the Chesapeake, and Washington and the French army followed. French ships cut off Cornwallis while the Americans and French laid siege to his position at Yorktown. In October 1781, Cornwallis was forced to surrender his entire army.

In battling for a vast territory on hostile soil three thousand miles from home, Britain had faced an enormous task from the outset. And with the defeat of Cornwallis, the nation lost its will to fight. Early in 1782, Parliament voted to abandon the war and open negotiations. The specific terms—which dealt with borders, fishing rights, and more—took months to resolve, but Britain had accepted that its former colonies were now the independent United States of America. The Treaty of Paris was signed in 1783, and British forces left their last foothold in New York. The colonists' rebellion had truly become an American Revolution, establishing an independent United States determined to build a new way forward—one led by a government founded on the consent of its citizens.

ERA 6: WE THE PEOPLE: BUILDING AN AMERICAN REPUBLIC *(1776 TO 1789)*

DEMOCRATIC EXPERIMENTS: THE ARTICLES OF CONFEDERATION AND THE STATE CONSTITUTIONS

Americans faced enormous challenges during the Revolutionary War. They were waging a complex war against a powerful enemy over vast territory. Soldiers often suffered poor conditions and received only promissory notes as payment. Some even threatened to mutiny. Amid these crises, Americans were constantly confronted with a difficult question: Who was in charge? Congress was in overall control of the war effort and the main Continental Army, but its powers were poorly defined. It had few means to raise revenues and no way to force individual states to cooperate.

America needed an overarching government to unite its thirteen new states. Thus far, the only attempt to create an American confederacy had failed: Benjamin Franklin's 1754 Albany Plan had been rejected by the colonial governments. In 1777, Congress completed the Articles of Confederation, establishing itself as the permanent legislative body—composed of state delegates—for the United States. There was no president or bicameral legislature (a legislature with two houses, each balancing the power of the other), and the individual states managed virtually all of their own affairs.

When Congress had agreed on the articles, it sent them to the states for ratification. But just as they did for most major acts of Congress, the articles demanded unanimous support for ratification. The thirteen states each had their own interests and priorities, and unanimity was difficult to achieve. Several states claimed western lands on the basis of old colonial charters; others refused to ratify until those land claims were yielded to Congress. A 1781 compromise finally allowed ratification, but the land cession agreement soon broke down. It was a sign of struggles to follow.

The revolutionary crisis had left people deeply suspicious of powers beyond local control, and the Confederation government was left deliberately weak. Congress could not impose direct taxes and was largely limited to dealing with foreign affairs. Every state had one equal vote, and unanimous agreement was required for any major action or for an amendment to the articles. The articles, in short, created exactly what their name implied: a confederation of individual states, as opposed to a national government.

Meanwhile, states each had to create their own new governments. Most had to replace obsolete colonial charters, which granted key powers to royally appointed governors or royally authorized proprietors. Even as the Revolutionary War raged, states began to experiment with elected republican systems by passing a variety of new constitutions.

Like the Articles of Confederation, the new state governments generally kept central power weak. Most authority was placed in the elected assemblies. The executive branch had little power: governors typically served for short terms and could only run once, because frequent elections were seen as an important check on government abuses. Over time, though, people's fears of centralized government were trumped by their realization that government needs strength to function and move forward. The early constitutions were eventually replaced or heavily modified, but the first experiments were crucial steps as Americans learned to build elective, representative systems.

The Articles of Confederation had some success. For instance, Congress finally managed to take control of the western lands that some states had claimed, despite the disintegration of the 1781 deal. Though it took a long time, Congress organized the new lands into nationally controlled territories. One of the final acts of the Congress established by the Articles of Confederation was the Northwest Ordinance of 1787, which set up a major section of territory for settlement and eventual statehood. The ordinance followed a 1784 proposal from Thomas Jefferson and banned slavery in the Northwest Territory.

These successes, however, were overshadowed as the disadvantages of a weak central government under the articles became clear. Congress had no power of direct taxation and could raise revenues only through trade duties and fees. And with unanimous votes required to do or change virtually anything, it proved immensely difficult for the states to agree on significant matters. As states went their separate ways, foreign powers saw America as divided and weak.

Dissatisfaction and calls to revise the articles and expand the government's powers grew, but still Congress could hardly agree on any positive steps. The situation was worsened by Shays' Rebellion (from 1786 to 1787), during which debt-ridden farmers rose up against the state of Massachusetts and attacked a federal arsenal in Springfield. Congress was unable to respond effectively, and the rebellion was finally put down by the state government. The need for revision was clear, and calls for reform increasingly sounded.

Around the same time, in September 1786, a convention of state delegates met in Annapolis, Maryland, to discuss interstate commerce. While there, they urged Congress to call a new convention in Philadelphia to consider changes to the articles. Several states agreed and appointed delegates. Members of Congress tentatively endorsed the plan in early 1787, envisioning a convention that would only consider revisions to the existing articles.

Fifty-five delegates from twelve states assembled in Philadelphia that spring and summer. Notoriously uncooperative Rhode Island, which had often blocked action in Congress, did not attend. It refused even to discuss changes that might leave it with less influence than larger states.

Although many delegates played key roles in the convention debates that followed, particularly important participants included James Madison of Virginia, a learned student of government who greatly influenced the proceedings; Benjamin Franklin of Pennsylvania, now eighty-one years old, a peacemaker and elder statesman; and Alexander Hamilton of New York, who pushed for a strong government—almost an elected monarchy that would look more like Britain's. The delegates elected Revolutionary War hero George Washington of Virginia as the convention's president. His reputation instantly enhanced the legitimacy and magnitude of the proceedings.

THE CONSTITUTIONAL CONVENTION OF 1787

The convention in Philadelphia was designed to propose revisions to the Articles of Confederation. Those revisions would then be submitted to Congress and the state legislatures for consideration. But the delegates quickly went further. Meeting under a pledge of secrecy (debates were recorded mainly in a private journal kept by Madison), they were soon discussing plans to replace the articles with an entirely new plan of government. The assembly moved beyond its original purpose and would be called the Constitutional Convention.

As the delegates debated a new federal system, the convention's key challenge was to balance increased central authority with the individual powers of the states. The Virginia Plan, which was largely Madison's work, was favored by the bigger states. It stated that each state's representation in the federal legislature would be proportional to population, and would thus grant the largest states the greatest power. The smaller states responded with the New Jersey Plan; although it accepted many of the Virginia Plan's tenets, this plan gave states equal representation, which they had held in Congress under the articles. The result was deadlock.

A compromise proposal from the Connecticut delegation finally broke the stalemate. Under the Connecticut Compromise, the legislature would be bicameral, as Madison had urged. In the lower house, each state's representation would be proportional to its population. But in the upper house, each state would have an equal vote. The delegates decided that the lower house, which they named the House of Representatives, would be popularly elected every two years. This would help ensure representatives' accountability to the people. In the upper house, each state would select two senators for six-year terms. Only the popularly elected lower house could introduce tax bills, thereby upholding the principle of taxation with representation.

During the sweltering Philadelphia summer, in an airless room closed off for secrecy, the delegates worked through a string of contentious issues. The government would consist of legislative, executive, and judicial branches—a new Congress, a president, and a Supreme Court that would check and balance one another to prevent abuses of power. But how would the president be chosen, and how long would he serve? How much power would Congress have over commerce, or to levy taxes? How could the new Constitution be amended? Would slaves—who could not vote—be counted as part of the population in assigning representation to the states?

Compromises gradually emerged. The president would serve a four-year term, and could be reelected. He would be chosen by an electoral college: each state would have electors equal to its total number of senators and representatives, and each state government would decide how to choose its electors (for example, by popular vote, or by the state legislature). The new Congress would control foreign and interstate commerce, and it would be able to impose taxes. The amending process was made deliberately difficult to avoid frequent and disruptive changes. Unlike the articles, however, the new system would require only three-quarters of the states to agree on any amendment.

As already noted, some questions proved difficult: Should slaves be counted as part of a state's population? To give their states more representatives and consequent weight in Congress, southern states wanted them counted. Northern states—which had far fewer slaves and had, in several cases, moved to abolish slavery—did not wish to see the South gain so much influence. Therefore, they did not want slaves counted at all. An awkward compromise finally emerged, granting much of what the slaveholders demanded: three-fifths of a state's slave population would be counted in determining its representation.

Slavery itself was a contentious issue. Many Americans were uncomfortable with the institution, even if they were unwilling to give it up. The new Constitution avoided the words *slave* and *slavery* entirely. One clause required all states to return fugitive slaves, but referred to them as persons "held to service or labor"; the three-fifths clause distinguished between free people and "other persons." The document also prohibited any federal interference with the African slave trade until after 1808, but described it only as the "Importation of such Persons as any of the States . . . shall think proper to admit." The Constitution thus protected the rights of slaveholders without openly endorsing the institution of slavery. It was a delicate balance.

THE BATTLE FOR RATIFICATION AND THE CALL FOR A BILL OF RIGHTS

The convention had met in strict secrecy; its debates would actually remain secret for decades. Madison's notes were not published until 1840, four years after his death. By mid-September 1787, the convention was ready to present its plan. Americans were suddenly confronted with an entirely new model of government and nationhood—a far stronger central government with multiple balanced branches, elected both directly and indirectly. Though states would still have significant internal power, the Constitution was to become the "supreme Law of the Land." The people now had to decide whether they would accept or reject this radical proposal.

Some members of the old Congress protested that the convention had exceeded its powers, but most soon agreed to submit the new document to the states. The Constitution included rules for its own ratification. To ensure that ratification was a decision of the *people*, not only of current state governments, each state was to elect a special ratifying convention. Those normally allowed to vote by the various states, generally adult males who met a minimum property requirement, were allowed to elect the conventions (a remarkable degree of popular participation by the standards of the time). Once nine states had ratified it, the Constitution could take effect.

Supporters of the new Constitution—that is, advocates of increased federal power—came to be known as Federalists. They insisted on the need for a strong, centralized national authority that could manage U.S. affairs without being blocked by a few local interests (as had so commonly happened under the articles). The proposed system's opponents, who came to be called Anti-Federalists, were more swayed by memories of the American Revolution. They feared the loss of local control and thought that the new federal government would be too far removed from the people; they worried that it could come to threaten liberty as Britain had before independence. Federalists answered that unfettered local democracy, without broader checks and balances, would fragment the United States and allow factional majorities to tyrannize minorities.

Many states were deeply divided over ratification. Some ratified easily, even unanimously. Delaware was first, ratifying unanimously in early December 1787; Pennsylvania ratified a few days later by a two-to-one margin, followed by several more states. But some states witnessed far greater battles. Rhode Island rejected the Constitution, and would long refuse to reconsider. Debate raged not only in the ratifying conventions but also in the popular press. For months, newspapers and pamphlets were dominated by essays on the Constitution's virtues or dangers. For several months between 1787 and 1788, there appeared in New York the period's most distinguished and widely circulated series of essays: *The Federalist*, an influential defense of the Constitution by James Madison, Alexander Hamilton, and New York politician John Jay.

A major Anti-Federalist concern was the new Constitution's failure to explicitly guarantee basic rights. Federalists found such guarantees unnecessary, because the new government's powers were strictly limited; some even feared the idea and worried that lists of specific rights could lead to the trampling of any rights not mentioned. But Federalists were prepared to compromise, and their promises to add a Bill of Rights once the Constitution took effect swayed enough opponents to win major ratifications. In Massachusetts, such arguments won over the influential Samuel Adams and helped secure a close vote in favor. Several conventions attached to their ratification vote recommendations for specific amendments.

The ninth state, Maryland, ratified in April 1788 and allowed the Constitution to take effect. But everyone knew the system would fail without the support of such important states as New York and Virginia. Virginia's Federalist forces, led by Madison, were challenged by Patrick Henry's Anti-Federalists, but Madison's promise to pursue a Bill of Rights helped secure a narrow vote for ratification in June. Hamilton led the Federalists in New York, winning a narrow victory in July. (The twelfth state, North Carolina, did not follow until November 1789, when the new Congress proposed a Bill of Rights. Rhode Island would not ratify until May 1790.)

The old Confederation Congress prepared to transfer power to the new government, which would be based in New York City. Although Patrick Henry and other fiery Anti-Federalists pushed for a second convention, the states proceeded late in 1788 to choose their senators and elect their representatives. Early in 1789, the states selected their presidential electors. George Washington, without doubt the most revered man in America, was unanimously chosen by the electors. John Adams of Massachusetts–chief author of his state's constitution and Confederation Congress diplomat–was chosen as vice president. It was time to put the new system into practice.

ERA 7: DEMOCRACY MADE REAL: AMERICA PASSES THE TORCH *(1789 TO 1800)*

CREATING THE NATIONAL GOVERNMENT

The new federal Constitution was pieced together in a series of complex compromises. Many important clauses were written in broad, general terms to satisfy different priorities and to give the new government much-needed flexibility. As a result, important questions about the nature and extent of federal power were often left open to considerable interpretation.

The first great task facing the newly elected Congress and president was the creation of a working system from the Constitution's general outline. Basic issues still had to be resolved, such as the fundamental rules on which the two houses of Congress would operate. For example, the Senate met in secret session for its first five years, a practice that Americans would later consider inconceivable.

The Constitution assumed there would be "executive departments" but did not define them; it stated only that the president's nominees for executive offices would require Senate confirmation. Congress was left to decide what departments were necessary and to create them through legislation. The idea that the heads of the various departments would form a presidential cabinet largely came from President George Washington, who began to consult with and depend on the counsel of department leaders.

There was even a lengthy dispute over the president's formal title. Some senators and Vice President John Adams favored elaborate concoctions, such as "His Highness, the President of the United States of America, and Protector of the Rights of the Same." But such suggestions smacked of royalty and were deeply unpopular with the public and many congressmen, who preferred the simple "President of the United States" and "Mr. President." The controversy's main effect was to damage Adams's standing with Washington, and to help block vice presidents—whose only official duty under the Constitution is to preside over the Senate—from participating in Senate debates.

During his presidency, Washington's greatest achievement was leading the government through these early trials. His firm, steady, and dignified leadership, coupled with the near-universal high regard in which Americans held him, helped overcome divisions and hold the government together as it gradually assembled itself.

In September 1789, as soon as the executive departments were established, James Madison turned his focus to the amendments he and other Federalists had promised in the ratifying conventions. Congress submitted twelve amendments to the states, ten of which were ratified by 1791. The resulting Bill of Rights guaranteed freedom of speech, freedom of the press, and freedom of religion; the right to bear arms for militia service; freedom from unreasonable search and seizure; the right to a jury trial; and freedom from cruel or unusual punishments. The ninth amendment, addressing Federalist concerns about the dangers of listing only certain freedoms, protected rights that were not specifically enumerated; the tenth reserved to the states or the people all powers that were not specifically granted to the federal government by the Constitution.

Congress then had to establish the federal judiciary. The Constitution specified only that there would be a Supreme Court and "such inferior courts" as Congress established. Even the number of Supreme Court justices was (and today remains) left to Congress. Yet the exact role of the Supreme Court remained unclear. It was not until 1803, in *Marbury v. Madison* under Chief Justice John Marshall, that the court ruled an act of Congress unconstitutional. This began a long process by which the court established its power to review the constitutionality of both federal and state laws.

THE FIRST PARTY SCHISM

The new government was created carefully and methodically, but a completely unplanned phenomenon also emerged: the rise of political parties. Different groups of politicians and citizens inevitably had divergent visions for the country's direction, and many began dividing into factions. President Washington tried to discourage factionalism by promoting compromise and accord, but the differences were too great. Two nascent parties were soon identified with two rival members of Washington's cabinet: Secretary of the Treasury Alexander Hamilton and Secretary of State Thomas Jefferson.

Hamilton's faction, which believed in strong federal power, called itself the Federalist Party (this should not be confused with the Constitution's Federalist supporters, who split their loyalties between the new parties). The new Federalists aimed at a powerful central government that would promote industry and commerce, and in turn create moneyed classes. These classes would invest in government debt and fund government operations, including permanent and potent military forces. In essence, they aimed for an elected, representative version of wealthy and powerful Great Britain.

The Federalists' rivals were known as the Democratic-Republicans, or simply Republicans, and Jefferson was widely seen as their leader. They embraced a strict constructionist vision, pressing for a far weaker federal government whose powers were limited to those explicitly granted by the Constitution. They wanted state and local governments to retain considerable power because they were closer to the people and thus more democratic. The Republicans, or Jeffersonians, also envisioned an agrarian society of independent small farmers, as equal in wealth and influence as possible. They feared that extensive commerce and industry would foster inequality between owners and laborers, leaving the latter unable to resist the political will of the former. They particularly resented financial speculators (or investors) who reaped profit at others' expense while never producing goods of their own.

The party divide was heavily sectional (that is, regionally divided between the different sections of the country). Federalist support was strong in commercially developed New England and the mid-Atlantic region, whereas the agrarian South, and its plantation-owning elite, was primarily Republican. Sectional priorities and economic interests thus further exacerbated the increasingly bitter party divide.

Conflict erupted as early as 1790, when Hamilton offered a fiscal program to strengthen America's credit and economic standing. Some tenets of his plan, such as one honoring the Confederation's debts to foreign powers, were uncontroversial and widely accepted. But his insistence that the new federal government honor the states' Revolutionary War debts sparked a crisis. Much of that debt, including pay still owed to soldiers, had been bought up by speculators at a fraction of face value. The Jeffersonian South vehemently objected to increasing federal power and raising taxes to enrich speculators (mostly northern) with money properly owed to others.

In the end, a compromise was reached. A strong lobby wished to move the nation's capital from New York to Philadelphia (which served as the capital from 1776 to 1787). Jeffersonians, however, did not want the government based in either city, because both were so tied to powerful commercial interests. Hamilton, Madison, and Jefferson reached a deal: Jeffersonians would support Hamilton's debt plan if the capital were moved to a patch of reclaimed swampland along the Potomac that was far removed from northern commercial cities. The government would move to Philadelphia only while construction of the new federal city, soon named in honor of Washington, was under way. The government would finally move to Washington, DC, in 1800.

THE NEW NATION'S PARTIES AND POLITICS

The debt compromise did nothing to relieve the fundamental split between the parties. Despite President Washington's efforts to mediate, partisan conflict only deepened, especially as members of the press aggressively began to take sides. In 1791, seeking to stabilize the currency and promote development, Hamilton persuaded Congress to charter a national Bank of the United States. Jefferson insisted that the Constitution did not authorize such an act, but Hamilton countered that Congress's "implied powers"—those necessary to meet the Constitution's stated aims—allowed the bank's creation. Washington signed the bill, but the bank remained deeply unpopular among Jeffersonians.

The parties also broke sharply over the French Revolution that erupted in 1789, especially when the new French government deposed and executed King Louis XVI in 1792. Federalists, on the one hand, feared France's atheistic and populist radicalism; they also wished to maintain close ties with Britain, which was soon at war with revolutionary France. Many Jeffersonians, on the other hand, admired the French cause despite its growing violence. They were wary of British influence, and considered Britain's enemy their friend.

Washington kept the nation neutral, but in 1793 a new French envoy, calling himself "Citizen Genêt," tried to bypass the government and appeal directly to the people for support. He and the French cause proved widely popular. The "Citizen Genêt Affair" widened the party breach, even though Jefferson, Madison, and others soon found his excesses embarrassing. Genêt's faction meanwhile fell in France; called home to face trial, he took asylum and became a U.S. citizen. In the wake of Genêt's meddling, Washington shifted toward Hamilton's anti-French position, and Jefferson resigned as secretary of state.

Despite deepening partisan feuds, the new government proved its strength. At Hamilton's urging, Congress had enacted an excise tax on distilled liquors. This tax, along with trade duties, served as the government's main source of revenue. Western Pennsylvania distillers rebelled against the tax in 1794's Whiskey Rebellion. Unlike the Confederation government, which had not been strong enough to quell Shays' Rebellion in 1786–1787, Washington's government was able to put down the rebels. And it did so with strong public support: because the tax had been passed by the people's representatives, few saw rebellion as a legitimate response. Rebellion was valid only before the American Revolution, when the people had lacked any say in Britain's actions.

Relations with Britain also brought controversy. Even after independence, America and Britain clashed over the continued presence of British forts on the northern U.S. border. Seeking to isolate revolutionary France, the British also began to seize American ships and even press American sailors into the British navy. The threat of war loomed, but America was heavily dependent on British imports (duties on which provided a major source of federal revenue). In 1794, Washington sent Chief Justice John Jay to negotiate.

Jay managed to defuse the crisis and negotiate a treaty, but he tacitly acknowledged America's dependence on British trade. Although he secured a British guarantee to abandon its forts along the border, he acquiesced to Britain on many points. Republicans were outraged and stirred up popular clamor against the treaty, but Federalists swallowed their own doubts and defended it as tactically wise. The Senate narrowly ratified the Jay Treaty. But debate had been very divisive, and the dispute further alienated the parties from one another.

In 1796, Washington retired after two terms; he thereby set another important precedent, as no president would win a third term until 1940 (after which time a constitutional amendment would make the traditional two terms in office the legal limit). Washington's famous 1796 "Farewell Address" (published, rather than delivered as a speech) explained the rationale for his retirement and warned against permanent alliances with Europe's feuding powers. He also cautioned strongly against the dangers of partisanship and warned that sectional divisions were especially perilous.

But even Washington could not suppress the schism. The party split differed from the divide in the American party system that emerged in the nineteenth century, in which two parties competed in successive elections to shift policy in one direction or another. The first party schism was a battle over the fundamental nature of the country—each party believed that only one could survive and ultimately prevail.

THE REVOLUTION OF 1800

The presidential election of 1796 was the first truly contested race, and it became an openly partisan battle. The Constitution made no allowance for party candidates: as the Electoral College then stood, the top finisher became president, and the candidate who placed second became vice president. Adams, who had served as Washington's vice president, won the election. But the Jay Treaty had strengthened the Democratic-Republicans: Jefferson, Adams's chief opponent, finished a close second and thus became vice president. Jefferson, the de facto opposition leader, would have a very limited role in the Adams administration.

Under Adams and the pro-British Federalists, relations with France quickly deteriorated. Like Britain, France interfered with American shipping to war-torn Europe. Adams dispatched ambassadors, but French negotiators (identified as X, Y, and Z in diplomatic reports) demanded a hefty bribe to engage in negotiations. The "XYZ Affair" caused a scandal, and negotiations collapsed. Hawkish Federalists pressed for war, which Adams resisted. As a result, an undeclared quasi-war erupted at sea from 1798 to 1800. Adams eventually defused the crisis through diplomacy—and stoked the fury of Hamilton and other war hawks.

At home, however, Adams was more amenable to strong measures. With his approval, the Federalist-dominated Congress passed the Alien and Sedition Acts in 1798. Some prominent Republicans were recent European émigrés; the Alien Act and other related measures made it much more difficult to win citizenship, and allowed the president to expel politically suspect aliens. The Sedition Act made it a crime to oppose the execution of federal laws or to publish "false" writings that brought the government into disrepute. This was used to target Republican newspapers, and Republicans knew that the act was set to expire just when Adams's term would end.

Republicans were furious at these partisan attacks on personal liberty and free expression. Resolutions passed in the legislatures of Kentucky (drafted by Jefferson) and Virginia (drafted by Madison) assailed the Alien and Sedition Acts as unconstitutional and insisted that the states had the right to judge the validity of federal laws. Northern states, most of which were still Federalist, objected that only the federal courts had that authority. In response, Kentucky insisted that states not only could judge but also could nullify, or strike down, federal laws they deemed unconstitutional. Kentucky stopped short of challenging the federal union of the states, but notions of state power and nullification would prove potent, and divisive, in coming decades.

The unpopular Alien and Sedition Acts helped undermine the Federalists in the election of 1800. But as the party system became more fixed, the flaws in the electoral process were further exposed. Each elector cast a vote for two different candidates for president. Now there were not only party candidates but also party *tickets*, complete with presidential and vice presidential candidates. The Republicans finished first, with seventy-three electoral votes to Adams's sixty-five. But each of the seventy-three Republican electors cast one of his votes for Jefferson and the other vote for Jefferson's running mate, Aaron Burr. The result was a tie, and the ambitious Burr refused to step aside.

In the event of an electoral tie, the House of Representatives was to decide the election (with each of the sixteen states' delegations getting a single vote). But the newly elected Republican House had not yet taken office, and the outgoing Federalists were determined to thwart Jefferson. With two states evenly divided, neither candidate could secure the nine states needed for a majority. However, Hamilton thought Burr was potentially dangerous. So, despite his hatred toward Jefferson, he finally threw his support to his rival and broke the deadlock. Jefferson was declared president on the thirty-sixth ballot, and Burr assumed the vice presidency.

Ugly though the process was, the new government had passed a crucial test in the 1800 election. The system had survived a serious crisis with neither violence nor disruption, and Jefferson was inaugurated without incident. This peaceful transfer of power from one party to the other marked a momentous achievement for the new nation, coming to be known as the Revolution of 1800.

ERA 8: GOING WEST: OPPORTUNITY AND PERIL ON AMERICA'S FRONTIER *(1800 TO 1830S)*

A YOUNG AND FAST-EXPANDING NATION

The electoral stalemate of 1800 was disruptive for the young United States, and everyone agreed that such a crisis must never happen again. The electoral system had to change to allow for party tickets before the next election. In 1803, Congress passed the twelfth amendment, which gave each elector separate votes for president and vice president. The system had thus passed another test: the amendment process worked and would provide an effective framework for making changes in the future.

The 1800 election marked a political watershed. Both the Federalists and the Democratic-Republicans had believed that only one party could survive. At least for the immediate future, they were right. After the turbulence and public suspicion of the Federalists' aristocratic elitism that wracked the 1790s, most Americans shifted their allegiance to the more populist Jeffersonians. The Federalists lost Congress as well as the presidency in 1800. As the country expanded, they were increasingly confined to New England and fell into permanent decline. The Federalist vision of an America closely modeled on Britain's fiscal and military state was clearly the losing perspective, and would gradually all but vanish.

Yet the pure Jeffersonian vision—an agrarian America with a weak central government, limited industry, and a small military—would not suffice either. As its commerce and industry grew rapidly, the new nation was changing irreversibly. The Democratic-Republicans, who had a growing monopoly on power, were forced to adapt. Although many party members remained hostile to the building commercial boom, other factions began to support pro-growth government policies and to represent commercial interests.

The young nation also began expanding west, just as Native Americans had long feared. The U.S. population was rapidly growing, and most of the country was still dependent on farming (an economic reality that would hold for over a century), so Americans' appetite for more land was insatiable. During the colonial period, Americans had looked east (toward Europe, and Britain in particular) and had viewed the West as a sort of backcountry. Now the image of an expanding American frontier became increasingly tantalizing. Soon, Americans would begin to see a divinely ordained right and need to expand the nation across the continent—by the 1840s, they would come to call it "Manifest Destiny."

West of the Mississippi River, the continent was still in foreign hands. In 1800, French emperor Napoleon Bonaparte won back the vast Louisiana Territory (which had been under Spanish control since the 1760s), and intended to revive France's colonial efforts in America. French ambitions alarmed President Thomas Jefferson. Fearing loss of access to the Mississippi River, he sought to buy New Orleans from France in 1803. To the astonishment of the American negotiators, Napoleon—mired in European troubles and reconsidering new colonial ventures—instead offered to sell the entire Louisiana Territory. Jefferson's emissaries, ignoring their instructions to make a much more limited purchase, immediately agreed.

Jefferson was in a bind. He had long insisted on a strict constructionist view of the Constitution, which said nothing about purchasing foreign territory. But the acquisition would double the size of U.S. territory with one stroke. For Jefferson, whose vision of a nation of independent farmers depended on land, this prospect was irresistible. (The Federalists had always taken a loose constructionist view. But they feared that an even greater westward expansion would further damage their dwindling northeastern base, and so they assailed Jefferson's move on strict constructionist grounds.) Jefferson quickly arranged an expedition (from 1803 to 1806) under Meriwether Lewis and William Clark to explore the new territory and lay the ground for future settlement.

Jefferson was also prepared to be flexible on foreign affairs. Even as he sought to reduce government spending and debt (for example, by scaling back the military forces that John Adams had expanded), his foreign policy grew more aggressive. Like George Washington, he was keen to avoid "entangling alliances" with European powers—that phrase, often attributed to Washington's "Farewell Address," is in fact Jefferson's.

But independent American strength was another matter. North Africa's Barbary States had long exacted tribute by threatening American ships. Washington and Adams had continued to pay the ransom. Tripoli, one of the Barbary powers, increased its demands and finally declared war in 1801. Jefferson responded forcefully, and dispatched warships to the Mediterranean in 1803. Americans blockaded Tripoli, and Tripoli was forced to make peace in 1805. Even though other Barbary States continued to demand tribute, the American victory was significant in that the United States had shown that it could exercise power abroad.

AMERICA DEFIES THE EUROPEAN POWERS

Conflict with Europe was also brewing. As the Napoleonic Wars dragged on, both Britain and France tried to block neutral ships from trading with their enemies. Yet compared with the French navy, the British fleet was far more powerful. It seriously threatened American commercial shipping. Britain not only ramped up its seizures of American ships after 1805 but also pressed American sailors into its navy by claiming they were Royal Navy deserters.

The conflict revived many of the issues that the unpopular Jay Treaty of 1794 had left unresolved. The United States attempted to negotiate with Britain, and threatened to block British imports from entering America. (Though such boycotts had been tried in the Revolutionary War era and were considered successful, their impact on Britain had never been as powerful as Americans believed: if faced with a U.S. embargo, Britain could simply sell its goods elsewhere.) Britain was unbending, and negotiations failed. In 1807, the British warship *Leopard* opened fire and killed several sailors aboard the U.S. Navy's *Chesapeake* near the Virginia coast. Sailors on the *Leopard* claimed they were searching for British deserters.

Jefferson responded with the Embargo Act of 1807, which essentially banned all trade (that is, both imports and exports) with foreign nations. Britain was the intended target, but America emerged as the measure's real victim. Denounced by Federalists and commercially oriented Republicans alike, the embargo was widely evaded by rampant smuggling. Public pressure forced Congress to ease the embargo, but the British government refused to make concessions. Pressure for war mounted. In 1812, President James Madison–Jefferson's ally and successor–asked Congress to declare war. Despite opposition from New England and other eastern commercial states that favored a negotiated settlement to protect trade, southern and western support pushed the vote through Congress. The War of 1812 had begun.

The war began badly for the United States. American forces launched a poorly planned, inadequately armed invasion of Canada. Despite the fact that British resources were tied down in Europe, America made a weak showing. The United States did have notable successes at sea–for example, the famous exploits of the *Constitution* and a major victory on the Great Lakes that blocked a British push from Canada. But the 1814 defeat of Napoleon allowed the British to commit greater forces to America. British troops pushed into the mid-Atlantic and burned Washington, DC. Nonetheless, American forces made a crucial stand at Baltimore, stopping the British advance. A huge battle flag, flying over Baltimore's Fort McHenry at dawn, showed that the city had withstood the British assault, inspiring eyewitness Francis Scott Key to write "The Star Spangled Banner."

Despite these sporadic successes, America's resources were strained, and its citizens were bitterly divided by the war. New England, in particular, remained violently opposed. Efforts at peace talks began, and both sides finally signed the Treaty of Ghent in late 1814. With news of the treaty still en route, General Andrew Jackson won a major American victory at New Orleans in January 1815, blocking British attempts to seize the Mississippi River. Ultimately, the Treaty of Ghent resolved very few of the issues that had sparked the war. But the end of the Napoleonic Wars in 1815 allowed Britain to relax its harassment of American ships, and tensions between the two nations gradually eased.

Despite the war's inconclusive ending and the overall poor performance of American land forces, Americans were emboldened by the naval victories and Jackson's New Orleans triumph. In 1816, a naval expedition under Stephen Decatur forced the remaining Barbary States to end their attacks on American ships. The United States would never pay foreign tribute again. By 1823, President James Monroe was prepared to declare the entire Western Hemisphere a uniquely American sphere of influence. Many of Spain's Central and South American colonies had recently rebelled and declared independence. The Monroe Doctrine also indicated that the creation of new European colonies or interference with the newly independent Latin American states would be considered an act of aggression toward the United States.

THE ECONOMY TRANSFORMS AS COMMERCE EXPANDS

The young American republic was marked by dizzying commercial development. New urban factories turned out textiles and other manufactured goods, while ever-expanding rural territory and the growing plantation system produced masses of crops. There were markets both at home and abroad: Europe needed goods and raw materials to fight the Napoleonic Wars, then demanded more imports to rebuild the continent at the wars' end.

A major requirement for growth was the construction of modern roads and canals, which would allow efficient movement of goods across the country's huge distances. Such projects depended heavily on private and government investment. The Erie Canal, for example, opened in 1825 to connect Lake Erie with the Hudson River, and was built by the state of New York at government expense. This project, and others like it, provided entirely new avenues for crops and goods to reach urban centers and trading ports. Commercial development dramatically increased in once-isolated inland communities.

Despite the political unease felt by some Democratic-Republicans, commercial growth was unstoppable. As the Federalists faded and the Republicans' political hold became unbreakable, elements of the party came to represent the nation's commercial and pro-development interests. Tension between the party's different factions increased as the demand for economic investment intensified. Despite considerable political resistance, the federal government slowly began to promote such internal improvements as roads and canals in the 1820s. This policy would remain a major point of controversy in the coming decades.

Another source of political dispute was the still-controversial national bank. Although many continued to believe a nationally chartered bank was unconstitutional, the bank helped fund expansion and stabilize the currency, and it offered money for borrowing and investment. A divided Congress had let Alexander Hamilton's First Bank of the United States expire at the end of its charter in 1811. But without a central body to coordinate national economic policy, the War of 1812 sparked a currency crisis. Congress was forced to create a Second Bank of the United States in 1816, complete with another twenty-year charter.

The Supreme Court under Chief Justice John Marshall was crucial in establishing the federal government's power to promote economic development. In 1819's *McCulloch v. Maryland*, the court upheld the constitutionality of the national bank against a challenge by the state of Maryland. Marshall's decision endorsed Hamilton's "loose construction" and "implied powers" arguments of the 1790s, which insisted that Congress could enact whatever laws were necessary to achieve the Constitution's broad aims. This was an enormously influential decision, in that it cemented the growing power of the federal government. In its other decisions, the Marshall court consistently backed broad federal power to aid and develop commerce.

Economic change also presented many Americans with new perils. Rural farmers had long relied on local farming and barter economies. But industrializing cities and the growing European market for American exports increased demand for food and raw materials. Farmers were asked to supply those goods in exchange for cash, and now they needed that cash to fulfill their own needs and wants. Tied into new trading networks and a vast money-based market economy, rural areas were thus exposed to new and frightening risks if the larger economy stumbled.

And stumble it did. Fevered growth and heavy borrowing from the national bank spurred risky investment in insecure up-and-coming ventures, and the complex economy became dependent on unpredictable exports and bank policies. The Panic of 1819 illustrated for rural farmers how vulnerable to outside forces they had become. Many of them were now mired in crippling debt. They blamed the Second Bank of the United States for these new problems (mismanagement in the bank had contributed to the 1819 panic), demonizing it as a monstrous predator on ordinary citizens. The old Jeffersonian prejudice against "speculators" took on new urgency and fueled a wave of popular fury, laying the groundwork for a populist political backlash.

ERA 9: FREEDOM FOR ALL: AMERICAN DEMOCRACY BEGINS TO TRANSFORM *(1820S TO 1840S)*

THE NEW PARTY SCHISM AND THE JACKSONIAN ERA

By 1820, the Federalists were virtually extinct—in that year's presidential election, they did not even field a candidate. Four years earlier, the overwhelming victory of Democratic-Republican James Monroe had ushered in the Era of Good Feelings, a supposedly nonpartisan period of Republican dominance. Yet with the collapse of the Federalists and their vision of a more aristocratic America, the Democratic-Republicans inevitably grew more diverse. The party now included Americans from many regions who had competing priorities. And because there was no opposition party, members were not motivated to strive for unity within their own. Republican factions formed, and members of Monroe's cabinet battled over policy and influence (much as they had during George Washington's presidency).

As the national government became more heavily invested in promoting internal transport routes, the deepest political divisions revolved around the federal government's role in fostering economic growth. One faction supported protective tariffs and government-funded internal improvements. Henry Clay, an influential Kentucky congressman (and later senator), called this the "American System." But others in the party held a more traditionally Jeffersonian populist line. They feared the growth of federal power at the states' expense; they resented the economic crises, which they blamed largely on speculators; and they assailed the banks—especially the ever-controversial national bank—for providing those speculators with loans.

The dramatic expansion of voting rights fueled the growing partisan split. Since the Revolutionary War, Americans' notions of popular rights had gradually changed. As the frontier moved west in the early nineteenth century, new states increasingly rejected property requirements for suffrage (the right to vote). Federalists had argued that power should be restricted to a more educated and prosperous elite, but their decline was echoed by a rapid expansion of suffrage in the older states. By the 1820s, most states had given virtually all white males the vote. On the world stage, this was nothing short of extraordinary: in Britain, the democratizing Great Reform Act of 1832 still left fully 80 percent of men without the vote.

As popular power grew, the means by which American presidents were elected also changed. Since the republic's beginning, states had differed on how they chose electors (that is, selection by state legislatures versus election by the voters). By the late 1820s, voters chose their electors directly in all but two states. The president was, in essence, now popularly elected by all adult white men. The transformed political landscape came to be known as Jacksonian Democracy in honor of Andrew Jackson, the Tennessee frontiersman, politician, and War of 1812 hero who led and symbolized the populist movement.

In the absence of an opposition party, the 1824 election pitted four rival Republicans against each other. Jackson finished first in both popular and electoral votes, but fell short of a majority in the four-way race. Members of the House of Representatives were required to choose between the top three finishers; Henry Clay finished fourth and threw his support behind John Quincy Adams of Massachusetts, who finished second nationally but secured the backing of the House. When Adams named Clay secretary of state, rumors swirled that the two men had made a corrupt bargain.

Widely seen as illegitimate, Adams's election further fractured the party. Jackson, whose supporters now called themselves the Democratic Party, decisively defeated Adams in an 1828 rematch. Whereas Adams—from the commercially active Northeast—had favored a strong government role in economic development, the aggressively populist President Jackson challenged that role. He targeted speculators, blocked federal spending for internal improvements, and vetoed the renewal of the national bank on the grounds that it was unconstitutional. The bank expired in 1836.

Yet despite his insistence on limited federal powers, Jackson used his own executive powers with ruthless force. He bullied the other government branches and appointed his personal friends and allies to federal offices (the so-called spoils system). He also fiercely defended westward expansion by any means necessary. Determined to push Native Americans out of the way, Jackson aggressively backed Congress's Indian Removal Act of 1830. He ignored a Supreme Court decision that upheld the sovereignty of Native American nations, and he aided states' efforts to remove Native American peoples from the South. The difficult and deadly migration of the Cherokee and others to the Oklahoma Territory was called the Trail of the Tears by the dispossessed tribes.

Jackson's opponents called his policies wrong-headed and his use of power tyrannical, and the opposition press branded him "King Andrew the First." In the face of his growing Democratic Party, pro-development Democratic-Republicans began to form their own rival party in the early 1830s. Led by Clay and his allies, the Whig Party took its name from a British term, widely used in the American Revolution, that referred to opponents of unchecked monarchical power. The Second American Party System, the real start of the permanent two-party system that would come to define American politics, had arrived.

A MORE PERFECT SOCIETY: SOCIAL CHANGE AND THE REFORM MOVEMENTS

In the 1820s and 1830s, the new nation was gripped by a surge of Protestant evangelical fervor. The Second Great Awakening, like the first a century earlier, was marked by revivalist meetings and proselytizing churches that sought to save American souls (particularly those along the western frontier). Baptists, Methodists, and other evangelical sects grew rapidly, and new movements emerged. For example, upstate New York's Burned-Over District (named for the revivals that swept over it like wildfire) was the birthplace of Joseph Smith's Mormon movement.

Revivalist leaders wanted to achieve a perfect society through moral reform. This was a particularly urgent aim for many old-stock Americans, who were concerned about the morals of the growing waves of immigrant laborers. Germans arrived in large numbers in the 1830s and 1840s, and Ireland's potato famine drove many Irish to move to America in the late 1840s. In eastern cities, the surging immigrant population changed the political landscape. Democrats courted their votes, whereas anti-immigrant, nativist parties warned of the dangers posed by the newcomers' supposedly inferior stock. Revivalist reformers believed that they were charged with improving immigrants' morality.

Coupled with a broader post–Revolutionary War push to expand and improve social justice, revivalist beliefs drove a host of reform movements. The temperance crusade battled alcohol and the social ills surrounding it. Immigrants were considered particularly vulnerable to degrading saloons and especially dangerous when they were under alcohol's influence. Other efforts sought to expand public education opportunities, including those for women. Still other reformers worked to transform the American prison system, hoping to create model prisons, or reformatories, that would rehabilitate instead of merely punish those who were incarcerated.

The reform movements also sparked the country's first concerted push for women's rights and suffrage. Led by Elizabeth Cady Stanton, women's activists held a convention at Seneca Falls, New York, in 1848. Its "Declaration of Rights and Sentiments" was carefully modeled on the Declaration of Independence, and insisted on the self-evident truth "that all men and women are created equal." The women's rights movement grew and became a long-standing element of the country's reform efforts. Although it had little immediate effect on women's status, the movement also promoted other reforms of the period and laid a strong foundation for the successful women's suffrage push of the late nineteenth and early twentieth centuries.

The North's growing abolitionist movement would have the greatest immediate impact. Even before the Revolution, some Americans (particularly Quakers, who also became heavily involved in the women's rights movement) had challenged the morality of slavery. But the Revolution pushed the issue to the forefront: Could a free people continue to enslave others? The Second Great Awakening fostered a heavily religious abolitionist movement, which denounced slavery as a moral evil and demanded its immediate elimination throughout the United States. Though some southerners certainly had doubts about slavery, the organized abolition movement was almost entirely a northern phenomenon.

Condemnation of slavery did not necessarily imply concern for blacks' rights. Most abolitionists viewed blacks as natural inferiors in need of protection, whereas others regarded them with blatant contempt and hostility. Many backed so-called colonization: a plan to resettle freed slaves in Africa that was already promoted by such ambivalent slave owners as Thomas Jefferson and James Madison in the 1810s. One early effort created the African state of Liberia as a home for emancipated slaves. Relatively few abolitionists advocated anything approaching racial equality. True abolitionism, demanding the full and immediate abolition of slavery, was always a minority position—even in the North. Yet the movement was powerful, helping focus the North's attention on the growing grip of slavery in the South. In turn, southerners grew alarmed as they pondered northern intentions to interfere with the cornerstone of their labor system.

AFTER ITS POST-REVOLUTION DECLINE, SLAVERY GAINS STRENGTH

In the wake of the Revolutionary War, doubts about slavery were particularly strong in the North, where the system was less entrenched and could more easily be dismantled. Many southerners—including Presidents Washington, Jefferson, and Madison—also expressed concerns. Yet few plantation owners were actually prepared to emancipate their slaves: they simply did not know how to live without them. They also wondered what would happen to large populations of freed slaves in a white society.

The North began to act against slavery even before the Revolution ended. Mainly in the South, many slaves heeded British calls to cross the lines and fight for their freedom. But several thousand, mainly from the northern states, fought on the American side in exchange for liberty; free blacks also fought for the American cause. Their example—fighting alongside white Americans in a broader struggle for freedom—made it particularly difficult for the northern states to defend slavery.

Pennsylvania, with its strong Quaker antislavery sentiment, was the first state to act, passing a gradual emancipation law in 1780. The 1780 Massachusetts Constitution stated that all men are created free and equal. In 1783, Massachusetts's highest court ruled that slavery was a violation of that guarantee, and slavery in Massachusetts collapsed. Gradual emancipation laws, like those passed in Rhode Island and Connecticut, were more typical, ordering that all slaves born after a given date would become free once they reached a given age. Slavery was more firmly entrenched in New York, but that state too passed a gradual emancipation act in 1799 (though its slow workings delayed slavery's final end in the state until July 4, 1827). New Jersey was the last northern state to act, enacting gradual emancipation in 1804.

Even in the upper South, where slavery was deeply rooted, emancipation was seriously considered. A Virginia state convention only narrowly defeated gradual emancipation proposals in 1832; had emancipation won, the region's future would have been profoundly different. As it happened, emancipation's defeat marked a turning point. Powerful, prominent Virginia would remain part of the slaveholding South. And southerners, who were terrified after the bloody insurrection led by Virginia slave Nat Turner in 1831, now tightened their control over the slave population. They restricted movement, meetings, education, and voluntary manumission (the freeing of slaves by their masters) by individual slave owners.

In the deeper South, some had also questioned slavery in the wake of the Revolution. But few planters, or even political leaders who harbored doubts about human bondage, could accept the total demise of their labor system. Most southerners were unwilling even to consider the idea. For a time, it seemed nature might force the question: by the 1790s, soil degradation had begun to undermine traditional cash crops and reduce the value of slave labor. But by 1800, new technologies like Eli Whitney's cotton gin made the once labor-intensive harvesting of cotton—which was in heavy demand in northern and European textile mills—highly profitable.

Thus, even as slavery was phased out in the North, and as Virginia hung in the balance, the institution became an even more integral part of the southern economy. In 1808, Congress abolished the trans-Atlantic slave trade. Though there would later be calls in the South to reopen the trade, many slave owners supported the ban. American slave populations were increasing rapidly through natural growth. As the demand for slaves grew and cotton plantations quickly spread south and west, planters knew that the ban on new imports would increase the sale value of their own surplus slaves.

Even as manufacturing and commerce expanded in the rest of the United States, the South became more reliant than ever on its plantation system. At the same time, it lagged behind the rest of the country in terms of industrial development. In the North, abolitionist voices like those of William Lloyd Garrison and his influential newspaper, *The Liberator*, were growing louder. Most northerners were not abolitionists, but they felt threatened by slavery's implications for white society. Although they did not push for an end to slavery in places where it already existed, they were determined to stop it from spreading. The North was turning firmly against slavery, just as the South was rallying behind its "peculiar [that is, unique] institution." Collision was inevitable.

ERA 10: A HOUSE DIVIDED: NORTH VERSUS SOUTH *(1820 TO 1859)*

A LINE IN THE SAND: SLAVERY IN THE TERRITORIES

Most northerners were never abolitionists: they did not demand an immediate end to slavery in the South or focus on slaves' suffering. Nonetheless, many of them turned strongly against slavery—not on moral grounds, but because of its impact on whites. A majority believed that slavery degraded free labor, lowering all laborers to the status of slaves. They looked angrily at the South's undemocratic slaveholding aristocracy, with its outspoken contempt for all working men: indeed, some planters openly equated white laborers with slaves. Many feared this lordly class of southerners would seek to dominate all Americans. As the South clung more and more fiercely to its slave system during the first decades of the nineteenth century, more northerners came to see slavery as a direct threat. Antislavery sentiment escalated rapidly.

Although they did not represent mainstream northern opinion, abolitionists helped stoke such attitudes. Their tracts and newspapers circulated widely, graphically publicizing the brutality of slavery and its degrading social impact. Adding to their influence were a growing number of black abolitionists, many of whom had experienced slavery firsthand; they bitterly challenged the still-popular notion of colonizing freed slaves in Africa, and firmly pointed out that slaves were Americans, not Africans. Frederick Douglass, having escaped from bondage to come to the North, became prominent in the 1840s and 1850s. Books by Douglass and others revealed the horrors of enslavement to a wide audience. Most northerners saw abolitionists as fanatics—yet the abolitionist portrait of slavery stuck in many minds.

Though typical antislavery northerners did not demand southern emancipation, they were determined to keep slavery from expanding. The nation had turned its eyes westward: by the mid-1840s, Americans had begun to talk of their "Manifest Destiny" to expand all the way to the Pacific. The crucial issue was not slavery in the South, but the status of the burgeoning western territories. The North's increasingly powerful antislavery movement was fixed on one goal: keeping the territories as "free soil" for free white labor. Slavery—and in the view of most whites, all blacks, whether slave or free—had to be excluded absolutely: most free-soilers bore deep racial hostility to blacks. So, indeed, did many white abolitionists: though they denounced slavery as a moral evil and decried the suffering it caused, most viewed blacks as natural inferiors in need of protection, not as potential equals.

The status of the territories also had immediate political implications, for it was key to the balance of power in the federal government. Many northerners feared the aristocratic "slave power" exerted in Washington, DC, by the slave states—particularly in the Senate, where the equal allotment of two seats to each state blocked the North's rapidly growing population from giving free states any advantage. Keeping slavery out of the territories would mean many new free states and no further slave states, guaranteeing a solid free-soil majority in both houses of Congress.

Slaveholders, however, were just as determined to keep the territories open to slavery. There were commercial reasons: new territories with expanding plantations meant an ever-growing market for slaves and a permanent boost to their market value. But there were also more fundamental motives. Southerners, seeing slavery as the foundation of their society, felt besieged by the North's surging antislavery movement. They feared that new free states—with no new slave states to balance them—would undermine southern power in Washington and allow antislavery interests to dominate, strangling slavery everywhere. The West quickly became each section's battleground.

Sectional divisions were not, of course, entirely consistent or predictable. Some northerners sympathized with the South and its slave system—motivated by racial prejudice, by an aristocratic outlook, or by cultural or commercial ties with the South. Urban immigrants were particularly likely to reject antislavery views, fearing that free blacks would compete for the low-skill jobs on which they themselves largely depended. Such attitudes helped make the northern wing of the Democratic Party (which attracted many immigrants) a frequent ally of the slaveholders, making immigrant neighborhoods dangerous for the North's free blacks and helping give antislavery and anti-immigrant parties common cause.

At the same time, some southerners—particularly poor farmers in the backcountry, where slavery barely penetrated—looked at the slave-owning elite with distrust and hostility. Much like the northern Free-Soilers, they resented the aristocratic pretensions of the "slaveocracy" and believed that slavery degraded the standing of all laborers. Like many antislavery northerners, most of the South's antislavery whites were nonetheless violently antiblack, fearing competition from black labor and seething at comparisons between their own status and that of an "inferior race."

THE SECTIONAL DIVIDE GROWS

The sectional split was already plain in the first decades of the nineteenth century, and the status of the territories was quickly emerging as the flash point. In 1819, Missouri—part of the territory gained in the Louisiana Purchase—sought to join the Union as a slave state, triggering a battle over the future of slavery in the West. There were then twenty-two states—eleven slave and eleven free. Free-state populations not only were larger but also were growing more quickly: their influence in the House of Representatives was greater and was poised to grow further. The slave states were determined at least to maintain equal power in the Senate.

In 1820, Congress struck the Missouri Compromise. Missouri was admitted as a slave state. At the same time, Maine (until then a part of Massachusetts) was admitted as a free state, to preserve the equal balance between slave states and free states. In the future, the compromise declared, new states above the 36°30′ line of latitude (Missouri's southern border) would be free states, and those below the line would be slave states. The issue, for the moment, seemed settled.

But sectional tensions continued to rise as the North and South eyed one another with growing suspicion. In the 1820s, northern industrial interests pressed for higher protective tariffs on British and European imports to shield American manufactures from outside competition. But the South, dependent on crop exports to Europe and with few industries to protect, painted protectionism as a northern plot against southern interests—even against the South's slave society. A small number of radical southerners began to suggest secession from the federal union if northern policies won out.

In 1828, pro–Andrew Jackson, antitariff forces in Congress plotted to discredit tariffs (and embarrass pro-protection President John Quincy Adams before the 1828 election) with a bill so extreme that no region could support it. But to the horror of the plotters, protectionist forces chose to uphold the tariff principle even with an unattractive bill, and the so-called Tariff of Abominations passed. Stunned, several southern legislatures denounced the law as unconstitutional. John C. Calhoun of South Carolina, Adams's vice president, anonymously published his "South Carolina Exposition and Protest," in which he asserted the right of affected minorities to challenge majority rule—and the right of states to nullify federal laws.

The crisis worsened under President Jackson, who defended the tariff's constitutionality even while working to soften it. Calhoun, now Jackson's vice president, began openly promoting nullification. A gentler 1832 tariff changed little; a South Carolina convention declared the tariff acts void and barred collection of duties within the state. Jackson, though urging further tariff compromise, threatened to answer nullification with military force; Calhoun resigned as vice president and moved to the Senate. In 1833, Congress passed a compromise tariff—and the Force Bill, which authorized military action against the nullifiers. South Carolina backed down and accepted the new tariff (to save face, it also declared the Force Bill nullified). Tensions temporarily eased, but sectional conflict was reaching alarming heights.

Faced with a rising stream of northern antislavery petitions in the mid-1830s, Congress overwhelmingly voted that it lacked any authority over slavery, and passed a gag rule barring the reading of such petitions. Former president Adams—now a Massachusetts congressman—led an annual battle against the gag, finally defeating it in 1844; ominously, the congressional vote increasingly fell on sectional rather than party lines, with northern Democrats beginning to split from their southern colleagues to vote with Adams and the northern Whigs.

But it was the new territories that remained the key battleground—especially as the nation's western possessions grew and rapidly expanding railroad networks raised the prospect of faster western settlement. In 1836, American settlers in Texas declared the territory independent of Mexico and sought annexation to the United States. Being below the 36°30′ line, Texas would become a slave territory under the 1820 Missouri Compromise, and northern Whigs strongly opposed annexation. In 1845, ignoring threats from Mexico and antislavery objections, Congress finally voted in favor of annexation.

The dispute over Texas erupted into war with Mexico in 1846. Nurturing blatant territorial ambitions, many in Washington welcomed the conflict. American forces captured Mexico City in 1847, forcing Mexico to cede vast southwestern lands, including California, in 1848. Inevitably, the huge new acquisitions opened a fresh battle over slavery's expansion. As early as 1846, northern congressmen pushed the Wilmot Proviso, barring slavery from any territory the United States might gain in the Mexican-American War. Southern interests killed the measure, but the principle would be repeatedly pressed by northern congressmen in the coming years. Southern forces, led by Calhoun, declared their section under attack. In the face of growing northern strength, they insisted on the inviolability of state power.

THE DIVIDE BEGINS TO REND THE COUNTRY

By 1850, the crisis over the territories had become an obvious threat to the federal union of the states. Kentucky's Henry Clay returned to the Senate; desperate to rein in the conflict, he proposed a series of compromise resolutions meant to forge a permanent peace. California would be admitted as a free state, but the rest of the territory won from Mexico would be open to slavery; slavery in the District of Columbia—a common target of antislavery opposition—would be protected; and a stronger fugitive slave law would be passed, enforcing the Constitution's requirement that free states return runaway slaves.

The Compromise of 1850 barely passed Congress; each element had to be voted on separately, with majorities cobbled together from different interest groups. At best, the resolutions offered little more than a truce. Calhoun, though near death, denounced the entire scheme, essentially demanding a southern veto over federal measures. Meanwhile, northern states were infuriated by the new fugitive slave law, openly defying it (even declaring it nullified) and actively protecting runaway slaves. The so-called Underground Railroad, a network of sympathizers who helped slaves escape the South, was never as organized or as coherent as later legend made it out to be—nonetheless, it grew more so in the 1850s after the passage of the Fugitive Slave Act.

In another attempt to defuse the impending crisis, Democratic senator Stephen Douglas of Illinois (who also hoped to profit from railroad construction by encouraging settlement) promoted a new principle of popular sovereignty, by which a majority of settlers would choose their territory's status as slave or free. Congress passed Douglas's Kansas-Nebraska Act in 1854, overturning the Missouri Compromise—and the status of Kansas and Nebraska, above the 36°30′ line, would be decided by their settlers. But many southerners were determined to block northern antislavery settlers by force.

Since at least 1840, there had been efforts to organize an antislavery political party. The Liberty Party ran presidential candidates in 1840 and 1844, with little impact. The stronger Free-Soil Party followed in the 1848 and 1852 elections; attracting disaffected northern Whigs and Democrats, it ran second in some northern states. By the early 1850s, the Whig Party was disintegrating, divided between North and South over slavery while struggling with anti-immigrant nativism and other issues. In 1854, a new Republican Party was organized, thus capitalizing on northern anger at the Kansas-Nebraska Act. The new party quickly absorbed the Free-Soil Party, most northern Whigs, the nativist parties, and the North's antislavery Democrats. Southern Whigs meanwhile crossed to the Democrats, who were left as the South's sole effective party.

Sectional tensions were swelling everywhere. Harriet Beecher Stowe's 1852 novel *Uncle Tom's Cabin*, a sentimentally tragic account of slave life, became an enormous northern best-seller by the mid-1850s, helping deepen northern hostility to the South's "peculiar institution." The Kansas-Nebraska experiment had swiftly degenerated into chaos: free-soil Kansas settlers were overwhelmed by organized pro-slavery forces from Missouri. By 1856, the territory, enmeshed in guerilla warfare, was lamented as "Bleeding Kansas." When abolitionist Senator Charles Sumner of Massachusetts denounced southern politicians' efforts to impose slavery on Kansas, he was savagely beaten on the Senate floor by Congressman Preston Brooks of South Carolina; the South's gleeful celebration of Brooks's attack shocked the North even more than the assault itself.

The new Republican Party came to dominate the North, sweeping northern congressional seats in 1856. The Republicans were the main challenger to the pro-southern Democrats in the 1856 presidential election, carrying eleven northern states (though losing the election). The crisis over Kansas, meanwhile, only worsened. Efforts to force through a pro-slavery constitution culminated at Lecompton, Kansas, in 1857, succeeding through a combination of intimidation and fraud. The tame acceptance of the rigged Lecompton constitution by Democratic president James Buchanan and his congressional allies—determined to appease the South at almost any cost—enraged even Douglas, who considered it a betrayal of the popular sovereignty principle. Another attempt at compromise had devolved into sectional turmoil.

In 1857, the Supreme Court, dominated by southerners, ruled in *Dred Scott v. Sandford*, the case of a slave who claimed his freedom after his owner took him into free territory. The court did not merely deny Scott's claim—it ruled that slavery could not be barred from any territory without destroying property rights, making the Missouri Compromise unconstitutional. It also ruled that blacks could not attain U.S. or state citizenship and, in even more absolute terms, that under the U.S. Constitution blacks had "no rights which the white man is bound to respect." The North, racist though it was, found the ruling shocking. Many feared the court might next force slavery even on the free states—and such a case, challenging free states' right to deny a slave owner his property, was in fact making its way through the appeals process to the Supreme Court.

Some northern radicals—a fringe of the abolitionist movement—were now prepared to turn to violence. John Brown, a religious zealot who had committed violent atrocities while battling pro-slavery forces in Kansas, led a raid on Harpers Ferry, Virginia, in 1859, hoping to spark a general slave insurrection. The raid, put down by federal troops under Colonel Robert E. Lee, failed utterly, and Brown was hanged for treason by the state of Virginia. The South, always terrified of "servile insurrection," looked on Brown with horror—but many in the North, though unwilling to condone his methods, admired his stance; at the very least, many would not entirely condemn him. Southerners were more alarmed by the northern reaction than by Brown's actions themselves, and they became further convinced that antislavery agitation endangered their very survival.

ERA 11: BLUE VERSUS GRAY: CIVIL WAR AND RECONSTRUCTION *(1860 TO 1877)*

SECESSIONISTS AND UNIONISTS

By 1860, the sections were near rupture. The outgoing president, Democrat James Buchanan, had tried to appease the South and settle the dispute over the territories by colluding with the Supreme Court on the Dred Scott decision and by supporting Kansas's rigged pro-slavery constitution. But in spite of such concessions, the breach only widened. The Democrats' 1860 presidential nominating convention split into northern and southern factions: northern Democrats nominated Stephen Douglas, whereas southern Democrats chose Buchanan's vice president, John Breckinridge, as their candidate and demanded unlimited expansion of slavery into the territories. Another group, the Constitutional Union Party, fielded John Bell of Tennessee, who pledged to unite the North and South.

The only group with a solid power base was the young Republican Party, which dominated the northern states with a platform that embraced westward expansion into free-soil territories. At the Republican convention, delegates argued over well-known (and controversial) potential candidates. Abraham Lincoln of Illinois emerged as their compromise candidate. He was a rising figure in the new party, having garnered national attention when he challenged Douglas for his Illinois Senate seat in 1858. The two had engaged in a series of widely followed debates on slavery in the territories, and Lincoln's cogent arguments and powerful speeches had made him a strong voice for the antislavery Free-Soil movement as it fought to keep slavery out of the territories.

Lincoln swept the solidly Republican northern states, crushing Douglas. Yet southern ballots did not even list his name. Because the rest of the country was divided, Lincoln won the four-way race with 40 percent of the vote. Lincoln was fiercely opposed to slavery, believing that it must eventually disappear. But he was confident it would die on its own—probably within another century—if it were blocked from expanding. Lincoln vowed not to interfere with the southern system, so long as slavery was barred from the territories. And although he defended the humanity of blacks and their basic right to freedom, he in no way argued for social or political equality. For much of his presidency, in fact, he favored proposals to colonize freed slaves in Africa.

Lincoln's careful assurances did nothing to calm most southerners, who saw him as a dangerous fanatic out to destroy them. He was, as they loudly objected, a president who had been elected without a single southern vote. Dark rumors swirled throughout the South: Lincoln and his "black Republicans" would send in the army, hand all property to the slaves, and force white women to marry black men. Although most southerners did not own slaves, they resented outside interference with their local affairs and way of life—and they were terrified by the supposed Republican plots to imposc "Ncgro rule."

South Carolina had repeatedly threatened to secede from the Union since the nullification crisis of the 1820s, in which it had first proclaimed a right to invalidate federal laws. As soon as Lincoln was elected, the state called a convention for the following month. Delegates declared the new president "hostile to slavery" and voted unanimously to secede from the Union. By February 1861, eight states—the entire lower South—followed suit. They agreed to form the Confederate States of America, with a constitution that would permanently enshrine slavery. The states in the upper South did not yet follow, but they warned the North not to attack the new Confederacy or attempt to force the seceding states back into the Union.

Struggling to reassure the secessionists, outgoing president Buchanan backed a constitutional amendment that would protect slavery in all territories below the 36°30′ line. President-elect Lincoln strongly opposed the idea. He was prepared to support an amendment that would protect slavery solely in the southern states where it already existed, but southerners were dissatisfied. A last-ditch peace conference met in Washington that February, but agreement was impossible. Meanwhile, southern states demanded the handover of federal forts within their territory. Buchanan refused, but was unwilling to use force to defend the installations. Charleston's Fort Sumter in South Carolina was besieged, and southern batteries drove off federal resupply vessels.

Many northerners, however, were ready to fight to preserve the Union. They worried that if a losing minority—the arrogant and aristocratic southern slaveholders—could reject the results of a legitimate election, democracy was dead. Its demise would signify the failure of the American Revolution and its great experiment in popular self-rule.

At the same time, southerners believed that in fighting for local control and state-level democracy, *they* were defending the Revolution's legacy against the tyranny and aggression of an outside power—and they were ready to battle for those freedoms. Both sides readily invoked George Washington and the founding generation. Many northern Democrats also opposed war against the South, blaming Lincoln and the Republicans for the crisis; the most extreme faction openly supported the southern cause (Republicans would derisively call them "copperheads" after the poisonous snake). Even pro-war northern Democrats sought only to restore the Union as it was, and would tolerate no broader moves against slavery.

Lincoln refused to accept secession, and he would not give up Fort Sumter. Determined not to fire the first shot, he sent ships in early April to peacefully resupply the fort—forcing the secessionists to decide whether they would open an armed conflict. On April 12, 1861, South Carolina opened fire on Fort Sumter, which was soon forced to surrender. Lincoln now called for seventy-five thousand volunteer soldiers to quell the rebellion. Virginia and three other states declared Lincoln's order an act of aggression against the South. Although several of these states harbored strong unionist movements, majorities now voted to secede and join the Confederacy. Four border slave states remained in the Union, although several had to put down their own secession movements (federal troops helped keep Maryland in line, lest Washington, DC—between Maryland and Virginia—be surrounded by Confederate states).

THE WAR FOR THE UNION: 1861–1862

The American Civil War had begun. The North's larger industrial base and population were huge military advantages. But it was fighting for the more abstract aims of preserving the Union and protecting democracy. The South, in contrast, was fighting on its own soil to protect its independence—the stakes were concrete and very high. It hoped to make a Northern victory so costly that the Union would lose its will to continue. Both sides expected a quick victory.

The Union hoped to starve out the Confederacy with a naval blockade that would cut off its crucial cotton exports to Europe (known as the Anaconda Plan). Union forces sharply curtailed the South's outside trade, but Confederate blockade runners kept the sea routes open and smuggled out cotton while they imported weapons and supplies. The blockade was not enough to decide the war.

In July 1861, Union troops marched on the new Confederate capital at Richmond, Virginia. However, Southern forces soon bested them at Bull Run, driving them back to Washington in confusion. The Confederates had shown they would not be easily beaten, yet the Union showed no signs of giving up. This war would be neither brief nor easy.

Confederates sought recognition and aid from Britain and France, with whom they had strong trading ties. "King Cotton," they hoped, would bring Europe aboard—and many upper-class Britons would have been delighted to see America's democratic experiment fail. (In contrast, however, the middle and working classes, including those in the cotton-dependent textile trade, were often sympathetic toward democracy and the Union.) Britain debated whether it should support the Confederacy, and nearly came to blows with the United States in late 1861 when a Union warship seized Confederate emissaries from a British steamer. Europe, however, was strongly opposed to slavery. Indeed, despite demands from many Southerners to reopen the African slave trade, the Confederate constitution banned it—in a diplomatic gesture to Europe. Yet the European powers ultimately refused to openly align with the Confederacy.

After their humiliating defeat at Bull Run, Union forces continued to gather and train troops, so as to take advantage of their enormous manpower and industrial resources. By early 1862, Union troops had seized coastal enclaves along the Carolinas and Gulf of Mexico, and they had begun to push down the Mississippi River from the North. In April, the Union took New Orleans and won a bloody, close-run victory at Shiloh, Tennessee. In the coming months, Union forces tried to push farther down the Mississippi and north up the river from New Orleans. Setbacks would leave the front stalemated until the end of the year, but Union troops began to push south toward the strategic town of Vicksburg, Mississippi.

The Virginia expanse between Washington and Richmond was the key military theater. After Bull Run, the Union's Army of the Potomac was put under General George B. McClellan, who molded it into a professional force. But once he began his push on Richmond, McClellan proved painfully hesitant, exaggerating Confederate strength and refusing to press his advantage. And he soon faced a dangerous new opponent: General Robert E. Lee, commander of the new Army of Northern Virginia. Lee, a former U.S. Army officer, had refused Lincoln's offer to command Union forces. When Virginia left the Union, he immediately followed. Though he was reluctant to endorse secession, Lee's first loyalty was to his state.

Lee invaded Maryland in September 1862, hoping to threaten Washington and force the North out of the war. After a fierce and bloody battle at Antietam, Lee had to abandon his Northern invasion and retreat to Virginia. But the Union's victory was hardly decisive: McClellan failed to commit his full forces or to pursue Lee's retreating army. In November, Lincoln permanently removed him from command. But the battle nonetheless proved critical. Until now, Britain and France had been thinking about recognizing the Confederacy and pressing a negotiated peace. Lee's defeat made them lose confidence in Confederate strength. The appearance of Union strength also allowed Lincoln to take a step he had been contemplating for months: making an attack on slavery into a fundamental aim of the war.

THE WAR AGAINST SLAVERY: 1863–1865

The North had entered the war in singular pursuit of defending the Union, not of attacking slavery—the Union even contained four slave states that bordered the Confederacy. But slaves were now fleeing to Union lines in search of freedom, and in summer 1861, the United States declared them contraband (confiscated enemy property). In spring 1862, Congress abolished slavery in the District of Columbia and throughout the territories, the Homestead Act opened western land to settlers for minimal fees, and Congress soon financed a transcontinental railroad to further open the West. These measures fulfilled popular Republican pledges and solidly established the West as free soil. In July, Congress declared all rebel-owned slaves behind Union lines to be permanently free. But Lincoln was already planning to go further.

By summer 1862, Lincoln was seeking to target the entire Confederate slave system, which would undermine the Southern war effort and make it impossible for antislavery Europeans to support the Confederacy. And though the four unionist slave states continued to reject even compensated emancipation, Lincoln also had a growing sense that the war must settle the issue of slavery once and for all. His cabinet feared that a bold move would look desperate while Union arms were struggling, and it urged him to wait for a victory before acting. Victory came at Antietam, and Lincoln issued a preliminary Emancipation Proclamation just days after the battle. The final version, issued on January 1, 1863, declared all slaves in rebel territory free. Union-occupied areas were excluded (as were the border slave states that stayed in the Union)—but Congress had already moved to free rebel-owned slaves behind Union lines.

Union troops could now liberate entire slave populations as they advanced, and slaves in the Confederate interior would be encouraged to resist their masters. The proclamation also urged freed slaves to enter Union armies, an opportunity that free blacks and so-called contrabands had sought since the war's beginning. Recruitment of black regiments (though under white officers and at reduced pay) began in early 1863. At that time, the Union was implementing a highly unpopular draft to raise troop levels; now the Union had a million black men eager to fight. Furious Southerners vowed to enslave all black prisoners and execute their white officers. Lincoln promised retaliation against Southern prisoners, and the Confederate policy was shelved.

White Union troops were often hostile to black soldiers, and generals often used them for manual labor. Some Northerners, especially Northern Democrats, rejected the war on slavery entirely, and lashed out against blacks: in July 1863, New York workingmen and immigrants rioted against the draft law and killed dozens of blacks. Yet the war also changed minds. Lincoln slowly abandoned his earlier support for colonization of freed slaves. When given the opportunity, black troops performed with bravery and distinction. Their performance impressed many Northerners; more began to wonder if the Northern cause should extend beyond preserving the Union and look to end the moral evil of slavery. Although racist attitudes still pervaded the North, many people were forced to confront prejudices that had long gone unchallenged.

As Northern perspectives evolved, war raged. Lee continued to hold off the Army of the Potomac in Virginia into early 1863. But Union forces, led by General Ulysses S. Grant, advanced down the Mississippi and laid siege to Vicksburg in May. In June, Lee's army pushed through Maryland into Pennsylvania—again seeking a decisive blow with a second invasion of the North. The Army of the Potomac met Lee at Gettysburg. Fighting on their own home soil, Union forces finally dealt a devastating blow to Lee during the first three days of July. Although Union troops were too exhausted to pursue and destroy his army, Lee was forced to retreat. Gettysburg marked a turning point in that going forward, Lee would be on the defensive as he worked to hold back and wear down Union forces.

The same day Lee retreated from Gettysburg—July 4, 1863—Vicksburg fell to Grant. The entire Mississippi River was soon in Union hands, and the Confederacy was cut in two. In early 1864, Grant assumed command of all Union armies and pressed into Virginia with a series of costly battles. But unlike his predecessors, Grant refused to retreat even after he suffered heavy losses. He maintained pressure on Lee and pushed toward Richmond. To the west, Union armies had pushed south into Georgia; in May 1864, General William T. Sherman began a drive toward Atlanta.

The 1864 election was the South's last hope. But preserving democracy was the Union's chief cause, and Lincoln was determined to hold the election even during wartime. His challenger was George McClellan, his one-time general. If elected, McClellan was expected to concede Southern independence and negotiate peace. The brutal war, capped by Grant's slow and bloody Virginia campaign, had deeply strained the North. Sherman took Atlanta in September, however, and gave Northern morale a timely boost. Lincoln won 55 percent of the popular vote, and he dominated the electoral vote. Soldiers who had once adored McClellan now supported Lincoln—they refused to see their sacrifices thrown away. Grant continued his relentless push toward Richmond, while Sherman began a drive to the sea across Georgia and South Carolina, devastating the towns through which he passed.

By early 1865, the South was imploding: wracked by shortages and internal unrest, its slave system was eroding from within. Some desperate Confederates even urged that slaves be recruited as soldiers in exchange for their freedom. In the North, Republicans now dominated Congress. In January 1865—after furious debate and pressure from Lincoln—Congress passed the Thirteenth Amendment, which banned slavery in the United States. This would have been unimaginable four years earlier when the war began. Richmond fell on April 2, 1865; seven days later, Lee surrendered his army at Appomattox, Virginia. Within a week, Lincoln was assassinated at Washington's Ford's Theater by a small conspiracy of Confederate sympathizers led by actor John Wilkes Booth. But the Union pressed on, and remaining Confederate forces soon surrendered. The Civil War was over.

THE RISE AND FALL OF RECONSTRUCTION

Now the United States was left with the massive challenge of Reconstruction, which would involve rebuilding the southern states and readmitting them to the Union. The states ratified the Thirteenth Amendment by December 1865, including many southern states, which understood they had no choice: slavery was dead, and readmitted Southern states would have to accept that fact. Yet the government was divided. Congress was dominated by Republicans determined to remake the South. The new president, Andrew Johnson, who had served as Lincoln's 1864 running mate, was a pro-Union Tennessee Democrat—antislavery, but virulently racist. His hatred of slavery had stemmed from his hatred of aristocratic slave owners. With those same plantation magnates now paying him homage, he quickly shifted ground. And he shared their aim of keeping the black population harshly subordinated.

Lincoln had envisioned lenient terms for readmission of the South, and Johnson followed through with enthusiasm. He swiftly returned political power to ex-Confederates in exchange for oaths of allegiance. Major property owners and other prominent ex-Confederates were required to apply to him personally, but Johnson readily granted pardons as the once-hated plantation lords humbly appealed. By the end of 1865, virtually the entire Confederacy had returned to the Union, under governments run by the former rebels. Although many northerners were unsatisfied, Johnson declared the Union restored.

In the final months of his life, Lincoln had been moving toward bolder positions on race. He had contemplated granting full citizenship to African Americans—a concept utterly repugnant to Johnson. In 1865, southern states began to impose Black Codes. To control former slaves, these laws imposed harsh restrictions: blacks were denied freedom of movement, could not leave their former masters' employment without permission, and could be sentenced to "penal servitude" for vagrancy (that is, leaving their respective plantations without a pass). Johnson enthusiastically backed such laws, which precisely matched his racial ideas—and which restricted free blacks almost as much as had their previous enslavement.

During this early Presidential Reconstruction, the heavily Republican Congress was not in session. When its members assembled in December 1865, they immediately turned on Johnson and began to implement "radical" Reconstruction. In early 1866, Congress overrode Johnson's veto and empowered the new, military-backed Freedmen's Bureau to protect the rights of southern blacks. Determined not to cede power to former rebels, the Republicans sought instead to enfranchise the South's large—and inevitably Republican—black population. In July, Congress passed the Fourteenth Amendment. Dismantling the Dred Scott ruling, the amendment granted full citizenship to all Americans, and allowed the federal government to protect citizens' rights against state interference.

Although Johnson campaigned aggressively against Republican radicals, northern voters viewed his lenient Reconstruction plans as a surrender that squandered the Union's costly victory. In the 1866 elections, Republicans took even firmer control of Congress. Again over Johnson's veto, they placed the South under martial law and ordered the army to enroll new voters. Many of these new voters were African American, whereas many ex-Confederates were barred from voting. New state constitutions were enacted that protected black rights while limiting the power of ex-Confederates. In the coming years, due to large black electorates allied with pro-Union whites, a number of African Americans were elected to public office—even to seats in the U.S. Congress and Senate.

Congressional Republicans, who were easily able to override Johnson's regular vetoes, worked to strip the unwanted president of his powers. Even the army, still commanded by Grant, was placed virtually outside of Johnson's control. When a new law barred him from removing cabinet members without Senate permission, Johnson denied its constitutionality (the Supreme Court later agreed) and fired the Lincoln-appointed secretary of war. In 1868, the House impeached Johnson for defying its laws, though the Senate fell one vote short of convicting him and removing him from office. Aided by half a million newly enfranchised African American voters, the far more sympathetic Grant was elected president that fall.

Southern white anger remained a dangerous problem. Vigilantes, including members of the new and violent Ku Klux Klan, terrorized blacks, northern officials and activists (whom they derided as parasitic carpetbaggers), and their southern allies. Trying to safeguard Reconstruction, Congress passed the Fifteenth Amendment in 1869, guaranteeing the right of African Americans to vote. But ex-Confederates were regaining power. Southern states officially accepted the Fourteenth and Fifteenth Amendments, but only the army kept the South in check—and the army could not stay forever. Anti-Reconstruction southerners—called Redeemers, as they strove to restore the white antebellum order—gradually won control. And in 1874, amid a struggling economy, corruption in Grant's cabinet, and growing suspicion among northerners of "radical" pro-black policies, Democrats took the House of Representatives.

Fierce southern resistance and waning northern will had undermined Reconstruction, and the 1876 election delivered the final blow. With the southern black vote already widely suppressed, Democrat Samuel Tilden won the nation's popular vote. But Republicans, who still controlled three southern states, manipulated the count to give Rutherford B. Hayes the Electoral College by a single vote. After months of conflict, Democrats agreed to accept Hayes's election. But in exchange, they demanded the final withdrawal of troops from the South and the acceptance of its Redeemer governments. The Compromise of 1877 restored white control to the South, and the status of African Americans there would quickly sink. Yet the Fourteenth and Fifteenth Amendments remained, and they would be invoked again in the future.

ERA 12: RESISTANCE AND RECOVERY: REBUILDING A WAR-TORN NATION *(1870S TO 1890S)*

INDUSTRIALIZATION, IMMIGRATION, AND EXPANSION

An estimated seven hundred fifty thousand Civil War soldiers died in combat, and many more succumbed to poor sanitation and camp disease. Although the South suffered less than half of the war's fatalities, its smaller population made those losses more severe. Further, because the majority of the battles were fought on Confederate soil, the South endured more home-front shortages, disrupted agriculture, civilian casualties, and overall devastation. The North also suffered massive loss of life, but its larger population and undamaged industrial base made it well poised for recovery. Indeed, the North was already moving into a post-war boom as the South battled through Reconstruction.

Westward movement—boosted by the 1862 Homestead Act and expanding railroads—continued to accelerate. American farm production surged. But foreign production also increased, flooding world markets and cutting demand for American exports. By the mid-1880s, crop prices had slid, and many farmers were plunged into debt. In the cities, post-war industrial mechanization took firm hold. Earlier in the nineteenth century, inventors had experimented with interchangeable parts—simple mass-produced components that could produce virtually any product. Now factories churned out such products on assembly lines, and skilled artisans were no longer necessary. The new factory system pushed them aside in favor of unskilled laborers who were willing to work for low pay in dismal and dangerous conditions.

Meanwhile, large monopolies called trusts took control of entire industries. The magnates who led these trusts amassed unprecedented fortunes. In the 1870s and 1880s, Pittsburgh's Andrew Carnegie greatly improved the manufacture of steel and soon controlled much of the country's steel production. The discovery of oil just before the Civil War created a new and fast-booming industry, displacing whale oil as the country's chief lighting source; John D. Rockefeller's Standard Oil Company was formed in the 1860s and controlled 90 percent of the U.S. oil refining industry by the 1880s. The trusts targeted smaller rival companies with incredible ruthlessness, removing them by whatever means necessary, including smear campaigns, beatings, and even bombings. As competition was eliminated, laborers' wages were driven lower—but workers had few alternatives.

Across the Atlantic, Europe was also under strain. As its population grew, there were too few farming opportunities for too many would-be laborers. They moved to the cities for work, but factories there also had limited jobs to offer. With little to lose, many were driven to seek new opportunities in America. Until this point, the U.S. immigrant population had consisted mainly of Western Europeans. Now, as the population in eastern and southern Europe swelled, Catholics and Jews increasingly immigrated to the United States. America's well-established Anglo-Saxon majority responded with hostility as new waves of culturally alien immigrants crowded the cities' tenements and dominated the low-wage employment market.

Other routes to wealth proved more difficult than Americans had anticipated. Many had rushed to California after the discovery of gold there in 1848. After the war, even more fortune seekers moved westward in pursuit of precious metals. But rich and easy finds were rare, and forced increasingly complex underground mining. Although a few entrepreneurs became fabulously wealthy, the vast majority of miners worked dangerous, low-wage jobs deep under the earth.

The American West enticed those who wished to escape the crowded eastern cities. Many were lured by open, available land and jobs in western mining towns (although farming, overproduction, and the corporatization of mining made neither a sure bet). Post-war railroad construction finally linked the coasts and opened the vast U.S. interior to the rest of the fast-growing nation. Like factories, the railroads needed cheap labor and attracted more immigrants. On the West Coast, railroads relied heavily on Asian immigrants—who endured prejudice from and tension with the white population as well as open legal discrimination.

The westward push also sparked violent campaigns against Native Americans. The Plains Indians' nomadic culture depended on vast spaces and the West's enormous buffalo herds—both of which were incompatible with white settlement and railroad expansion. The U.S. government tried to force Native Americans onto fixed reservations, but even the treaties granting such lands were readily violated whenever the government wished the tribes moved elsewhere. A Native American alliance led by Sitting Bull and Crazy Horse destroyed a U.S. cavalry force under General George Custer at Little Bighorn, Montana, in 1876, but the United States soon gained the upper hand. The Dawes Severalty Act of 1887 aimed to push native people into farming, ending native groups' land claims in exchange for U.S. citizenship and personal land grants. But the land was poor, and speculators often tricked Native American families into losing it.

The final large-scale Native American resistance effort, the religiously inspired Ghost Dance, arose on the western reservations in the late 1880s. It promised to remove white settlers and restore the Plains Indians' traditional culture. American troops were sent to squelch the movement. In late 1890, troops captured a large group of Lakota Sioux and brought them to Wounded Knee, South Dakota. When the soldiers tried to disarm the Native Americans, shots were fired. The soldiers launched a furious attack; even their officers lost control, and many of the Native Americans, including women and children, were massacred. The slaughter effectively marked the end of active Native American resistance in the West, and left a bitter, enduring wedge between Native Americans and the U.S. government.

THE STRAINS OF THE GILDED AGE

The last decades of the nineteenth century were hard. Farm prices dropped, and the American economy grew more susceptible to international crises. Urban wage labor surged, but for low pay and in poor conditions; and with immigration also increasing, there were often fewer jobs than prospective workers. Republicans and Democrats battled in a series of hard-fought elections, feuding over protective tariffs, immigration, civil service reform, and veterans' benefits. Both parties were corrupt and internally divided; often, they focused on little more than factional gains and the interests of their most powerful supporters. Urban political machines all but controlled working and immigrant communities, providing protection in exchange for votes. Many Americans felt ignored by the political process entirely.

A handful of industrialists—branded "robber barons" by their many critics—had ruthlessly amassed vast wealth. Self-made men, these determined, aggressive, and hard-working businessmen exemplified the opportunity so many sought in America; the corporations and infrastructure they pioneered were crucial to the country's rapid industrial expansion after the Civil War. But their success came at a high price for many: most of their numerous laborers worked for low wages and in poor conditions, and rival businesses were cold-bloodedly suppressed or destroyed.

Satirist Mark Twain dubbed the era the "Gilded Age": gold-plated rather than golden, with a thin, glittering veneer that masked the seething troubles beneath. By the 1880s, some of the corporate giants, led by Carnegie, began to contribute large sums to philanthropy, endowing libraries, museums, and other institutions. Carnegie came to preach a "gospel of wealth," arguing that vast fortunes must be used to better society. Such efforts somewhat improved the magnates' image and made dramatic contributions to public culture and the arts—but conditions for their employees scarcely changed.

A rising labor movement sought to improve wages and working conditions. Many found inspiration in such radical European ideas as Marxism and Socialism, which insisted on communal ownership of property (that is, Communism) or, less radically, on a larger government role in promoting social welfare. One group, the Knights of Labor, helped organize influential labor strikes in the 1880s. Industrial leaders pushed back, limiting labor's gains. In May 1886, as a multicity strike pressured industry for a standard eight-hour workday, anarchists rallied in Chicago's Haymarket Square to protest deadly police attacks on strikers. When police tried to subdue the protest, someone threw dynamite into the police ranks. The Haymarket Riot helped discredit labor organizers by casting them as dangerous radicals.

Later that year, Samuel Gompers formed the American Federation of Labor (AFL). As the AFL merged groups from across the country to increase political pressure for reform, clashes between labor and industry only worsened. In 1892, Carnegie refused to recognize a steelworkers' union. When his Homestead, Pennsylvania, factory went on strike, the company brought in private detectives to suppress the workers, and the strikers opened fire. With support from the state militia, the union was defeated. Carnegie's reputation was tarnished, but steel unions were effectively blocked until the 1930s. In 1894's Pullman Strike, unions shut down railroad networks, and the federal government directly intervened. Declaring it illegal to interfere with interstate commerce and the U.S. mail, the government sent troops to suppress the strike and restore order. Now facing direct federal suppression, labor had suffered another blow.

In rural areas, a new populist movement gained ground as farmers fell further into debt. Farmers' unions and political organizations lashed out at banks, eastern businesses, and railroads. They demanded inflationary silver-backed currency (as opposed to a pure gold standard) to increase the money supply and drive down the value of their debts. The Populist (or People's) Party ran a presidential candidate in the 1892 election, and although the party finished a distant third with just a handful of electoral votes, it succeeded in familiarizing Americans with its grievances. The silver issue, in particular, gained traction. International financial moves had reduced the country's gold reserves, and now many Americans looked to "free silver" as a popular check on the eastern big-money magnates.

The free-silver movement was especially popular among Democrats. In 1896, Nebraska's William Jennings Bryan was nominated by both the Democrats and the Populists. Delivering a rallying call for free silver at the Democratic convention, Bryan famously proclaimed that the people must not be crucified on a "cross of gold." Bryan broke with the tradition of candidates' saying little before the election, instead actively campaigning across the country. Despite dominating the West and South, Bryan lost the election. Republicans had successfully painted him as a dangerous, anarchy-loving extremist. Bryan ran again in 1900, but populism's large following fast faded. The agrarian movement, like the labor movement, was left angry and largely powerless.

Although the trusts dominated oil, steel, beef, sugar, whiskey, and other industries across the United States, political pressure yielded a few victories. In the late 1880s, western and southern states began to pass antitrust laws that sought to limit the huge monopolies. The states, however, had no power over interstate commerce. An 1890 federal law, the Sherman Antitrust Act, banned conspiracies "in restraint of trade." But the courts ruled that the act did not apply to most multistate conglomerates. Instead, they used the law to brand the unions as conspiracies against trade. The trusts emerged largely untouched, whereas the unions were deeply hampered. Further action would be needed to address growing public discontent.

THE NEW SOUTH AND THE RISE OF JIM CROW

After Reconstruction, with the former slaveholding aristocracy largely restored to power, the South sought new routes to prosperity in a world without slavery. Southern leaders poured their energy into industrialization, and the region modernized and became more integrated with the national economy. The "New South" was untroubled by labor agitation and thus attracted some northern industrialists. Yet despite the growing industrial boom, low pay and unproductive farms created a sharp divide in wealth. A few leading men became extremely rich. At the other extreme, many southerners were desperately poor. Rural and urban poverty would become a chronic southern problem.

With few exceptions, African Americans were pushed to the bottom of the economic pile. As slavery collapsed, most southern blacks had dreamed of independent land ownership and true freedom from others' control. Such dreams proved illusory. Although Congress overturned the 1865 Black Codes, with their virtual reimposition of slavery, any dramatic post-war gains quickly faded. Black rights were rarely recognized, and the withdrawal of federal troops made antidiscrimination laws unenforceable. Social and economic advancement was thwarted by oppressive discrimination. And although blacks fared the worst economically, they bore the brunt of poor whites' resentment.

Once slavery ended, planters needed to replace the labor force. Their attempt to keep hold of their former slaves through the Black Codes had failed, but by the late 1860s, a new pattern was emerging: sharecropping. Under this system, families were allotted their own plot on a plantation's land, farming it themselves in exchange for a small share of the profits from the crop. Both black and white laborers were forced into sharecropping, but African Americans often found it to be their only option. This was not slavery: individuals could not be sold, and families could not be divided. But it fell far short of full economic freedom.

More direct threats to freedom also lurked. Sharecroppers were forced to buy food and supplies from plantation owners at exorbitant prices. This often forced them into debt, and planters demanded labor in return. This peonage (or virtual enslavement based on unpaid debts) was technically illegal. But poor farmers—black or white—had little access to legal assistance, and they easily fell victim to the powerful and well connected.

African American political rights barely survived Reconstruction. By 1876, the black vote was widely suppressed, and the situation only worsened as federal troops permanently withdrew and the white so-called Redeemer governments took hold. The Fourteenth and Fifteenth Amendments were evaded with poll taxes and literacy tests, undermining blacks' citizenship and voting rights. Poor southern whites, and immigrants throughout the country, were also disenfranchised by such methods. But the discrimination against blacks was systematic and widespread. Vigilante groups, such as the Ku Klux Klan, enforced exclusion and repression through lynching, intimidation, and other acts of terror.

By the 1890s, black suffrage in the South was effectively dead, and the Republican Party had all but vanished from the region. White social pressure routinely forced blacks into segregated spaces, and they were almost entirely excluded from public education, juries, and virtually everything else. As public transit offered Americans new travel options during the 1880s, blacks were legally restricted to separate cars. African American resistance met with little success, and discrimination became even more systematic as employers and unions barred blacks from skilled professions. By the 1890s, all ex-Confederate states had legally imposed segregation, a system that came to be known, after a caricatured black character in pre–Civil War minstrel shows, as Jim Crow.

In upholding southern segregationist legislation, the Supreme Court turned a blind eye to black disenfranchisement. In the civil rights cases of 1883, the court rejected discrimination complaints and struck down a Reconstruction-era civil rights law: the justices ruled that the Fourteenth Amendment protected citizens only against discrimination by the state, not by individuals. In its 1896 *Plessy v. Ferguson* decision, the Supreme Court ruled in favor of state discrimination as well, upholding Louisiana's segregated railroads. The court held that the maintenance of separated yet equal facilities for blacks and whites fully satisfied the Fourteenth Amendment's guarantee of equal protection under the law. This "separate but equal" doctrine would form the legal framework of segregation for the next six decades.

ERA 13: THE NEXT BENCHMARK: AMERICA IS A GLOBAL LEADER *(1890S TO 1920)*

THE UNITED STATES LOOKS OVERSEAS

Since George Washington's presidency, the United States had pursued an isolationist foreign policy that avoided what Thomas Jefferson called "foreign entanglements." Although the 1823 Monroe Doctrine had asserted U.S. strength and declared the Western Hemisphere a uniquely American sphere of influence, it mainly aimed to keep Europeans out of the region. But the nation's foreign policy began to shift even before the Civil War, showing the first signs of a broader global reach.

In 1854, a naval expedition under Commodore Matthew Perry forced Japan, which had for centuries been closed to most foreigners, to open its borders to Western trade. In 1867, the United States purchased Alaska from Russia and commenced occupation of Pacific islands, such as Midway. In the 1870s, the United States began to exert influence over Hawaii and to devote significant resources to the construction of a powerful modern navy. By the late nineteenth century, the nation's economy was strong, and its foreign dealings were fast increasing. Many Americans began to see their nation as a natural global power.

The events that truly catapulted America onto the world stage began in Spanish-held Cuba, one of the last European footholds in the New World. In the mid-1890s, Cuba rebelled against Spanish control. Spain's brutal crackdown on Cuba, coupled with sensationalist coverage in William Randolph Hearst's *New York Journal*, earned the Cubans considerable American sympathy. Spain offered concessions, but unrest continued, and relations with the United States deteriorated. Prominent U.S. politicians saw an opportunity to expand American influence in the Caribbean, and early in 1898, the battleship *Maine* arrived at Havana Harbor in a show of American force. On February 15, the *Maine* exploded, killing more than two hundred of its crew. Although the explosion was probably accidental, Americans—goaded by Hearst's "yellow press"—believed a Spanish mine had destroyed the ship. "Remember the *Maine*!" became a national rallying cry.

Alarmed, the Spanish offered further concessions, and President William McKinley sought a peaceful solution. But American pro-war pressure was powerful. McKinley issued an ultimatum that demanded Spain's withdrawal from Cuba, and he asked Congress to declare war even before Spain's reply arrived. As war erupted, America's Pacific ships destroyed the Spanish fleet at Manila Bay in the Philippines and soon seized the islands. Spain's Cuban fleet was blockaded and finally destroyed. American ground forces (which included Theodore Roosevelt's famous volunteer cavalry, the Rough Riders) quickly conquered the island. American battle casualties were few; many more soldiers succumbed to disease than to combat. By the end of 1898, the brief Spanish-American War had ended, and Spain was forced to seek peace.

Victory triggered an identity crisis: Should America abandon isolationism completely and assume its place as an imperialist power? The United States had annexed the Hawaiian Islands during the war, and a powerful lobby argued that the nation was destined for global leadership. They invoked an increasingly popular ideology of racial strength, which asserted that the Anglo-Saxon elite had a duty to "civilize" inferior races. (Inevitably, such ideas also questioned the racial fitness of the ever-rising immigrant tide.) Crudely distorting Charles Darwin's new ideas on evolution through natural selection, theories of Social Darwinism lent pseudo-scientific credence to the domination of "weaker" nations, races, or economic classes by "racially superior" elites.

Anti-imperialists meanwhile denounced conquest as expensive, unwise, and fundamentally un-American. Pushed and pulled by rival factions, American actions abroad proved inconsistent. The peace treaty with Spain granted independence to Cuba and ceded Puerto Rico to the United States; America also purchased the Philippines from Spain. Over the strong objections of the newly founded Anti-Imperialist League, the United States quashed a Filipino uprising. The government also recommended that the islands ultimately gain independence—at some future point, when the United States deemed them ready. Further, America sought influence in China, even though it made no territorial claims there. Determined to evade the European powers' competing claims to China and open Chinese markets to Americans, the United States worked to create an Open Door Policy for all foreign powers and helped suppress China's anti-foreign Boxer Rebellion in 1900.

Becoming president after McKinley's assassination in 1901, Theodore Roosevelt sought a navy capable of dominating both the Atlantic and the Pacific. Roosevelt helped engineer a revolution in Panama that created a friendly regime and allowed the United States to build a canal across the isthmus—thus linking the two oceans. The ever-ambitious president bolstered America's influence in the Western Hemisphere with the Roosevelt Corollary to the Monroe Doctrine, which authorized an American police power to intervene in Latin American countries to stop "uncivilized" behavior and protect U.S. interests. Roosevelt further enhanced American might and prestige by helping negotiate an end to the 1905 Russo-Japanese War (making him one of the first Nobel Peace Prize winners) and sending the U.S. Navy's Great White Fleet—a group of dazzlingly white battleships—on a two-year tour around the world.

SOCIAL STRAIN AT HOME AND THE PROGRESSIVE PUSH FOR REFORM

By the turn of the century, industrial leaders had reined in some of their more aggressive practices and poured money into philanthropic causes. But labor conditions were only slightly improved, and unions made little progress after the setbacks of the 1890s. The courts consistently turned antitrust laws against the unions and rejected attempts at reformist legislation. In 1905's *Lochner v. New York*, for example, the Supreme Court struck down a New York law that limited bakery workers to ten-hour shifts, ruling that the state had violated employers' right to negotiate contracts. Critics decried the decision as an abuse of judicial power, but the labor movement continued to face stiff headwinds. And as immigration increased, anti-Catholic and anti-Jewish discrimination blocked union aid to unskilled workers who faced some of the worst conditions.

Alarming social strain, pressure from traditional religious social campaigners, and the growing power of the popular press all led to calls for new and bold reforms. Whereas the "yellow" journalism of Hearst and his imitators sought mainly to sell newspapers through cheap sensationalism, others wanted to expose injustice and inspire change. Aggressive journalists—branded "muckrakers" for the dirt they uncovered—revealed rampant corruption in business and government, also drawing attention to slum conditions, failures in public education, and other shocking social ills that most had chosen not to notice.

As outrage over these widespread injustices grew, and as the courts continued to block many attempts at reform, the rising Progressive movement sought to enact change at the federal and state levels. Progressivism had an ally in President Roosevelt, a Republican, who channeled his activist policy instincts into correcting society's blatant wrongs. First, he launched a new attack on the trusts that aimed to dissolve or otherwise reform the conglomerates. In the face of increasingly widespread logging and mining, Roosevelt also pressed for the protection of natural resources and scenic wonders with the establishment of the National Park System and other pioneering conservation measures.

Meanwhile, Congress also began to promote reformist legislation. In 1903, it took a major step toward government economic oversight as it created the Department of Commerce and Labor (split a decade later into two separate departments) to regulate interstate business. In 1906, muckraker Upton Sinclair published *The Jungle*, which exposed Chicago's shockingly unsanitary meat industry. With measures like the Pure Food and Drug Act, Congress banned the sale of tainted products and mandated government inspection. Despite fierce opposition from private banks, the Federal Reserve Act established a system of government-controlled banks to stabilize the currency. Another measure granted immunity to business officials who exposed corporate abuses. And at the state level, reforms allowed the recall of elected officials and the proposal of referendums by popular initiative.

Because it was impossible to enact all reforms through legislation, Progressives sought constitutional amendments to implement more fundamental changes. One major demand was a national income tax system: a progressive tax—drawing most heavily from higher earners—would fund expanded programs to benefit the less fortunate. The courts had ruled income taxes unconstitutional, but in 1909, Congress passed the Sixteenth Amendment (ratified by the states in 1913) to legalize such levies. Progressives also sought to increase the people's power; in 1912, Congress passed the Seventeenth Amendment (also ratified in 1913), which established direct popular election of senators. The people had previously elected only their representatives, and state legislatures had chosen senators.

Many Progressives also embraced the long-standing and powerful temperance movement. Casting saloons as evil destroyers of men and of families, anti-alcohol or "dry" forces had gradually built a power base that bolstered politicians who helped them or defeated those who hindered them. By 1900, many states and counties had passed dry laws. A federal ban on alcohol was more difficult to secure, as the excise tax on liquor was one of the main sources of federal revenue. However, the income tax amendment shifted the balance and freed the government from its dependence on the excise. The dry lobby turned its power on Congress, winning passage of the Eighteenth Amendment in 1919 and securing state ratification with dramatic speed. The production or sale of most alcoholic beverages was now illegal.

Another major part of the Progressive cause was women's suffrage. At the Seneca Falls Convention in 1848, some women had begun to demand public equality. But the majority of Americans, both male and female, continued to see the home as a woman's natural place. After the Civil War, Susan B. Anthony and other activists worked to shift perceptions of women's roles. Families also needed more income, and there was a massive demand for unskilled labor; thus, more women joined the workforce, challenging traditional definitions and barriers. Local politics led the Wyoming and Utah Territories to enact women's suffrage in 1869 and 1870, respectively, which encouraged an active lobbying push across the country. Other states had held referendums on women's suffrage by the 1890s, but most failed.

The rise of Progressivism helped reinvigorate the women's rights movement. Although an 1896 suffrage referendum had been defeated in California (saloon owners feared the onslaught of so many potential temperance voters and fiercely opposed the measure), a new initiative narrowly passed there in 1911. Attitudes began to shift, and other western states followed California's lead. Politicians sensed the shift, and were eager to win the support of women soon-to-be voters. In 1918, under political pressure, President Woodrow Wilson endorsed national women's suffrage; Congress passed the Nineteenth Amendment a year later. Most southern states, worried that the reformist wave would also challenge their disenfranchisement of African Americans, opposed the amendment while virtually every other state endorsed it. American women could now exercise a right to vote.

THE LIMITS OF PROGRESSIVISM AND THE CALL FOR CIVIL RIGHTS

Despite their forward-looking achievements, Progressives had their own blind spots, centered on the issues of socioeconomic class and race. Progressives were often suspicious of the capacities and morals of the poor—especially the increasing number of poor Catholic and Jewish immigrants. Even as they worked to extend the franchise to women and improve working conditions and labor rights, many Progressives supported—or at least accepted—measures to limit the rights of the poor. Progressive-backed laws made it more difficult for immigrants to achieve citizenship, and other measures made it far more difficult for the poor to vote.

The Progressive record on race was similarly problematic. Southern Progressives supported or turned a blind eye to the many barriers (that is, poll taxes, literacy tests, and property qualifications) that denied African Americans the vote. Racial prejudice was reinforced by broader Progressive suspicions of the "ignorant poor," and southern laws that barred blacks from voting mirrored those that Progressives endorsed elsewhere to keep the poor from voting. Indeed, southern voting laws disenfranchised many poor whites as well as blacks—leaving power comfortably and unquestionably in the hands of the white elite. Southern states feared the women's suffrage push would undermine Jim Crow voting laws, yet many Progressives who backed women's suffrage were actually quite sympathetic to the South's racial restrictions.

The Jim Crow South barred African Americans from skilled professions and consigned many to a tenuous and degrading life of sharecropping and debt. Opportunities for economic advancement were scarce, and a growing number of blacks began to move to northern cities in search of greater opportunity and prosperity. But the barriers they faced in the North were nearly as serious as those they had left behind in the South. Although explicit segregation laws were rare in the North, widespread discrimination had much the same effect.

In the North, blacks were largely forced into separate—and squalid—urban neighborhoods. Living conditions were poor; those African Americans who could afford to leave these grim conditions and move into more prosperous, mainly white areas were threatened and even assaulted when they tried to do so. As migration from the South caused the black population in northern cities to swell, discrimination only deepened. Northern blacks were driven from skilled professions they had once occupied. Unions—among the few allies that most laborers had in improving their lot—often barred blacks from membership. In terms of wages, living conditions, and opportunities, black workers consistently fared worse than their white counterparts.

Isolated by society's prejudices, many African Americans viewed their communities as separate islands of refuge in a hostile world. African American leader Booker T. Washington and others urged a focus on commerce, prosperity, and self-betterment within black communities. Washington argued that if blacks built visible achievements and proved their worth through quiet, nonconfrontational accomplishments, they would ultimately win respect and acceptance from whites. But to many activists, Washington's arguments sounded defeatist, counterproductive, and even servile. They noted that even the most successful blacks endured savage prejudice.

Determined to fight for what they saw as the basic rights of all Americans, these activists—men and women, black and white—united to form the National Association for the Advancement of Colored People (NAACP) in 1909. The creation of the NAACP marked the beginning of the modern civil rights movement, which demanded full social and legal equality through legislative and judicial action. A generation of skilled young African American lawyers was integral to the NAACP's mission. One of the organization's founding leaders was Dr. W.E.B. Du Bois, a Harvard-educated African American scholar.

Du Bois produced several serious historical works on Reconstruction, in which he documented the black struggle for political equality. He was one of the first to challenge the orthodox view, which had evolved since the 1880s, of Reconstruction as an "unnatural" tragedy. The orthodox narrative stated that conniving northern "carpetbaggers" had tried to invert the natural social order by goading and misleading blacks—who were painted as simple, credulous, even bestial racial inferiors. In saving white honor, driving blacks back to their proper place and expelling the vile carpetbaggers, vigilantes like the Ku Klux Klan served as the tale's chivalric heroes.

Du Bois offered a compelling scholarly counterblast, documenting African Americans' push for political rights in the wake of the Civil War. But the orthodox caricature of evil carpetbaggers, deluded blacks, and heroic Klansmen (enshrined by D. W. Griffith's epic 1915 silent film, *The Birth of a Nation*) was firmly engrained, and would dominate America's image of the Reconstruction era for decades to follow.

ERA 14: THE GREAT WAR: RALLYING AMERICAN PATRIOTISM *(1914 TO 1929)*

AMERICA ENTERS EUROPE'S WAR

By the late nineteenth century, a newly unified and aggressive Germany had helped divide Europe into rival blocs. The British were wary of Germany's autocracy and colonial ambitions, and they looked to ally with their former enemies: France and the United States. In 1914, Britain, France, and Russia faced off against Germany and its chief ally, Austria-Hungary, the other great Germanic power. As Austria expanded into the Balkan Peninsula, nationalists from the small Balkan state of Serbia struck back by assassinating Austria's imperial heir in June 1914.

Russia warned Austria not to attack its ally Serbia, but Germany was convinced that its European enemies were waiting to pounce and supported Austria unconditionally. By August 1914, Europe was at war. Germany pushed through neutral Belgium into France, and it combined forces with Austria to press against Russia. The result was a long and bloody stalemate. Each side hoped to shorten the war by starving out the other. Britain's navy blockaded trade to Germany, and Germany used its recently developed submarine force, the U-boats, to attack Britain's maritime supply lines. In sinking merchant vessels without warning, the U-boat campaign disregarded the established rules of war.

Despite their country's growing international role, few Americans wanted to take part in a devastating war thousands of miles away. Most clung to traditional U.S. isolationism, yet Great Britain, tied to the United States by commerce and a common language, had America's obvious sympathies. The U-boat war raised the stakes by disrupting Anglo-American trade and fueling Americans' anti-German sentiment. In May 1915, a U-boat sank the British passenger liner *Lusitania* en route from New York; 1,198 people, including 128 Americans, died. The United States demanded that Germany abandon unrestricted submarine warfare. Germany feared American intervention in the deadlocked war and backed down; it agreed to offer fair warning to merchant vessels and avoid attacks on neutrals.

As war dragged on, the Germans became more convinced that starving Britain was their only pathway to victory. They wagered that they would win the war before Americans could intervene effectively on Britain's behalf. Early in 1917, Germany announced that it would resume unrestricted submarine warfare. President Woodrow Wilson, who had tried to broker peace between the European nations—and who had centered his 1916 reelection campaign on keeping America out of war—severed U.S. relations with Germany. Tensions sharply escalated when British intelligence intercepted a telegram from Germany's foreign secretary, Alfred Zimmerman, bound for the German ambassador in Mexico. Germany suggested that if the United States should join the war, then Mexico should aim to reclaim Texas, New Mexico, and Arizona.

In March 1917, the U.S. government publicized the Zimmerman Telegram. The telegram inflamed anti-German and pro-war feelings, including those in Congress. Now most Americans saw intervention as a crusade for justice and political freedom. In early April, Wilson asked Congress to declare war, emphasizing in his war message that "the world must be made safe for democracy." The United States hoped to promote a democratic post-war order throughout Europe, including in Russia—where democratic activists had recently overthrown the tsarist government and were now struggling to fight the war, even as they fended off radical Communist revolutionaries (Bolsheviks) who promised to make peace with Germany.

In late 1917, the Bolsheviks seized power and quickly pulled Russia out of the war. Germany transferred its forces west to try to crush Britain and France before America could mobilize. And as Germany had predicted, American mobilization was slow. As it had been since Thomas Jefferson's time, the peacetime army was small, requiring mass conscription to swell its ranks, and it took time to organize, train, and equip new recruits. Although Germany made gains, however, it failed to win a decisive victory before the Americans arrived. As U.S. troops bolstered Allied strength, German defeat became inevitable. Facing revolt from a war-weary populace at home and massive setbacks on the battlefield, Germany surrendered in November 1918.

During peace negotiations the following year, Wilson sought to impose his vision of a noble settlement. But the embittered Allies had borne far more devastating losses than had the United States, and they insisted on harsh punitive terms for Germany. The Treaty of Versailles stripped Germany of territory and colonies, limited it to a token military, forced it to accept sole blame for the war, and required it to pay significant reparations to the Allies. The only major concession to Wilson was the founding of the League of Nations, a multinational organization aimed at resolving international disputes. But Wilson refused to negotiate with skeptical Republicans in Congress, who led the Senate to ultimately reject the treaty and keep America out of the league.

THE WAR AT HOME: GROWTH AND GOVERNMENT, PATRIOTISM, AND REPRESSION

America suffered more than a hundred thousand deaths during World War I, but such losses were minor compared to those of the European combatants: a fraction of 1 percent of the total U.S. population was lost, as opposed to up to 4 percent of the populations of Britain, France, and Germany. America was also geographically far removed from the theater of war, so its cities and factories emerged from the war unscathed—unlike those of the European combatants. Nonetheless, the war had profound consequences for the United States and reversed long-held traditions of small government and a limited military. It also propelled the nation into an even greater global leadership role.

Progressives worked to strengthen federal power over economic affairs, including the war economy. Local control efforts were inefficient, and helped big-government advocates carry out their agenda. By 1918, federal umbrella organizations directed the war industries, controlled the production and distribution of food and fuel, managed the railroads, and decided labor disputes. Invoking powers granted by the Sixteenth Amendment, the United States also established a graduated federal income tax, and sharply increased taxes would serve as the war's main revenue source.

Under the new Selective Service Act of 1917, all men of military age had to be registered and classified fit or unfit for military service. More than twenty million men registered; for many rural Americans, it was the first time their lives were directly affected by the federal government. The classification system also offered a disturbing portrait of American public health, exposing widespread inadequacies in medicine and hygiene as well as lack of education. Three million men were found fit and called into military service, marking the largest enlistment since the Civil War.

As soon as war was declared, a federal Committee on Public Information was charged with rallying public support through newspapers, posters, and films. The publicity campaign's overt aim was to inspire patriotism, but it also helped spawn frenzied suspicion of foreigners and dissenters. All things German were vehemently rejected (for example, sauerkraut was renamed "liberty cabbage"). The federal government was given enormous power to suppress subversives—those suspected of disloyalty, such as German immigrants and labor organizations. The 1917 Espionage Act granted broad powers to pursue those suspected of hindering the war effort, and the 1918 Sedition Act—directed at Socialists and pacifists—extended the hunt to those accused of defaming the U.S. government, political system, or military.

The military's rapidly expanding needs placed enormous demands on U.S. industrial resources and helped create the fully modern, internationally dominant American manufacturing economy. The new economy required a huge influx of manpower, and as production increased and calls for more workers were issued, masses of rural workers migrated to northern and midwestern factory cities in pursuit of better-paying jobs. Because millions of men were away at war, more women were drawn into the workforce, further challenging traditional gender roles and giving another boost to the growing women's suffrage movement. With labor in such high demand, the bargaining power of unions surged (although federal crackdowns quickly targeted the unions for suspected subversive interference with the war effort).

The war also increased racial discord at home. Among the rural workers flocking to urban industrial jobs were half a million southern blacks. Wilson, the Virginia-born president, was no friend to racial integration. His academic work had glorified the Ku Klux Klan, and he promoted the then-orthodox view of Reconstruction as a crime against white society. Black leaders had supported him in the 1912 election, but Wilson soon ordered the federal government segregated. Although many African Americans served during World War I, the military was strictly segregated, and black units were largely excluded from combat.

Social tensions did not recede at the war's end. America's labor movement had always harbored radical elements, and the Bolsheviks' new Soviet Russia spurred fears that Socialist and labor groups might foment revolution in America—particularly because Soviet propaganda was actively urging them to do so. Strikes and agitation, together with a series of anarchist bombings that targeted government officials, judges, and businessmen, helped spark a full-blown Red Scare. From 1919 to 1920, Wilson's attorney general, Mitchell Palmer, launched mass arrests of leftist and labor figures. The so-called Palmer Raids targeted those suspected of subversive views, regardless of their actions. Thousands were arrested, and although many were eventually freed, hundreds of suspected radical immigrants were deported.

As urban black populations swelled, a series of severe urban race riots broke out in 1919. They reached a fever pitch in Chicago that summer. After police there treated white violence toward blacks with indifference, African Americans fought back—and dozens of blacks and whites died before the militia finally intervened. The government and press blamed the violence on leftist agitation. As they told it, the "Reds" were plotting to push black communities into open revolution.

Facing severe discrimination and de facto segregation even in the North, disillusioned African Americans increasingly lost hope in integration and the National Association for the Advancement of Colored People (NAACP). Some were attracted by the teachings of Marcus Garvey, a Jamaican activist who moved to the United States in 1916. Unlike W.E.B. Du Bois and the NAACP, which urged a continued legal and political push for racial integration in America, Garvey preached global black unity, self-improvement, and separation from whites in a new African republic.

POST-WAR AMERICA: PROSPERITY AND NEW FREEDOMS—FOR SOME

Despite its domestic turmoil, America entered the 1920s with great international stature: its standing as one of the world's great powers was cemented. After Wilson left office, a series of Republican administrations sought a return to peacetime normality—though the administration of Warren Harding, Wilson's immediate successor, was wracked by damaging crimes among his cabinet, including the infamous Teapot Dome Scandal, in which a top official took bribes in exchange for granting oil companies access to federal lands.

The Republican presidents of the 1920s—Harding, Calvin Coolidge, and Herbert Hoover—nonetheless had a strong effect on the direction of government policy. They halted the federal government's expansion, retreated from anti-Red persecution, tried to reduce the cost and size of the military, and embraced international treaties aimed at limiting an escalating global arms race. Although many Republicans of this era were not philosophically opposed to Progressive reforms (Coolidge had championed such causes as governor of Massachusetts), they were wary of expanding federal power. Generally, they preferred to let the states handle regulation and reform.

The 1920s were, for many, a time of spectacular prosperity. As the federal government retreated from its World War I expansion, business was left largely unregulated and taxes were kept low, resulting in a boost to short-term profits. Americans poured money into the soaring stock market and reaped fantastic profits in a seemingly endless economic boom. Industries emerged to supply novel demands, and a new consumer culture began to transform domestic life. Electricity, which had been used for lighting since the 1890s and was now available virtually everywhere (except in rural areas), triggered the creation of home conveniences. Radios provided nearly instant news access, leading to the rise of mass culture in music and entertainment.

This was also the Prohibition Era: although the Eighteenth Amendment aimed to eliminate drink from American life, it merely drove it underground. Prohibition promoted vast networks of illegal production, importation, and distribution, and drew millions to speakeasies: establishments that ranged from dirty holes-in-the-wall to elegant urban clubs where Americans could buy alcohol. Speakeasy culture helped fracture gender barriers, as women flaunted new freedoms in dress and lifestyle. To a lesser extent, racial barriers also shifted as jazz, a new African American music form, swept the nation. Great black jazz musicians played at high-end clubs—even though black customers were often barred. Giddy feelings of limitless prosperity filled the air, and the atmosphere of the Jazz Age created a looser popular culture that defied centuries of more restrained cultural mores.

For many other Americans, however, the period was anything but glittering. Although the surging consumer culture boosted industrial production and wages, rural migration to the cities increased competition for jobs. With too few jobs for the number of aspiring workers, many remained mired in poverty. Unions also suffered: an oversupply of labor weakened their leverage, and widespread mistrust of their objectives lingered after the Red Scare. African Americans, as they moved north, continued to face some of the worst prejudice and exclusion. Their wages were lower, and neighborhoods remained largely segregated. Antiblack harassment and violence were routine, as was discrimination in education, social services, and transportation. Nonetheless, black communities flourished culturally. For example, New York's Harlem Renaissance revitalized black music, literature, and arts—and attracted scores of white admirers and patrons.

To many religious traditionalists, the flamboyant culture of the 1920s seemed extremely alarming, apparently defying their most basic ideas of a decent society. As Protestant fundamentalism pushed back against threatening modern ideas, Darwinian evolution became a particular target. Fundamentalists saw the notion that humans had descended from "lower" animals as a serious threat to traditional morals and beliefs. Moreover, evolution was often used at that time to promote a callous Social Darwinism, which raised further religious objections. The most famous clash occurred in Dayton, Tennessee, where the Scopes trial pitted local activists and northern liberals against the state's antievolution law. Dayton drew ridicule in the national and international presses, and the situation was often subsequently painted as a humiliation for the fundamentalists. But higher courts evaded the issue of the law's constitutionality, and the religious furor in fact terrified many educators. Evolution was all but dropped from American textbooks until the 1950s.

Immigrants also continued to flood the United States, further alarming many traditionalists. By 1920, measures to reduce the flow were in place. These measures mainly targeted Catholic and Jewish immigrants in the East and Asian workers in the West. But as the pace of social change radically accelerated in the 1920s, old-guard elites and rural conservatives pushed back even harder on immigration. Quota laws passed in 1921 and 1924 sharply limited the number of immigrants. A rejuvenated Klan assailed blacks, Catholics, and Jews, especially (though not exclusively) in the South, and few politicians were willing to challenge the Klan's strength. Although more intense press coverage and important court convictions helped diminish the Klan's power over the course of the 1920s, lynching and racial violence continued unabated.

ERA 15: PROSPERITY HAS ITS PRICE: ECONOMIC COLLAPSE AND WORLD WAR II *(1929 TO 1945)*

CRASH, DEPRESSION, AND THE NEW DEAL RESPONSE

The investment boom of the Roaring Twenties was built largely on euphoria and blind optimism, rather than actual economic expansion. Financial speculation was barely regulated, and the value of shares grossly outstripped real corporate growth. Investment relied on borrowed money, and investors could only repay if stock values continued to surge—this was a classic economic bubble. As the heedless rush continued, questions were raised: Could companies grow at a pace that would justify the enormous sums invested? Would such risky ventures even survive? By October 1929, nervous creditors began to call in loans and demand repayment. The bubble burst, and the market crashed. In just a few hours, billions of dollars in investments were wiped out.

The Federal Reserve tried to rein in wild borrowing by raising interest rates, but it was too late. The ill-timed tight monetary policy now made it impossible for debtors to raise funds and smothered business spending. The 1930 Hawley-Smoot Tariff Act sought to protect American farmers and manufacturers from foreign competition, yet as many economists urgently warned might happen, the law sparked retaliatory tariffs abroad and stifled international trade. Banks failed, and many Americans' personal savings disappeared. Consumer spending plummeted, and the economy slowed even further. Because of their ties to U.S. bank loans, European banks also collapsed. With trade, jobs, spending, banking, and investment in free fall, the entire developed world plunged into crippling economic depression.

President Herbert Hoover wanted alliances of private businesses—not the federal government—to fix the economic crisis and promote recovery. As unemployment surged to 25 percent, however, Hoover finally took steps to support the banks. Although he hoped that these measures would stabilize credit and boost consumer spending, he still opposed direct federal assistance to the millions of unemployed. He did not want to breed permanent dependency, nor did he want to burden the government with large deficits.

In 1932, the Bonus Army—thousands of unemployed World War I veterans—marched on Washington, asking that a $1,000 bonus promised to veterans, meant to be paid in 1945, be paid immediately. A bill to grant their request died in Congress, but many protesters and their families refused to leave, setting up camp in the city. Federal troops finally attacked the protesters, driving them out by force and burning their encampment. Although the violent crackdown exceeded Hoover's orders, public outcry helped seal his fate. In that fall's election, the president was crushed by Franklin D. Roosevelt. Roosevelt, a Democrat, campaigned on a platform of active government intervention, promising "a new deal for the American people."

FDR quickly secured emergency legislation to stabilize the banks and protect private deposits, and he ordered direct federal assistance to the poor and mortgage relief for homeowners. He supported new programs to expand federal hiring, and he commissioned public works projects that created millions of new jobs. The Tennessee Valley Authority, for example, was an ambitious federal project that brought electricity and industry to a large rural area. Roosevelt had also campaigned on a pledge to end the increasingly unpopular Prohibition laws. In early 1933, Congress passed the Twenty-First Amendment, repealing the ban of alcohol; state conventions bypassed dry politicians to ratify it in less than a year. Restoring the massive alcohol industry also provided another boost to the national economy.

To raise farm prices, the government paid farmers to keep their fields partially unsown; lower production did bolster prices, but it hurt sharecroppers and farm workers—especially African Americans in the South. In the Great Plains, the Dust Bowl's crippling drought and storm-blown soil erosion spurred emergency federal measures to reclaim the soil through improved farming practices. But thousands of sharecroppers and poor farmers (mostly white in this region) were forced to abandon the area, migrating to California in search of opportunity. A new federal agency, the National Recovery Administration, sought to reorganize the economy by negotiating industry codes that would control wages, prices, and production. This was another attempt, with only limited success, to raise employment by limiting production.

The New Deal marked a drastic expansion of federal power. Conservatives denounced such policies as virtual Communism, whereas Socialist and Marxist radicals found FDR's plans totally inadequate and urged Soviet-style revolution. But most Americans idolized Roosevelt because of the relief programs he created and the hope that he inspired for the future. Resurgent unions led large-scale strikes and demanded the full benefits of New Deal programs. Voters handed Democrats increasingly massive majorities, and an emboldened FDR pushed harder: the second part of the New Deal, introduced in 1935, created Social Security, a national pension system funded by taxes on employers and wages; it required the states to offer assistance to the unemployed and disadvantaged; it bolstered the right to unionize; and it used revenues from increased taxes on the upper classes to fund further job creation, in fields ranging from industry to the arts, through the Works Progress Administration.

But unemployment was still high. Many Americans were alarmed by the growing power of unions and feared that FDR's policies encouraged dangerous radicalism. The Supreme Court, dominated by older, conservative Republicans, struck down the National Recovery Administration in 1935. Two years later, FDR, afraid that the court would overturn Social Security and his other major initiatives, proposed reorganizing the court by adding six justices who would uphold his policies. The court-packing threat helped prompt the conservative chief justice to shift ground: he voted to uphold Social Security and FDR's union measures. But FDR's court-packing struck many middle-class and conservative Democrats as an alarming power grab, sparking an angry backlash. Americans would not give unlimited leeway to any leader, not even one they admired so much.

New Deal measures had boosted the economy, especially since 1935. But they were never intended to be permanent, and the government started dialing back its support. Federal jobs programs were slashed. The new Social Security taxes hit wages, but Social Security pensions would not begin until 1941, so for now, the money did not reenter the economy. Growth faltered, stocks crashed again, and unemployment surged. Unhappy voters sent more conservatives to Congress in 1938 who blocked further stimulus measures. FDR was left politically weakened, and the economy continued to struggle; for some—especially women and minorities, who had little influence in Washington—the New Deal reforms had brought few benefits to begin with. Yet, despite its failings, the New Deal had already changed the role of government forever, creating innovative protections for millions of working Americans.

TOTALITARIAN EUROPE AND GLOBAL CRISIS: ALARM, EXTREMISM, AND ISOLATIONISM AT HOME

Even before the global economic collapse of 1929, totalitarian ideologies had been on the rise in Europe. Russia's Bolshevik revolution in 1917 had set off a civil war, and Vladimir Lenin's Communists had emerged victorious, imposing ruthless dictatorship in the people's name. Later, in the 1920s, Joseph Stalin, paranoid and murderous, imposed still harsher rule on the Russians. In Italy, which had fought with the Allies in World War I but suffered devastating defeats, Benito Mussolini's Fascist movement (called "Fascist" after an ancient Roman symbol of authority) seized power after his militia marched on Rome in 1922. Fascism, a form of dictatorship based on fierce nationalism and total subordination of the individual to the state, would come to define the era.

Germany's post–World War I Weimar Republic suffered economic collapse in the early 1920s, crushed by the reparations Germany was forced to make to the victorious Allies. As hyperinflation rendered German money worthless, foreign aid from the United States and other countries helped contain the crisis. But the Weimar government won little support from the German people, and extremism rose sharply. Adolf Hitler's National Socialist, or Nazi, movement fed on resentment toward the Treaty of Versailles. Although anti-Communism was an essential component of all Fascist movements, the Nazis added a layer of obsessive racial politics. They preached German racial supremacy—a belief that Germans were descended from a purer and superior ancient stock that racial theorists called "Aryan." And they demanded the enslavement, removal, or eradication of those they deemed racial inferiors—Slavs; Gypsies; and especially Jews, whom the Nazis blamed for all evils (including both Communism *and* capitalism).

The Great Depression sapped Europe's faith in the strength of its democratic governments and gave extremist parties a massive boost. Though Soviet-backed Communists were strong, the anti-Communist Right made the most dramatic gains. In Germany, the Nazis—now the country's largest party, backed by gangs of thugs uniformed in brown shirts—gained total control of the government in 1933. The Nazi state took control of the economy, creating new jobs and sparking growth; Hitler's domestic standing was greatly enhanced. However, the Nazis also blocked Jews from their professions and denied them basic civil rights. With Aryan supremacy as their aim, the Nazis began secretly rebuilding the German military. Their goal was military control of Europe, with the Slavic East seized for German settlement, and Slavs to be reduced to a slave race. The Nazis intended to eliminate Jews from Europe entirely.

For many who saw a world wracked by economic despair and faced with rising Fascist powers, democracy looked weak, inadequate, and doomed. Fascist movements arose throughout the West, including in the United States. Some Americans admired the Nazis' militarism, racism, and anti-Semitism: such prominent figures as automobile magnate Henry Ford and populist "radio priest" Joseph Coughlin embraced the Nazis' anti-Jewish propaganda. Yet many other Americans were horrified by Nazi ideology and aggression. Hitler's racially obsessed state loomed ever larger over Europe, annexing Austria, allying with Fascist Italy, and threatening to invade its neighbors. Nazi sympathizers were met with increasing suspicion and faced a rising backlash in America.

Regardless of their feelings toward the Nazis, however, many doubted that Germany could be stopped. Prominent American and British statesmen urged appeasement, a policy that would allow Hitler to take virtually whatever he wanted so long as it avoided war. Some, like Joseph P. Kennedy, U.S. ambassador to Britain, not only deemed Hitler unstoppable but even saw him as an ally in the mounting fight against Communism. Although Communist and Fascist dictatorships were both brutal, Communism's attack on private property and enterprise particularly appalled many Americans. The Great Depression had reinvigorated American Communists, who blamed capitalism itself for the economic collapse—and whose leaders, as their opponents accurately charged, were actively directed from Moscow.

In 1938, Hitler laid claim to a German-speaking region of Czechoslovakia. Britain and France, which were still attempting appeasement, met Hitler at Munich and yielded to him. But Hitler soon annexed all of Czechoslovakia, and then shifted his gaze toward Poland. Britain and France vowed war if Hitler attacked the Poles; in September 1939, after having cynically allied with the Soviets—the Nazis' chief ideological enemy—Germany defied Anglo-French threats and invaded Poland. Great Britain and France declared war on Germany.

Most Americans wanted no part in Europe's new war. A new isolationist movement, embraced by prominent Americans, gripped the country and dominated Congress (famous aviator Charles Lindbergh was a prominent isolationist—and an admirer of Nazi ideology). In 1940, Germany overran France and battered Britain with air raids. Britain was pushed to the brink of defeat, and FDR pressed Congress to build up the U.S. military—a burst of spending that would finally revive the U.S. economy. But Roosevelt was not content to guard America while Britain fell, convinced that a Nazi victory would doom democracy.

Although FDR kept the United States officially neutral, he was determined to aid the British. As he campaigned for an unprecedented third term that fall, he gave fifty destroyers to Britain in exchange for naval bases in Canada, Bermuda, and the Caribbean—and risked isolationist fury. In 1941, he pushed the Lend-Lease Act through Congress, a measure that allowed him to sell, trade, or lease war material to any power deemed essential to U.S. security. That summer, Hitler broke his insincere pact with Russia and invaded the Soviet Union (U.S.S.R.). FDR put American hostility toward Stalin aside and extended Lend-Lease aid. He also defied the U-boat war that Germany was waging against Britain's Atlantic supply lines by shipping goods to Britain and even defending its convoys by air and sea. Germany wanted to keep America out of the war, so it avoided direct attacks on U.S. escorts—but American ships were inevitably sunk, and anger rose.

In the Pacific, tension was also mounting. An actively modernizing Japan had emerged as a rising world power: it defeated Russia in 1905, annexed Korea in 1910, joined the Allies in World War I, and eyed a colonial hold in China. Japan's economy had also suffered during the Depression, and in the 1930s, the nation increasingly came under military control. Espousing doctrines of national and racial supremacy, Japan invaded Manchuria (in northeastern China) in 1931 and China as a whole in 1937. Japan's brutal expansionism badly strained relations with the West—on which Japan had depended for oil and other essential resources. Japan aimed for complete self-sufficiency and began contemplating a Greater East Asian Co-Prosperity Sphere. Despite the name, this vision consisted of a militarist Japanese empire that would conquer resource-rich Asian nations and seize Europe's Pacific colonies.

THE UNITED STATES JOINS THE SECOND WORLD WAR

As relations with Japan deteriorated, the United States imposed embargoes on oil and other materials that Japan desperately needed. Japan viewed these measures as threats to its very existence, and became convinced that conquest was necessary to guarantee its security. In 1940, Japan joined the Axis alliance with Germany and Italy, and plotted massive invasions throughout East Asia. Japan feared that America's enormous industrial resources and manpower would overwhelm it in a prolonged war, so it hoped to stun the United States into negotiating peace. To that end, Japan launched a surprise air attack on the U.S. naval base at Pearl Harbor on December 7, 1941. America's Pacific fleet was badly damaged, and Japan surged to a string of military triumphs. Japan invaded other Asian nations, Europe's Asian colonies, and the American-held Philippines.

But the United States did not crumble as Japan had hoped. Americans responded to the Pearl Harbor attack with fury and indignation. Hitler felt convinced that conflict with the United States was inevitable, and he was determined to stop American aid to Britain and Russia. He promptly declared war—the exact outcome Roosevelt and British Prime Minister Winston Churchill wanted. Churchill and FDR had agreed, before the United States entered the war, that German Fascism posed the greatest world threat; they planned on a "Europe first" approach. Although huge naval forces were prepared for a Pacific offensive, the Allies' priority was still Germany. The United States also joined Britain in allying with Stalin's U.S.S.R. This union was often awkward: temporary necessity forced the Western Allies to ignore Stalin's own brutality, as well as his obvious ambitions ultimately to expand Soviet power over eastern Europe.

As the United States joined the war, the situation looked grim. Although Britain had repelled German air attacks and ended the risk of invasion during the Battle of Britain, Germany occupied most of the European continent and had pressed deeply into Russia. U-boats stalked Allied convoys in the Battle of the Atlantic and sank masses of ships and supplies. In the Pacific, Japan seemed unstoppable as it rolled from victory to victory.

However, the tide was slowly beginning to turn. Germany's Russian offensive stalled in the face of Soviet counterattacks and the harsh Russian winter, and a German push across North Africa—aimed at Egypt and the oil-rich Middle East—was stopped by British forces in early 1942.

Later that year, American troops landed in North Africa and helped force a German withdrawal. Although the U-boat threat remained serious, the Allies improved their antisubmarine tactics and struck back hard. Allied air forces mounted a strategic bombing campaign that targeted Germany's industrial base and pounded its cities to sap civilian morale. In the Pacific, the U.S. Navy suffered a string of early defeats but smashed a major Japanese fleet in the June 1942 Battle of Midway. And after months of incredibly brutal jungle combat at

Guadalcanal, the Allies stopped Japan's advance toward Australia. These battles marked a turning point, and Japan was on the defensive from then on.

Germany imposed tyrannical control in the territories it conquered–forcing people into virtual slavery, stealing their wealth, and using its feared secret police to brutally suppress dissent. Communists, intellectuals, gays, Gypsies, and others were targeted and killed, but the Nazis' main objective was the extermination of Europe's Jews. From the rise of their regime, they had sought to strip Jews of all rights and ultimately to drive them out of Europe. But as the war expanded, Nazi leaders decided that total eradication was the "final solution to the Jewish problem." An increasingly mechanized extermination system, centered on slave labor and death camps, ran ceaselessly until the war's end. Six million Jews were murdered while millions of other Europeans were worked to death alongside them.

Axis forces were pushed slowly back in 1942 and 1943, but horrific battles were raging in the U.S.S.R. Stalin urgently sought a second front in Western Europe, which he hoped would divide and weaken German forces. But it took the United States and Britain years to build the forces necessary to invade Europe, leaving Stalin constantly furious. As the Russians stopped a German push at Stalingrad in early 1943, the Allies readied their first foray into Europe. That summer, as the Russians began a large-scale offensive, the Western Allies invaded Sicily and continued into Italy. The Italians soon surrendered and joined the Allies, but German forces swiftly took control of the country.

Finally, in June 1944, the Allies' D-Day invasion across the English Channel into Normandy opened their second full front. As the Western Allies began to consolidate their base in France and push outward, the Russians were driving toward Germany. By late 1944, U.S. and British forces were advancing toward Germany's western borders. The final German counterattack, the Battle of the Bulge, involved costly fighting that set the Americans back. But German gains were short-lived: the Western Allies pushed into Germany in 1945, while the Soviets drove across eastern Europe toward Berlin. With his forces crushed and his nation's defeat certain, Hitler committed suicide in April, and Germany agreed to unconditional surrender days later.

Meanwhile, the Pacific war became a slow grind of Allied naval and amphibious operations to drive the Japanese from their island strongholds. At the same time, Allied armies fought in China and pressed into Southeast Asia. By early 1945, the Allies had taken the Philippines, Iwo Jima, and Okinawa–thus establishing strategic bases for massive bombing raids on Japanese cities. Japan was willing to face a devastating invasion rather than surrender, but the Allies had a secret alternative: a new atomic weapon urgently developed by American and European physicists in the clandestine Manhattan Project. (Germany and Japan had also tried to develop atomic bombs, without success.) The atomic destruction of the cities of Hiroshima and Nagasaki, coupled with a Soviet declaration of war against Japan's empire, forced Japan's surrender in August.

THE WORLD WAR II HOME FRONT

Japan's attack on Pearl Harbor and Germany's declaration of war instantly shattered America's isolationist mood. Through the draft and widespread voluntary enlistment, young men everywhere were swept into war. A shared patriotic purpose united Americans, and civilians pledged to contribute to the war effort: millions donated domestic goods and willingly accepted the government's rationing of meat, sugar, and gasoline so that the military could be supplied. Children sacrificed their toys, which were recycled into military equipment.

To meet the war's demands, the U.S. economy swung into massive expansion, finally sweeping away the lingering effects of the Depression. Just as America's enemies had feared, the country's vast industrial and human potential was powerfully and rapidly mobilized. The American fleet had been outclassed by Japan's modern aircraft carriers, but now it grew at a dramatic pace that left the enemy far behind. Assembly lines churned out merchant ships, replacing losses more quickly than the U-boats could sink them; new guns, tanks, and aircraft fed the demands of U.S. and Allied forces.

The federal government took unprecedented control of the vast economic mobilization, and the government itself expanded to supervise the effort. New federal agencies managed industries' transition from civilian goods to war equipment, they regulated prices, they settled disputes between management and labor, and they controlled domestic rationing. Federal spending skyrocketed, and vast revenues were raised through taxation and the aggressive sale of government war bonds, through which citizens invested their money in the war effort, in return for interest payments after the war. Athletic icons and Hollywood celebrities helped spearhead war bond sales drives, part of the government's huge program of patriotic and morale-boosting *propaganda* (a term that had not yet taken on its wholly negative modern tone).

Federal money poured into industry and research. The war spurred dramatic advances in technology and medicine, as government agencies coordinated research projects in academic and industrial labs throughout the country. Cooperation with the British led to the refinement of radar (an essential Allied advantage in the war) and the development of antibiotics. Leading Jewish European scientists and those who opposed Fascism fled Nazi tyranny and came to the United States. Even before the war, Germany had driven Jewish scientists from its universities. Now some of the world's best physicists, such as Albert Einstein and Enrico Fermi, joined British and American scientists in the urgent Manhattan Project.

Large corporate empires benefitted greatly from the vast surge in spending and production. But the American labor force was rapidly changing. The flow of young men into the military and the massive labor needs of the war effort forced companies and government entities to look to new sources. Women not only filled secretarial and clerical jobs but also entered professions that had been closed to them until now: they welded ships and assembled aircraft and tanks. Images of the symbolic Rosie the Riveter graced recruiting posters and entered popular culture. When the war ended, society expected women to return to pure domesticity. But wartime experiences changed many women's expectations and ideas, with far-reaching implications.

The war's urgent labor demands also forced doors open to minorities. The migration of southern African Americans to the North's industrial cities accelerated, and federal regulators pressed industries to drop discriminatory hiring practices and train blacks for skilled positions. The demography of the western United States also began to shift, as the government recruited vast numbers of Mexicans into the country as guest workers (temporary farm laborers). As the urban black and West Coast Mexican populations swelled, there were outbursts of racial violence and widespread discrimination. Meanwhile, the military remained racially segregated. As the United States fought against racially bigoted regimes abroad, many Americans noted the blatant disconnect and argued for reform at home.

Populations linked to enemy nations were at the greatest risk of direct government discrimination. German and Italian immigrants were branded enemy aliens and faced restricted freedoms; some were imprisoned or deported. The many U.S. citizens of German and Italian descent were mostly left alone. On the West Coast, Japanese Americans faced accusations—often founded on blatant prejudice and encouraged by neighbors' schemes to seize Japanese American property—of disloyalty and sabotage. More than one hundred thousand Japanese living on the West Coast, over half of whom were U.S. citizens, were interned in federal camps (although men could win release to join the U.S. military, and many served with distinction). The Supreme Court upheld internment in 1944. The United States would formally apologize and offer reparations to surviving Japanese American internees in 1988.

ERA 16: THE NEW AMERICAN DREAM: FREEDOM FROM TYRANNY *(1946 TO LATE 1950S)*

THE SOVIET UNION AND THE EMERGING COLD WAR

The West's necessity-driven World War II alliance with the Soviet Union (U.S.S.R.) was neither easy nor natural. After overthrowing Russia's democratic revolution in 1917, the Bolsheviks had quickly proved themselves autocratic and ruthless. During the Russian civil war that followed, the World War I Allies had offered generally unsuccessful military assistance to anti-Communist forces (though an American relief effort, led by staunch anti-Communist Herbert Hoover, also saved millions of lives after a catastrophic Soviet famine from 1921 to1923). Vladimir Lenin had imposed Communist rule with savage determination. His successor, Joseph Stalin, created a tremendously brutal police state. In the late 1920s and 1930s, he slaughtered the *kulaks*, or landed peasantry, when they resisted his plan to strip them of their farms; fearing potential rivals, he savagely murdered thousands of fellow Soviet Communist leaders and Soviet Red Army officers; and he began to send dissenters to the feared Gulag labor camps—where millions would die at his orders.

From 1917 on, the United States remained deeply apprehensive of the Communists and their intentions—the Soviets not only blatantly brutalized their own people but also were openly determined to export their Bolshevik revolution to other nations. The Soviets actively controlled Communist parties in Western countries, hoping to incite Communist revolts. The United States was the last major power to recognize the Soviet government: seeking to open trade and increase his diplomatic options, Franklin D. Roosevelt established ties in 1933.

Even then, most Americans remained strongly hostile to Communism and suspicious of the U.S. Communist Party (CPUSA), which was—as many suspected—largely directed from Moscow. Stalin's coldly practical 1939 alliance with the fanatically anti-Bolshevik Nazis—which included a secret agreement to divide Poland between Germany and Russia—hardly improved the Soviet image in the West; nor did the CPUSA's overnight switch from anti-German to pro-German propaganda as soon as the pact was announced. But when the Germans threw aside the two-faced treaty and invaded Russia in June 1941, the Soviets allied with Britain against Adolf Hitler, and thus received FDR's anti-Nazi assistance. And when the United States entered the war, the Soviets by default became a major ally.

Yet Western and Soviet long-term aims were incompatible, and the differences could no longer be ignored once the war ended. The Soviets were paranoid, aggressive, and determined to expand their territory and influence. Stalin was driven by a mission to export Communism, and he was convinced that he faced a constant danger of a Western attack. Roosevelt, Winston Churchill, and Stalin met at the Yalta Conference in February 1945 to discuss terms of the post-war settlement. In exchange for Stalin's pledge to join the Pacific war once Germany fell, the U.S.S.R. would gain Asian territories and an occupation zone in Korea. The three leaders formally agreed that Eastern Europe would remain independent and hold free elections, but it was obvious that Stalin's ambitions would be hard to restrain.

Roosevelt, whose health was failing at Yalta, has been criticized for yielding too much—but realistically, with the Soviet forces already driving across Eastern Europe, he had few options. FDR died in April, and his vice president, Harry S. Truman, assumed the presidency. At that summer's Potsdam Conference, Truman and Stalin agreed that the Soviets would occupy eastern Germany and that America, Britain, and France would occupy zones in the western part of the country; Berlin, which was situated deep in the Russian zone, would be divided likewise. The new atomic bomb gave the Allied leaders leverage. But the Russians, with secrets provided by Communist spies in Western laboratories, were already at work developing their own bomb.

In 1945, the Western Allies and the Soviets managed some cooperation, joining together to create the new United Nations (UN)—a more potent body than the now-defunct League of Nations—to oversee occupied Germany and to try the leading Nazis in an international court convened at Nuremberg. But as Stalin used force to impose his dictatorial will on Soviet-occupied territory, the rift between East and West continued to widen. In March 1946, Churchill—though no longer prime minister—warned that an "Iron Curtain" had descended across the continent as repressive Soviet-controlled regimes cut Eastern Europe off from the rest of the world. In 1947, Truman presented an urgent containment plan, using American resources and influence to stop nations from falling to Soviet-backed Communist movements. The U.S. Marshall Plan committed billions of dollars to stabilize the war-ravaged democracies of Western Europe. The Soviets promptly denounced the president's policy, known as the Truman Doctrine, as warmongering. They branded the Marshall Plan an imperialist plot.

Some in the United States called for a more conciliatory approach to the Soviets, blaming American aggression for Stalin's paranoid moves. In 1948, Henry Wallace—who had been FDR's vice president before Truman—mounted a third-party presidential campaign on a Soviet-friendly platform. But most Americans, aware of Stalin's genuinely irrational and savage behavior, looked on Wallace with mistrust. The CPUSA, little more than a Soviet mouthpiece, endorsed Wallace—which hurt him still further in the eyes of most Americans. Wallace received just 2.4 percent of the vote. President Truman and his anti-Communist Truman Doctrine kept the support of most American liberals, and he won a second term in the 1948 election. In later years, when the true scope of Stalin's atrocities became clear, even Wallace would reject his own 1948 attitude toward the Soviets as dangerously naive.

In the face of Stalin's menacing expansionism, West Germany and U.S.-occupied Japan were swiftly rebuilt as anti-Communist bulwarks. In the rush to bury hostilities and build friendly governments, punishments for many wartime atrocities were scaled back or even shelved. In 1948 and 1949, the Soviets demanded full control of Berlin and blockaded the city's Western-occupied sectors. As a U.S.-led airlift kept West Berlin supplied, the Western allies formed a mutual defense pact called the North Atlantic Treaty Organization (NATO). The Soviets backed down, but East and West Germany were soon split between rival governments: West Germany (including West Berlin) was democratic, whereas East Germany—like other Soviet-occupied territories—fell under a Soviet-controlled dictatorship. The Soviets detonated their own atomic bomb soon after, in August 1949. The Cold War—tense hostility hovering just short of open conflict—had begun.

In China, Communists under leader Mao Zedong had sought power since the 1920s. Although Mao allied with the Western-supported Nationalists against Japan during World War II, civil war erupted again in 1946. In 1949, Mao's Soviet-backed forces drove the Nationalists into exile in Taiwan. The rise of so-called Red China fueled Western fears of a Communist wave in Asia. Korea, which had been divided between a Soviet-occupied North and a U.S.-occupied South since 1945, emerged as a flash point. The Soviets resisted UN efforts to unify Korea under an elected government, and Communist North Korea claimed control of the entire country in 1948. South Korea created a rival, U.S.-backed republic (which would itself prove dictatorial, corrupt, unstable, and unpopular).

In 1950, Soviet-armed North Koreans—supported by the Soviets and Chinese—invaded South Korea. The United States successfully called for a UN force to counter the invasion (the Russians, having boycotted the session, were not present to exercise their Security Council veto). The UN forces (which consisted mainly of U.S. and South Korean contingents) repelled the North Koreans after difficult fighting, and they made a daring amphibious landing behind enemy lines in the Battle of Inchon. But when UN troops pushed into North Korea, China entered the war. The result was stalemate, negotiation, and a permanent truce in 1953 that established a divided Korea. The Korean War illustrated America's refusal to tolerate Communist expansion, and showed the strength of both rival blocs of nations.

THE COLD WAR AT HOME AND THE NEW RED SCARE

As a Cold War mentality took hold in the late 1940s, Americans–with obvious justification–viewed Communism as a grave, direct, and imminent threat to freedom and the Western way of life. Many expected war between the United States and the Soviet Union, and many took a hard line against Communist expansion. General Douglas MacArthur–who had lost the Philippines in World War II, and then made himself a legend driving his army back across the Pacific to reclaim the islands–became an anti-Communist American hero as he led U.S. forces in Korea. President Truman fired MacArthur in 1951, after the general openly resisted Truman's orders to avoid an all-out war with China. Most people had no desire for a wider war, and MacArthur's insubordination had dangerously challenged the president's constitutional authority. Nonetheless, the public overwhelmingly sided with the aggressive general over Truman.

Truman's successor, Republican Dwight D. Eisenhower, completed the Korean peace talks Truman had begun. Having served as the top Allied general in World War II, he was mostly safe from charges of being "soft" on Communism. But anti-Communist crusading had become a core element of American politics: for many it was a sincere effort to combat a genuine threat, but it also provided a ticket to political advancement. Truman and Congress had both encouraged aggressive hunts for Communist agents and sympathizers. Labor unions–which were attacked even by some within the labor movement for putting pro-Soviet loyalties above the interests of their members–came under hostile scrutiny. In 1947, the House Un-American Activities Committee (HUAC)–which had pursued alleged Communists in New Deal organizations in the 1930s–began investigating suspected Communist Party members in Hollywood.

A year later, California congressman Richard Nixon gained national prominence for his work in HUAC's investigation of Alger Hiss, an aide to FDR at Yalta, for Soviet espionage in the 1930s (Hiss was convicted of lying about his activities, and the evidence strongly indicates that he was a Soviet spy). By 1952, Nixon was Eisenhower's running mate. Government agencies drove out employees on disloyalty charges. J. Edgar Hoover, the autocratic director of the Federal Bureau of Investigation, zealously pursued suspected Communists and Communist sympathizers, or "fellow travelers." He built massive files on liberal-leaning artists and intellectuals, civil rights activists, and others (as well as on the private scandals of political leaders, thus making himself untouchable). As the Cold War worsened after 1949, anti-Communist suspicions became a massive and consuming domestic concern.

The Soviet espionage threat was entirely real: the Venona Project (a top-secret effort to decrypt Soviet cables) revealed an extensive network of Communist spies in America. But unless other evidence was available, few could be prosecuted without revealing the clandestine code-cracking project and compromising U.S. intelligence. In 1951, in one of the few high-profile prosecutions, CPUSA members Julius and Ethel Rosenberg were tried and executed for giving nuclear secrets to the U.S.S.R.; Venona decrypts–not used in court due to security concerns–indicate that Julius, at least, was guilty. Many known spies escaped the legal process entirely.

By the early 1950s, fears of Communist infiltration threatened to drive the anti-Communist crusade out of control: the accused often had little or no connection to actual spies. Republicans and conservative Democrats accused the Truman administration–which had itself pursued aggressive anti-Communist policies–of shielding Communist agents. Hollywood, notorious for its left-wing and even pro-Soviet politics, had become the target of HUAC investigations in the late 1940s. Studio executives, fearing public backlash if they failed to act, created a secret blacklist to bar suspected Communists from employment. The number of blacklisted names rose sharply in the early 1950s; most could find escape only by "naming names"—pointing HUAC toward other suspected Communists.

Joseph McCarthy, a Republican senator from Wisconsin, became the public face of the anti-Communist crusade after 1950. With increasingly wild rhetoric, he declared that Truman's State Department was full of Communist agents—operatives who aided the Communist takeover of China and subverted the U.S. government. McCarthy's public hearings pursued current and former CPUSA members as well as leftist and Progressive organizations that he deemed to be Communist fronts. McCarthy knew nothing of the top-secret Venona decrypts, and his targets were rarely tied to espionage. Yet the Americans whom he targeted fell victim to public disgrace.

Rival politicians and others who challenged McCarthy's accusations were branded as Communists. McCarthy even accused President Eisenhower—a fellow Republican, but no friend of McCarthy's—of protecting Communists in his administration. At first, influential Republicans and conservative organizations stood by McCarthy. But changing circumstances helped undermine his influence: to the relief of the West (and of many Soviets), blood-soaked dictator Stalin died in 1953. The Korean War, America's first open battle with Communism, ended with an armistice soon after Stalin's death. As the Communist threat came to seem less urgent, McCarthy's excesses attracted greater scrutiny.

During televised 1954 hearings into alleged U.S. Army subversives, McCarthy's abusive and arrogant behavior soured his reputation. Newspapers and increasingly influential television reporting (whose investigations were quietly encouraged by Eisenhower) began to expose his lies and bullying tactics. The Senate voted to censure McCarthy that November, and his power collapsed. His zealous crusade to squelch freedom of speech and thought became infamous, and *McCarthyism* became a blanket term for ideological persecution. Nonetheless, the sense of an existential battle with antidemocratic global Communism was not an irrational concern, and it persisted as a major element of American politics and culture throughout the 1950s.

AMERICAN LIFE IN THE POST-WAR ERA

Roosevelt's New Deal dramatically expanded the federal government's role in America's economy after the Great Depression, and World War II demands expanded government power even further. The shift was permanent: with the rise of federal regulation, higher income taxes, and expanded national services and social programs, a return to the largely hands-off policies of the 1920s was impossible. Socialist "welfare states"—where basic services and economic guidance were provided by the government—arose in post-war Europe. In the United States, however, Socialist policies remained unpopular. Many pushed back against the government's growing powers, which they saw as a threat to individual liberty and initiative.

After the war, President Truman sought a balance between government oversight and private enterprise. To that end, he encouraged a partnership with the private sector that would help demobilized soldiers attain education and employment. The GI Bill, which gained passage during the war, helped former servicemen and servicewomen secure loans for home purchases and business investments, and it helped them pay for employment training and higher education. In his second term (from 1949 to 1953), Truman promoted his Fair Deal program—a policy that relied on the booming post-war economy to fund the government's growing social welfare obligations, including an expanded GI Bill of Rights that extended benefits to Korean War veterans. The Social Security system—withholding money from wage earners' paychecks to fund retirement benefits—was expanded and solidified.

Broader attempts at national reform, such as a push for a national health care system, struck many as too radical, too broad, and too reliant on further government expansion. Conservative resistance blocked these efforts. Also, demand for new housing soared. As GIs returned home after long absences in military service, a surge in pregnancies—the baby boom—brought pressure for wholesome new neighborhoods with open spaces and modern school systems. The Housing Act of 1949 aimed to build public housing, but funding was scarce. Private development proved the bigger impetus. Planned suburban developments, such as Long Island's Levittown, attracted growing numbers of buyers and triggered a boom of mass-produced suburban construction.

Government loan guarantees and tax deductions for mortgage interest payments helped builders and buyers, who began to envision a new American Dream: instead of urban renting, people aimed to own their own home in the suburbs, filling their houses with such new amenities as vacuum cleaners, washing machines, and refrigerators. The popularization of television had a particularly big impact. The technology had existed since the 1930s, but only a wealthy few had been able to afford it, and programming was limited. As TV ownership became widespread in the 1950s, it helped create a new popular mass culture that linked millions of households. Yet as popular programs offered idealized portraits of suburban families, some Americans began to feel confined by the safe expectations of uniformity on their screens.

As Americans moved from a wartime culture to the new American Dream, women came under enormous pressure to return to a purely domestic sphere. Family comedies on the new television networks emphasized tight-knight families managed by women who embraced the dual role of wife and mother. Advertising emphasized new home conveniences that reinforced women's wholly domestic position. Yet many women did not easily forget their wartime experiences. Meanwhile, the growing economy increased demand in lower-paid service professions, such as nursing, teaching, and secretarial work. These fields now actively recruited women. Even under the veneer of 1950s domesticity, tension between the pressures of home and work were building.

As employers adjusted to a more regulated economy, relations between management and labor unions improved. As Americans borrowed money and enjoyed increased incomes, standards of living continued to rise. Automobile ownership dramatically increased, allowing unprecedented personal and family mobility. Suburbs became more and more practical as work, shopping, and recreation opportunities spread farther from city centers. President Eisenhower was wary of additional increases in domestic spending, but he accepted the New Deal and Fair Deal programs that he inherited. He also endorsed infrastructure investment: a federally constructed highway network spurred further growth in the auto industry (it also bolstered national security by allowing rapid deployment of military forces).

THE RENEWED CIVIL RIGHTS MOVEMENT

Although class tension and labor agitation eased (or at least moved further from view) with the economic boom of the late 1940s and 1950s, the issue of race continued to divide Americans. The South clung fiercely to legal and social segregation, and African American migration to northern cities helped stimulate white migration to the suburbs—a phenomenon known as "white flight." Suburbs were virtually all white, whereas urban centers became increasingly black. At the same time, though, challenges to racist ideology were growing: World War II, a global campaign against racially bigoted regimes, provoked a fresh examination of old assumptions. Activists of all races demanded reform.

In 1947, baseball great Jackie Robinson joined the Brooklyn Dodgers, thereby shattering major-league baseball's decades-old color barrier—and the "national pastime" had a strong impact on national culture. In 1948, President Truman ordered the military to begin the process of desegregation. He also focused on civil rights during the 1948 presidential campaign. This helped cement black support for Democrats in the North (where, despite social discrimination, African American voting rights were largely intact), but it also risked fracturing the party. Democrats had controlled the South since the end of Reconstruction, but some angry southerners now bolted into the Dixiecrat Party—which vowed to protect the South's segregationist system. Strom

Thurmond, the Dixiecrat candidate, won only 2.4 percent of the national vote, barely more than Wallace earned in 1948—but he managed to carry four southern states. Although the Dixiecrats were short-lived, their segregationist aims endured.

Truman also worked to desegregate the federal government's own labor force. But a bitterly divided Congress stalled in other ways, failing to enact measures that were against lynching and for black voting rights in the South. Truman's Justice Department went to court to attack segregation in schools and housing. The courts began to question the "separate but equal" doctrine, the legal basis of segregation since the Supreme Court's *Plessy v. Ferguson* ruling of 1896. In 1953, President Eisenhower appointed Earl Warren (a moderate Republican) as the new chief justice. Warren's court would move in an increasingly activist direction, making strong use of judicial powers to pursue social justice. One case already pending before the court was a National Association for the Advancement of Colored People (NAACP) challenge to school segregation: *Brown v. Board of Education of Topeka, et al.*

The NAACP's case was developed by its lead lawyer, Thurgood Marshall, and was based on studies that showed the psychological harm inflicted on African American children by segregation. Marshall argued that such harm made "separate but equal" invalid and segregation a violation of the Fourteenth Amendment's guarantee of equal protection under the law. Attorneys for the segregationist states argued that deficiencies in black schools could be remedied, and insisted that flaws in implementation did not invalidate the "separate but equal" concept. In 1954, Warren's court unanimously declared segregated schools "inherently unequal" because of their demonstrated negative psychological effects. In further hearings the following year, the Supreme Court ordered local courts to oversee a consciously cautious implementation of desegregation "with all deliberate speed."

The *Brown v. Board* decision at first only affected the states named in the NAACP suit. But the ruling had, at least implicitly, struck down the legal foundation of all official segregation. Southern whites reacted with predictable fury. Southern congressmen and senators rallied behind a "Southern Manifesto" that defended segregation; the Ku Klux Klan launched new campaigns of terror and violence; and a new White Citizens' Council fought to beat back change. To many conservatives, the civil rights push also smacked of Communism: racial integration had been a prominent feature of Wallace's Soviet-friendly third-party presidential bid in 1948. But federal courts began to invoke the Fourteenth Amendment more consistently and forcefully. Black and white civil rights activists, meanwhile, risked the threat of violence to defy the Jim Crow system.

In 1955, Emmett Till—a black teenager from Chicago who was visiting relatives in Mississippi—was savagely murdered by white vigilantes, who claimed that Till had whistled at a white woman. An all-white jury acquitted the two killers, who then openly boasted of their crime. At his family's insistence, Till's brutalized corpse was publicly displayed; the shocking image helped rally demands for justice. Later that year, the NAACP recruited one of its members, Rosa Parks, to defy bus segregation in Montgomery, Alabama. The NAACP intended her arrest to challenge segregation in the courts and in public opinion. The local black community, a major source of bus revenue, boycotted the transit system. The boycott, which won the support of black communities nationwide, was led in part by the young Reverend Martin Luther King Jr., who emerged as a national figure.

In 1956, the boycotters won: federal courts struck down the segregation law, and the transit system changed its rules. But progress came slowly. By the mid-1960s, only a tiny fraction of southern schools had complied with *Brown v. Board of Education.* In Congress, most southern Democrats resisted civil rights legislation or sought to weaken it. But northern Democrats allied with Republicans to challenge the South's disenfranchisement of blacks. Eisenhower remained cautious; but in 1957, when Arkansas's governor used the National Guard to resist a federal court order desegregating Little Rock's public high school, Eisenhower placed the Arkansas National Guard under federal orders and sent in U.S. Army troops—the first such intervention since Reconstruction.

Other groups also pressed for civil rights in the 1950s. Japanese Americans fought with little success to regain property stolen from them during World War II internment (Warren, who was then the U.S. attorney general, had been prominent in arranging internment). Further, in Texas and the Southwest, the Hispanic population was growing rapidly. Temporary agricultural workers (*braceros*) often stayed beyond their program's expiration, and both legal and illegal immigrants came steadily from Mexico. They, like African Americans, faced systematic segregation. In *Hernandez v. Texas*—a case heard in 1954, the same year as *Brown v. Board of Education*—the Warren court upheld the right of Mexican Americans to equal treatment under the Fourteenth Amendment. The justices ruled that with nonwhites barred from jury service, a Hispanic defendant had not received a fair trial. The nation's courts were continuing to expand their definition of justice.

ERA 17: COMMUNISM AND COUNTERCULTURE: THE CHALLENGES OF THE '50S AND '60S *(1950S TO LATE 1960S)*

THE SUPERPOWERS FIND AN UNEASY BALANCE: DETERRENCE AND THE BATTLE FOR HEARTS AND MINDS

As Cold War tensions climaxed during the early 1950s, the United States and Russia pressed for every strategic advantage over one other. When the first atomic fission bombs were developed in the 1940s, scientists already knew that thermonuclear fusion—the sun's source of energy—could create a bomb that was far more powerful. In 1952, the United States detonated the first thermonuclear, or hydrogen, bomb (H-bomb), which was many times more powerful than those dropped on Japan in 1945. The Soviets followed suit in 1953. By that time, Joseph Stalin was dead, an armistice had been reached in Korea, and fears of immediate war had eased. Yet the growing H-bomb arsenals, and fleets of long-range bombers to carry them, made any hypothetical war vastly more dangerous. An all-out thermonuclear exchange would endanger all of humanity.

Such a war would probably annihilate both sides: a grim reality dubbed "mutually assured destruction" (or, fittingly, MAD). The two superpowers thus embraced a doctrine of deterrence, striving to ensure that whichever nation attacked the other would not survive the victim's counterstrike; a nuclear "first strike" would thus be suicidal. Both powers began to build intercontinental ballistic missiles (ICBMs), which were difficult to destroy on the ground—and impossible to stop once launched. In 1945, the Russians and Americans had both tried to capture the engineers behind Germany's feared V-2 ballistic missile. The top German engineers took pains to avoid Soviet captivity and soon formed the heart of the American missile program. Russia had its own rocket scientists, however, and also began to produce viable ICBM designs.

Although the deterrence policy aimed to prevent a deadly direct conflict, it required constant buildup and maintenance of forces and alliances to keep a strategic balance. West Germany joined the North Atlantic Treaty Organization in 1955, and the Soviets created a military alliance, known as the Warsaw Pact, with its Eastern European satellite states. The threat of thermonuclear war also made effective diplomacy more urgent. Premier Nikita Khrushchev was then rising to power in the Soviet Union. He kept a tight hold on Eastern Europe and lashed out with fiercely bombastic rhetoric, vowing to destroy capitalism and "bury" the West. But behind the bluster,

Khrushchev was a pragmatist, determined to maintain Soviet power but also to avoid a catastrophic war. The superpowers began conducting summits in 1955; the meetings aimed to limit the arms race and keep tensions under control. In 1956, Khrushchev denounced Stalin's violent crimes at a Soviet Party Congress.

East–West relations remained difficult and tense. In 1956, Hungary rose against Soviet control and appealed to the United States for help. The United States knew that American intervention in Hungary—practically in Russia's backyard—would inevitably have meant all-out war. The United States did not answer Hungary's calls for help, and thousands of Hungarians were killed as Soviet forces suppressed the revolt. The American response reflected the high stakes of political or military challenges to Russia because of the threat of thermonuclear war.

With Europe in an uneasy balance, attention shifted to "Third World" nations: developing countries that were not aligned with Communist or non-Communist blocs. Each superpower wanted to pull these nations into its own sphere of influence, providing aid and weapons and launching secret operations to install friendly governments. Determined to defend Western democracy against Communism, the United States was often willing to bolster anti-Communist Third World dictatorships to weaken Soviet influence.

In this battle for hearts and minds, appearances in the global stage were essential; each side fought to prove its superiority. The Soviets' October 1957 launch of *Sputnik*, the world's first man-made satellite, sparked a global sensation. Until this point, the United States had not made a satellite launch a major priority. Yet most Americans were stunned and humiliated by the unexpected Soviet feat. After the shock of *Sputnik*, the United States rushed to strengthen public science education and to prioritize technological investments.

The so-called space race would remain a propaganda battlefield for more than a decade. At first, the United States struggled to match Soviet efforts—and Americans knew that a rocket that could launch a satellite could also deliver a nuclear warhead anywhere on Earth. Khrushchev boasted of his country's ICBM production, and American politicians began to fret about a "missile gap." In fact, top officials knew from secret U-2 spy plane missions that the Soviets had few missiles, and actually lagged well behind the United States—a fact that Khrushchev carefully tried to conceal behind his boastful bluster.

In 1959, Khrushchev toured the United States to ease fresh tensions over Berlin. But relations soured again the following year, when Russia shot down an American U-2. President Dwight D. Eisenhower publicly denied conducting secret spy flights over Russia. His advisors assured him that the plane's pilot must have died when the plane was shot down and that the Soviets would be unable to prove the truth to the world. But the pilot, Gary Powers, had in fact survived and been captured; under interrogation, he admitted to committing espionage. The exposure of Eisenhower's lie embarrassed the United States, and the episode strained diplomacy between the superpowers.

Meanwhile, a Communist presence was taking hold only ninety miles from Florida. In 1959, Cuba's U.S.-backed dictator was overthrown by Fidel Castro and his rebels. But Castro soon emerged as a brutal, ruthless leader. Declaring himself a Communist, he turned to the Soviets—who were eager to gain a foothold so near to the United States. Before he left office, Eisenhower authorized a Central Intelligence Agency (CIA) effort to train anti-Castro exiles for an invasion of Cuba. President John F. Kennedy (who narrowly edged out Richard Nixon in the 1960 election) carried out the plan in April 1961. Anti-Castro forces landed at the Bay of Pigs, but the Cuban people failed to rise against Castro as the CIA had expected. As the invasion quickly floundered, the United States decided to pull back and cancelled the promised air support, and the American-supported exiles were badly beaten. The new Kennedy administration was humiliated and turned to secret efforts to topple Castro—or to kill him.

COLD WAR TENSIONS UNDER KENNEDY AND JOHNSON

In June 1961, Kennedy met Khrushchev in Vienna. The summit went poorly: Khrushchev, embarrassed by the steady flow of defectors from East Berlin into West Germany, demanded that the entire city be turned over to East Germany outright. Kennedy found him bullying and irrational; Khrushchev saw Kennedy as weak, despite JFK's refusal to yield on Berlin. In August, East Germany hastily constructed the Berlin Wall and alarmed Westerners by abruptly separating East Berlin from the West. Cold War tensions were rising again. The Soviets were also building up Cuba's strength, equipping Castro's forces with weapons and secretly sending large numbers of Soviet troops.

Khrushchev hoped to protect Castro from another American invasion, and in 1962 he placed nuclear missiles in Cuba that were capable of striking the United States. JFK had strongly warned the Soviets not to take such a step. That October, American U-2s found the missile bases—a discovery that sparked the most dangerous crisis of the Cold War. Although the United States had similar missiles in Turkey that were aimed at Russia, a failure to respond to Khrushchev's move would have been politically impossible: the acceptance of secretly installed Soviet missiles so close to U.S. shores would critically weaken the United States in the eyes of its allies and of nonaligned nations. Resisting his advisors' pressure for a military strike, JFK placed Cuba under naval quarantine and publicly demanded that the missiles be withdrawn. As U.S. warships confronted Soviet vessels on the quarantine line, any misstep could have escalated into all-out war.

Khrushchev was deeply alarmed, and he was just as determined as Kennedy to avoid a nuclear exchange. Khrushchev pressed against his own militarist advisors to find a peaceful solution. Even after Russia shot down an American U-2 over Cuba (without Khrushchev's authorization) and killed its pilot, both Kennedy and Khrushchev held back. Finally, after thirteen days of crisis, the leaders struck a deal. Publicly, the Soviets vowed to withdraw their missiles in exchange for an American pledge not to invade Cuba (this pledge was never actually given, because Castro—furious that the Soviets had agreed to withdraw the missiles without consulting him—refused to accept the terms of the deal). Secretly, the United States promised Russia to remove its missiles from Turkey (by this point, these weapons were already being replaced by newer submarine-launched ballistic missiles).

The world had survived its closest brush with nuclear catastrophe. For several days, a thermonuclear war had seemed imminent—and both superpowers had learned a sobering lesson. A direct phone link was established between the White House and the Soviet Kremlin to improve communication during future crises. Diplomacy improved; in 1963, Kennedy and Khrushchev signed the Nuclear Test Ban Treaty, which prohibited all above-ground nuclear tests. The treaty sought to protect the world from nuclear fallout and to limit the quest for more powerful bombs. Nonetheless, the superpowers continued to wage their battle for global influence. With both sides more wary than ever of direct confrontation, the focus shifted still further toward propaganda efforts and battles in the Third World.

The space race remained an important part of this struggle for global prestige. In the early 1960s, the U.S. space program stood in the shadow of seemingly endless Soviet firsts. But the Soviet advantage was weaker than it appeared. The Russians sent the first human, Yuri Gagarin, to space in April 1961. But America's technology was advancing rapidly, despite its relative lack of headline triumphs. Seeking a race the United States could win, Kennedy proposed to land a man on the moon by the end of the decade. Russia could not outdo America over the long haul; the Soviet lunar program was ultimately abandoned, whereas *Apollo 11* landed a man on the moon ahead of schedule in July 1969. Later *Apollo* missions developed into more serious scientific efforts, but Cold War rivalries lay at the program's heart.

In the ongoing battle against Communist expansion, the Southeast Asian nation of Vietnam became the focal point. Vietnam had been a French colony since the nineteenth century, but Communist and nationalist uprisings drove the French out in 1954, leaving the country divided into a Communist North and a Western-aligned South. Eisenhower feared a domino effect–that nations throughout Asia would fall to Communism if the North Vietnamese prevailed–and actively supported South Vietnam's government, despite its rampant corruption. Although he was wary of major military entanglement in the Southeast Asian jungle, JFK increased military support for South Vietnam. In 1963, the United States quietly backed a military coup that overthrew and murdered South Vietnam's unpopular ruler.

JFK's successor, Lyndon B. Johnson, escalated efforts to strengthen the vulnerable South Vietnamese. In 1964, a U.S. destroyer was attacked off the North Vietnamese coast; LBJ pushed the Tonkin Gulf Resolution through Congress, which essentially gave him a blank check to use force as he deemed necessary. By 1965, South Vietnam's government was near collapse, and Johnson had a dilemma. Despite a Communist insurgency in the South, which was backed by the North, most South Vietnamese clearly opposed a Communist takeover. Yet the South lacked effective government, which meant that the worsening fighting would fall mainly on the United States. Johnson was convinced that a defeat for the United States would weaken its position throughout the world. Thus, he continued to step up combat operations and deepen U.S. involvement, bombing Communist positions and steadily increasing U.S. ground troops.

REFORM AT HOME: THE CIVIL RIGHTS REVOLUTION AND LBJ'S GREAT SOCIETY

In the wake of *Brown v. Board of Education* and the successful Montgomery, Alabama, bus boycott, the push for civil rights and racial equality gained greater momentum in the early 1960s. The pressure for change came mainly from grassroots activists. In 1960, black students–who were soon joined by white sympathizers–sat at segregated department store lunch counters in North Carolina and demanded service. Such nonviolent sit-ins soon began throughout the South, with activists insisting–ultimately successfully–that the states accept court rulings against the segregation of buses, transit stations, and more. Equality advocates and student groups used buses to carry out mixed-race "freedom rides" across the South, facing down violent and dangerous segregationist backlash.

The strengthening civil rights campaign put JFK in an awkward bind. Since the 1930s, the Democratic coalition had included many New Deal liberals, who favored civil rights reform. But since Reconstruction, the party had also relied heavily on its massive southern base. And southern Democrats, the backbone of the region's white power structure, remained heavily pro-segregation. Kennedy, however, began to take bolder steps. In 1961, he sent federal marshals to protect the freedom riders; in 1962, he used National Guard troops to force desegregation of state universities in Mississippi and Alabama. That same year, Congress passed the Twenty-Fourth Amendment (ratified in 1964). The amendment abolished the poll tax, which had long been used to prevent southern blacks, as well as many poor whites, from voting.

The following year, antisegregation rallies in Birmingham, Alabama, led to brutal police crackdowns and antiblack violence. National demands for reform increased, and JFK began pressing for stronger civil rights legislation. That August, activists staged a massive march in Washington, DC, that climaxed in Martin Luther King Jr.'s eloquent "I Have a Dream" speech. In November, Kennedy was assassinated, and LBJ assumed the presidency. A master of legislative maneuvering and deal making during his years in the Senate, LBJ looked toward an even bolder reformist agenda. In 1964, he secured an expanded Civil Rights Act (which also offered women protection against discrimination) by bypassing southern Democrats and securing the support of moderate Republicans.

Meanwhile, the Republican Party also faced internal discord. That fall, a rising conservative movement dedicated to drastic reductions in government power (except for when it came to aggressive military policy) nominated Barry Goldwater, an Arizona senator, for president. To many Americans, Goldwater was a dangerous extremist: he seemed poised to use nuclear weapons in Vietnam and willing to threaten New Deal programs, such as Social Security. And although he was personally opposed to segregation, he rejected the Civil Rights Act as a dangerous federal intrusion on state power. Goldwater was crushingly defeated by LBJ, but the movement that he had ignited continued to gain strength. William Buckley, an editor and publisher, and actor-turned-politician Ronald Reagan were rising stars in the movement, and they gained prominence and power in the Republican Party.

Crucially, Goldwater's opposition to federal civil rights laws had helped him win five states in the Deep South (his only victories outside of his home state and the first Republican victories in the region since Reconstruction). Clearly, white resentment was fracturing the Democrats' former "Solid South." Fully aware of the threat to the old Democratic coalition, LBJ nevertheless continued to press for additional reforms. The Voting Rights Act of 1965 gave the federal government broad new powers to protect African American voting access in the South. At the same time, activists kept up popular pressure. King led a series of marches from Selma, Alabama, in support of black voting rights, and televised images of police brutalizing peaceful demonstrators helped galvanize national support for civil rights demands.

Defying the increasingly vocal opposition of small-government conservatives, LBJ was determined to expand federal power even further to advance his social justice aims. Before the 1964 election, he had already declared a "war on poverty," a push for economic development and job creation. After his landslide 1964 victory, Johnson called for programs to promote a "Great Society." Medicare funded medical care for the elderly, and Medicaid did the same for the poor. Other programs sought to renew decaying cities and promote low-income housing, expand support for education and cultural programs, increase the minimum wage, strengthen environmental protections, and continue to expand civil rights guarantees.

Johnson hoped to increase the New Deal's social supports to help those whom the prosperity of the 1950s and 1960s had left behind. The Great Society tried to create opportunity and help people help themselves, investing federal resources to assist Americans in achieving prosperity. Johnson argued that such efforts would bolster the prosperity of the entire society. But these expansions of federal power were expensive and controversial—especially when the 1960s economic boom faltered and the heavy taxes needed to fund the programs seemed too burdensome to many Americans. Nonetheless, some Great Society programs—particularly Medicare, which had been urgently denounced by the new conservative movement as a fundamental threat to American freedom—became firmly entrenched alongside Social Security as popular supports for the elderly and the poor.

THE '60S: WAR, COUNTERCULTURE, AND CONFLICT

As the 1960s advanced, a host of controversies deeply divided the country. The growing movement for racial equality, supported by Johnson's aggressive push for federal civil rights activism, sparked massive southern resentment and split the Democratic Party. LBJ's ambitious Great Society programs drew a strong backlash from a reinvigorated conservative movement determined to roll back what its members deemed wasteful "big government" spending. A rebellious, anticonformist youth culture challenged traditional social rules and authority structures and turned against the worsening war in Vietnam. And, faced with continuing poverty, prejudice, and only limited gains, some minority groups erupted in violent frustration against society's status quo.

The 1950s culture of conformity had already sparked a youth rebellion centered on the new craze for rock 'n' roll music. With its roots in predominantly African American jazz and blues, the music—and the uninhibited dancing that often accompanied it—greatly alarmed the period's parents, just as their children hoped that it would. In reality, though, the rebellion was limited and offered little real challenge to society's norms and expectations. Yet during the early 1960s, the backlash against 1950s conformism grew more serious. By mid-decade, "New Left" politics added fuel to festering antiauthority attitudes. Inspired by the civil rights movement, young Americans—particularly college students—increasingly attacked the country's political and corporate cultures and demanded radical social change.

Defiant students shunned adult authority and traditional values in regard to clothing, sexuality, drug use, music, and lifestyle. These so-called hippies and their counterculture became a vast campus phenomenon, heavily influencing the broader popular culture. Hippies sparked daring new fads in dress, popular music, arts, and design. Pressure also rose for other forms of social change. A new women's rights movement—arguing that women's social standing had hardly changed since they won the vote in the 1920s—launched a fresh push for social equality and female empowerment beyond the home. Many men on the New Left dismissed women's issues as secondary, but the cause would gain strength in the 1970s.

The Vietnam War served as the antiestablishment movement's primary focus, coming to symbolize all the evils of violence, oppression, social injustice, and authoritarian power structures that the counterculture denounced. Young American males were required to register for the military draft and carry a draft card. Although most college students received deferments to complete their education, they expired on graduation. Campus antiwar protesters rallied, burned draft cards, disrupted classes, and occupied campus buildings.

As America's involvement in Vietnam deepened, controversy grew across American society. Most South Vietnamese still opposed a Communist takeover, yet the South—facing North Vietnamese guerillas and South Vietnam's own determined Communist insurgency—had neither an effective government nor an able military. The combat burden fell increasingly on American draftees, while the harsh fighting also brutalized Vietnamese civilians. Communist centers in both the North and the South were bombed, and villages were razed, turning the South Vietnamese people ever more against the Americans who ostensibly were there to help them. For the first time, television brought vivid images of wartime carnage straight to American living rooms. Media reports grew increasingly hostile toward the war, criticizing the destruction and widespread loss of life.

Assailed by student radicals and media criticism, the war grew less popular as its costs rose. North Vietnam's massive Tet Offensive, in early 1968, turned even more Americans against the conflict. The offensive was, in fact, a serious defeat for Communist forces: their dramatic gains were only briefly held before they were pushed back with heavy casualties, and the pro-Communist rising the North had hoped to trigger in South Vietnam completely failed to materialize. But the aggressive attack nevertheless caught U.S. forces off guard and shocked the American public, who saw that the war was far from over, despite the thousands of lives already lost. With casualties mounting, the fighting seemed endless; hopeful generals so often saw "light at the end of the tunnel" that the phrase became a target of sardonic mockery.

Protests against the war and the draft grew more explosive and widespread. LBJ's credibility and popularity plummeted, undercut from the Right by attacks on his "big government" programs and from the Left by outrage at the war. Challenged for the 1968 Democratic nomination by the antiwar Senator Eugene McCarthy, LBJ chose not to seek reelection. He soon halted the bombing of North Vietnam and vowed to seek a peaceful settlement.

Growing racial agitation only added to the rising sense of national crisis. By the mid-1960s, such radical black activists as Malcolm X denounced the slow pace of reform and offered a "Black Power" philosophy of racial separatism (in 1965, Malcolm X was murdered by rival members of his

Black Muslim movement). Such groups as the Black Panthers attacked King's nonviolent, integrationist approach. Despite the steady progress in civil rights, frustration seethed dangerously in urban black neighborhoods, which were still mired in poverty and deeply suspicious of arrogant and often-abusive white police. Some urban blacks began to lash out in bursts of violence, looting, and arson.

In 1965, tens of thousands of local blacks rioted for several days in the Watts district of Los Angeles, killing more than thirty people and causing tens of millions of dollars in property damage. Similar riots broke out in Newark, New Jersey, and Detroit, Michigan, in 1967. Urban, working-class whites—many of whom lived in close proximity to the riots—grew fearful. Many failed to distinguish between the rioters and the moderates, such as King, turning apprehensively against all blacks. Many also grew dubious of traditional labor-driven liberalism, looking toward more conservative policies to restore order and prevent social breakdown. Many black activists, meanwhile, made increasingly radical demands for immediate change, dividing their communities and further weakening moderate leaders. In April 1968, King was assassinated in Memphis, Tennessee, by white supremacist James Earl Ray. In response, new and severe riots erupted in black communities across the United states, further worsening the racial divide.

Robert F. Kennedy, brother of slain president John F. Kennedy, sought the 1968 Democratic nomination on an antiwar platform, but was also assassinated. Hubert Humphrey, LBJ's vice president, won the nomination. Outside the Democratic convention in Chicago, violence erupted between police and antiwar, antiestablishment demonstrators. The agitation reflected a growing split among Democrats: radicals attacked the party as complacent and racist, whereas working-class Democrats grew ever more concerned at the radicals' threat to social order. Republicans pointed to the violence as proof of the danger posed by leftist extremists. George Wallace, Alabama's segregationist governor, also sought the Democratic nomination. But he soon abandoned the party, running a potent third-party candidacy against Humphrey and Republican nominee Richard Nixon.

Wallace's candidacy was unsuccessful, but it marked a political watershed. His defection from the Democrats reflected the hastening collapse of the old Democratic Solid South. Nixon, deliberately targeting frustrated southern Democrats, also made strong inroads in the region. And although Wallace's aggressive pro-war stance hurt him at the polls, his attacks on racial integration, the counterculture, and federal power helped him win several Deep South states. Widespread fears of domestic chaos and social decay bolstered Nixon's campaign. His promises to end the war in Vietnam also boosted his standing, and he narrowly won the election (recent evidence shows that his staff worked during the campaign to undermine Vietnamese peace talks, fearing progress would boost Humphrey's standing). But the 1960s left the country deeply divided: many Americans were frightened by racial tensions and urban riots, alienated by radical disaffection, and bewildered by rapid social change.

ERA 18: MODERN TIMES: PRESIDENTIAL SCANDALS, CONSERVATISM, AND UNREST *(1968 TO PRESENT)*

GLOBAL CONFLICT AND DIPLOMACY: DÉTENTE, CHINA, AND THE MIDDLE EAST

After the 1962 Cuban Missile Crisis and the close brush with nuclear war, direct communication between the superpowers improved. The following year, the United States and the Soviet Union (U.S.S.R.) negotiated the Limited Test Ban Treaty to end above-ground nuclear tests.

The treaty was an effort to control the nuclear arms race and to avoid dangerous nuclear fallout. But the rivalry between the superpowers continued through less-dangerous proxy conflicts, as the two sides battled for influence in the developing postcolonial nations of the so-called Third World. The longest, most divisive conflict was America's intervention in the extended war between North and South Vietnam.

Even as he struggled to resolve the war in Vietnam, President Richard Nixon moved to lessen the risk of conflict with the major Communist powers. Pursuing a policy of détente (or the easing of relations), Nixon hoped to slow the dangerous, expensive nuclear arms race through a diplomatic thaw with the Soviets. Greater cooperation resulted in the Strategic Arms Limitation Treaty (SALT), which directly limited the construction of weapons systems. This agreement between the superpowers marked a major shift in Cold War relations.

Even more dramatically, Nixon reached out to Communist China. The United States had refused since 1949 to recognize Mao Zedong's People's Republic, instead recognizing Taiwan's exiled Nationalist government as the legitimate Chinese state. Communist China also resisted Western ties and supported North Korea against United Nations (UN) forces in the Korean War. Mao's extremism in the 1950s and 1960s soured his ties even with the Soviet Union, and it made improved relations with the West completely impossible. By the 1960s, the Soviets were openly repudiating the oppressive brutality of Joseph Stalin. Mao, instead, continued to grow more radical. Purging his own party of more moderate elements, he unleashed the savage chaos of the Cultural Revolution. Western influences were denounced as counterrevolutionary; those with Western learning were in danger of harassment, imprisonment, or death. China's acquisition of nuclear weapons further increased tension with the Soviets as well as with the West.

But the full fury of the Cultural Revolution could not be sustained. Damage to factories and labor forces undermined the economy, and the terrorization of teachers and closure of schools threatened the entire system of education. China's ruling Communists began anxiously pulling back from the full extremes of the Cultural Revolution in 1969. Although Mao continued to push for a rigidly ideological society until his death in 1976, even he began to retreat from the intense xenophobia that had gripped China. By 1971, he tentatively reached out to the wider world. Later that year, the UN granted China's seat, which Taiwan had held since 1949, to the People's Republic. The potent Security Council veto, which China had secured in 1945 as one of the five leading Allied forces (the United States, the U.S.S.R., China, Britain, and France), was also transferred to the People's Republic. In 1972, Nixon paid a formal state visit to Beijing. His successor, President Jimmy Carter, established full diplomatic relations with China in 1979.

Other international problems remained. After escalating its involvement in Vietnam and failing to end the conflict, the United States and North Vietnam signed the Paris Peace Accords in 1973, which allowed withdrawal of American forces. But beyond the American pullout, the peace agreement had little effect. North Vietnam continued to press its attack on the South. South Vietnam tried to continue the fight, but it was weakly governed and wracked by internal Communist insurrection. It was defeated in 1975, unleashing savage Communist crackdowns and mass flight by South Vietnamese refugees. Instability had already spread throughout the region. In 1975, neighboring Laos fell to a Communist insurrection—and the pro-American Hmong minority was harshly suppressed. That same year, Communist Khmer Rouge rebels seized power in Cambodia. Dictator Pol Pot's regime murdered two million Cambodians in a fanatical effort to purge intellectuals, end Western influences, and force the nation back to an agrarian peasant society. In 1978, the nation was overrun by Vietnamese troops. In 1991, the UN finally reestablished the constitutional monarchy that Pol Pot had ousted.

Meanwhile, there was ongoing hostility between the Arab states and Israel. Under the leadership of Yasser Arafat's Palestine Liberation Organization (PLO), militant groups refused to recognize Israel's existence and demanded a Palestinian state in its place. In 1967, Israel launched a preemptive strike as Arab nations prepared to attack. In the swift Six-Day War, Israel seized East Jerusalem and the West Bank from Jordan, and the Gaza Strip and Sinai from Egypt. In 1973, Egypt and Syria attacked on Yom Kippur (a Jewish day of fasting and prayer). But after early setbacks and a difficult fight, Israel emerged victorious once more.

Western-Arab tensions had been high since Arab independence was denied after World War I, and many in the Middle East resented Western backing of often despotic governments in strategically important oil-producing states. But the West's support of Israel exacerbated tensions with the Arabs and caused rifts with their respective governments. After the Yom Kippur War, the Arab states recognized the PLO as the sole legitimate government of all Israeli territory and imposed an oil embargo against Israel's Western supporters. A first major step toward stability in the region was the U.S.-brokered peace treaty between Israel and Egypt in 1978. Under the terms of the Camp David Accords, Israel ceded the Sinai Peninsula—which it had taken from Egypt in 1967—and removed its settlements there. But PLO terrorism against Israel, and Israeli crackdowns in the remaining occupied territories, raged on. A 1982 Israeli invasion of Lebanon, a nation devastated by Christian-Muslim civil war since the mid-1970s, sought to deprive the PLO of a major base. However, the invasion mainly resulted in sparking further international dispute.

Increasingly influential followers of radical Islamic ideas aimed to purge Muslim nations of Western influence and create a strict theocratic system of Islamic rule. In 1979, Iran's dictatorial, U.S.-supported shah was removed by Islamic revolutionaries. Iranian radicals demanded that the shah, who was in America for medical treatment, return to Iran for trial. They seized dozens of Americans in the U.S. embassy in the Iranian capital of Tehran, holding them hostage for months; their actions were part of a wider ideology of Islamic *jihad*, a doctrine of holy war for the defense and expansion of Islam that extremists claimed sanctioned acts of terror against Western civilians. Jihadists intended to force the West to withdraw support for Israel and to replace Western-backed Middle Eastern regimes with Islamist rule. But the West persisted in supporting Israel, and tensions between the West and Islamic radicals continued to rise.

THE COLD WAR ENDS, AND EUROPEAN COMMUNISM FALLS

By the 1980s, the Soviet Union was in serious economic trouble. After World War II, Stalin had promoted large, impractical schemes to transform the Soviet landscape—forcing crops into unsuitable climate zones and severely damaging agriculture in the process. By the 1960s, the state-controlled economy was focused on heavy industry; there was constant pressure to increase output, and attention to safety and quality standards decreased. The Soviets strained to maintain control of Eastern Europe and to preserve their massive military. In 1979, they invaded Afghanistan to defend a new Communist regime against Islamist rebels. The Soviets were opposed by American-supported and -equipped Islamic Mujahidin guerrillas, who saw the war as holy jihad. The war soon turned into a quagmire that further drained the Soviets' overstretched resources.

Meanwhile, major Western powers were growing both more conservative and more militarily aggressive. Since World War II, many Western European nations had built complex state-supported social welfare systems. But over time, the expense of such policies grew, and taxation reached extremely high levels that many feared would stifle economic growth. In 1979, the Conservative Party's Margaret Thatcher became Britain's prime minister. Remaining in power until 1990, she worked aggressively to reduce massive government spending and to rein in taxes. Opponents accused her of callousness as she cut taxes and reduced government-funded social services, but her supporters argued that the cuts were necessary to prevent government bankruptcy and economic collapse. She also firmly promoted a hard line against Soviet and Eastern European Communism.

U.S. president Ronald Reagan was elected in 1980 on a similar platform of shrinking the federal government and assuming a more aggressive foreign posture. He, too, focused intensely on eradicating Communism from the world—and he brought the dominant resources of the United States to bear on the issue. Reagan bolstered support for anti-Communist movements around the globe—including that of the Islamic rebels in Afghanistan. He also pushed for dramatic boosts in military spending to strengthen America's defenses. The Soviets were overburdened, and their economy was struggling. American policymakers did not just intend to bolster the U.S. military; instead, they hoped that forcing the U.S.S.R. to match U.S. spending would undermine the Soviet economy and bring down the Soviet Communist regime.

Although America's massive military spending created enormous budget deficits, the policymakers' predictions were correct: the Soviets' efforts to keep pace crippled them. Growing economic crisis in the U.S.S.R. boosted an internal Soviet reform movement. In 1985, Mikhail Gorbachev took power. The reformist premier quickly moved to modernize the economy, liberalize internal politics, expand free speech and personal rights, and retreat from aggressive foreign ventures. He called these policies *glasnost* (openness) and *perestroika* (rebuilding). In 1987, Gorbachev began preparing for withdrawal from the disastrous war in Afghanistan. Sensing a historic opportunity, Reagan pivoted to a strategy of diplomacy. He startled many as he proposed a dramatic arms reduction treaty, which the United States and the U.S.S.R. signed that year. In 1989, the U.S.S.R. withdrew completely from Afghanistan.

Eastern Europe had also been hit hard by economic decline, particularly as the cash-strapped Soviets cut back on supports, such as subsidized oil. As Gorbachev liberalized the Soviet Union and the threat of Soviet crackdowns eased, pro-democracy movements gained strength in nations that had long been under the Soviet thumb. Poland's Solidarity movement, led by labor activist Lech Walesa and openly encouraged by Polish-born Catholic Pope John Paul II, began openly opposing Communism in the mid-1980s. Unrest rose elsewhere, and as relations with the West improved, Gorbachev loosened the Soviet hold on Eastern Europe and allowed states to shift away from Communism. In 1989, rebellious East Germans broke down the Berlin Wall. The Communist East German government collapsed shortly thereafter.

Other pro-democracy movements soon spread across Eastern Europe. In Hungary and Poland, Communist governments negotiated settlements with opposition forces and transitioned to free elections. In Czechoslovakia, public demonstrations forced the republic's Communist regime to yield; in November 1989, dissident playwright Vaclav Havel became president of a free Czechoslovakian government. Bulgaria's Communist government fell to a coup, and Romania's fell to an armed insurrection. The Soviet sphere quickly crumbled—and Soviet acceptance of these developments marked the effective end of the Cold War. Within months, the global political order changed profoundly.

The Soviet Union itself began to dissolve. The U.S.S.R. included the large Russian state and more than a dozen smaller, once-separate republics. As Soviet policy liberalized and Communism crumbled in Eastern Europe, the republics began pushing for local control—and for the primacy of their own local languages, religions, and ethnic identities. Gorbachev tried to hold the U.S.S.R. together by force, but he was gradually compelled to yield greater autonomy to the republics. In August 1991, hard-line Communists attempted a coup to reassert Soviet control. Boris Yeltsin, the recently elected president of the Russian Republic (which was the central component of the U.S.S.R.) led a popular street uprising that defeated the coup plotters. That December, the Soviet Union dissolved and was replaced by the loose Commonwealth of Independent States.

Since 1919's Treaty of Versailles, the eastern part of Europe's many disparate ethnic and religious groups had been awkwardly joined together within often arbitrary national borders. Soviet control had kept these schisms forcibly submerged. But now the collapse of Communism allowed them to resurge. Czechoslovakia split into the Czech Republic and Slovakia in 1993. Yugoslavia, an uncomfortable amalgam of Slavic peoples that had been created in the ever-divided Balkans after the First World War, had begun to fragment by 1990; bitter fighting between ethnic groups soon followed. Long-buried splits also emerged in the Russian Republic. The Muslim province of Chechnya tried to break away, sparking a harsh Russian crackdown and a cycle of violence that is still unresolved. Germany was an exception: Cold War geopolitics had split a single people, who were reunited in a single German democracy in 1990.

Pressure against authoritarian Communism was not confined to Europe. China, which had opened to the West in the 1970s, was increasingly affected by Western economic and political ideas. As Russia enacted liberal reforms under Gorbachev, popular pressure rose in China. Citizens, especially the educated young, wanted similar changes. Even China's ruling Communist Party was divided between those who resisted reform and others who favored concessions toward democratic change. The removal of a top reform-minded official sparked urban pro-democracy demonstrations in early 1989. In May, youth-led protesters captured the world's attention as they occupied Beijing's Tiananmen Square. In early June, the government sent the army to suppress the protests. Hundreds died in a crackdown that heralded a wave of arrests and executions. The pro-democracy movement was broken, but Chinese authorities were left with the difficult task of addressing widespread discontent without yielding their power.

THE CHANGING POST–COLD WAR WORLD

The post–Cold War world created a new mosaic of international challenges, and U.S. president George H. W. Bush helped form new relationships and alliances between nations. From 1990 to 1991, Iraqi dictator Saddam Hussein (whom the United States had supported during his long, bloody war against Iran in the 1980s) invaded Kuwait and menaced Saudi Arabia. The invasion threatened America's allies, global oil supplies, and the entire world economy. Bush skillfully assembled a broad international coalition against Hussein. He was also able to keep Israel—whose involvement would have alienated Arab states—from joining the war, even after Hussein launched unprovoked missile strikes against Israeli cities.

Western Europe continued a long-standing post–World War II push toward unity and economic integration. In 1993, the European Union (EU) was formed, which tightened political ties and harmonized foreign and economic policies—despite continuing conflicts over the extent of individual member nations' sovereignty. In 1999, a new single European currency called the Euro took effect (although Britain, always cautious about strong European ties, refused to use it).

Eastern Europe struggled in its transition to unfamiliar democratic institutions. Eastern European nations gradually moved toward EU membership in the early 2000s. Poland, Hungary, and the Czech Republic joined the North Atlantic Treaty Organization in 1999. Other Eastern European nations followed suit, signaling a greater shift toward unified European policymaking. The single market and unified currency have created ongoing opportunities and ongoing challenges, as the EU has tried to balance Europe's stronger and weaker national economies within a stable and coherent single system.

Despite the push for unity, nationalism and ethnic separatism persisted—particularly in the regions that had constituted the former Yugoslavia. In 1914, Serbian demands for control of Bosnia, with its large population of ethnic Serbs, had helped spark the First World War. In 1991, Serbians in Bosnia-Herzegovina launched a genocidal campaign of "ethnic cleansing" (or targeted extermination) against the Bosnian Muslim population. Their aim was to create ethnically "pure" areas, which Serbia could then annex. The resulting Bosnian civil war unleashed savage violence, war crimes, and civilian slaughter. In the southern part of Serbia itself, the province of Kosovo witnessed uprisings against Serbian rule later in the decade. In 1998, Serbia responded with a new campaign of ethnic cleansing in Kosovo, aimed at ethnic Albanians and Kosovar Muslims. In 1999, the United States led a NATO intervention: airstrikes and NATO troops drove the Serbians back, and Kosovo was placed under UN control. Kosovo declared independence in 2008, but its status remains disputed.

As the world struggled to achieve post–Cold War political balance, its economy was quickly shifting. Globalization—the trend toward an integrated worldwide economy in which production and consumption are spread across the globe—had gradually been taking hold. For instance, factories had increasingly relocated to developing nations where labor costs were far lower and regulations were far weaker. In the 1990s, the world was no longer divided into rival Cold War camps. Thus, globalization accelerated dramatically. Beyond the United States and Europe, new centers of economic growth were rapidly emerging.

India, the world's most populous democracy, focused heavily on economic development after achieving independence from Great Britain in 1947. The nation was a quickly expanding center for manufacturing and technology by the 1990s, even though its government struggled to deal with widespread poverty. Hindu India and Muslim Pakistan have remained hostile toward each other. Although the nations have not been at war since 1971, border incidents and diplomatic clashes have continued. India attained nuclear weapons in the mid-1970s, and Pakistan followed a decade later (although it did not openly test a bomb until the late 1990s). In spite of the tension, there have been periodic thaws and increases in cross-border trade.

Development has been difficult in Central and South America, which had long been under U.S. and European economic domination. In 1994, the North American Free Trade Agreement (NAFTA) cut restrictions on cross-border commerce. Since NAFTA, Mexico has produced more goods for the U.S. market and has developed close ties with the United States. But Mexico has also been severely hit by organized crime, drug trafficking, and lawlessness: there are large areas where the government barely has authority. Elsewhere in the region, post-war industrialization efforts have often failed, and heavy borrowing led to debt crises in the 1980s.

Political instability led some nations into successive dictatorships. The United States sometimes supported these dictatorships, so long as they were anti-Communist. In 1973, the United States covertly helped Augusto Pinochet overthrow an elected Socialist government in Chile, a move that ushered in fifteen years of corrupt, brutal rule. Juan Perón, president of Argentina, flirted with Fascism after World War II. In 1976, Argentina fell to a military *junta* (a group of military officers in charge of a dictatorship), which murdered thousands of dissenters. The regime's unsuccessful 1982 attempt to wrest the disputed Falkland Islands from the British—aggressively fought off by Britain under Thatcher—finally led to its demise, and a new democratic government took power in 1983. South America's rich raw material resources—particularly oil and agriculture—today serve as a springboard for future growth. However, the profits rarely reach large portions of the expanding populations, and serious ecological damage has been done. The destruction of vast areas of rainforest to create agricultural land has global environmental implications.

Development across Africa has been extremely uneven since post–World War II decolonization. For some countries, oil and other raw materials offered a path to rapid prosperity. As in South America, however, a drop in oil prices during the 1980s left many nations in debt. Some of them have successfully established democratic governments, but ethnic conflicts and political turmoil have continued to ravage the continent. During Nigeria's civil war in the late 1960s, nearly one million people died of starvation. Outbreaks of ethnic cleansing in Rwanda in the 1990s and in Darfur in the 2000s have drawn international attention but defied straightforward solutions. Poverty, HIV and AIDS, political crises, environmental decay, and continuing debt continue to impede new reform and economic development efforts.

International pressure and internal resistance helped bring down South Africa's white-dominated Apartheid regime of racial segregation. In 1990, South African President F. W. de Klerk began to repeal the country's Apartheid laws, freed Nelson Mandela—leader of the anti-Apartheid

African National Congress—after twenty-seven years of imprisonment, and moved to enfranchise black South Africans. In 1993, de Klerk and Mandela shared the Nobel Peace Prize. The following year, Mandela was elected president of South Africa. His Truth and Reconciliation Commission sought to address the crimes of the old regime and avoid new divisions and further violence. South Africa, despite ongoing problems of poverty and ethnic tension, remains one of Africa's most successful democracies.

The Pacific Rim has experienced dramatic economic growth since World War II. During the post-war American occupation, Japan's growth was encouraged so that the nation might act as a bastion against communist expansion. Industry and technology had skyrocketed by the 1960s, as Japan became a major manufacturer of consumer goods and electronics. Within three decades, Japan had become one of the world's dominant economic powers. Although a serious fiscal crisis blunted its growth in the 1990s, Japan's economy remains powerful. Other nations in East and Southeast Asia—including South Korea, Indonesia, and the increasingly reformist Vietnam—have also become major players in manufacturing and agriculture and have received heavy Western and Japanese investment because of their lower labor costs. But there, too, destruction of rainforests and other natural landscapes for palm tree plantations, other agricultural products, and urban expansion has done serious environmental harm.

RECENT TRENDS: GLOBAL TIES AND CONFLICTS

One of the most dramatic recent global developments has been China's emergence as a dominant economic power. By the 1980s, China was bending its Communist economic doctrines as it invited foreign investment through free-enterprise zones. In the wake of 1989's Tiananmen Square crackdown and growing popular unrest, the Chinese government recognized that it needed to improve the lot of its younger, more educated citizens. In the 1990s, the nation relaxed its rigid economic restrictions further, allowing free markets to develop and privatizing many state-run industries. When the British colony of Hong Kong was returned to China in 1997, China maintained its globally connected investment markets. The result was an economic boom for the educated classes—even though the boom's sustainability depended on poor working conditions and meager pay for a large part of the Chinese population.

China's dramatic productivity and low labor costs have encouraged Western companies to outsource manufacturing to China, which in turn has become a major supplier of goods throughout the world. Although it has liberalized its economy, however, China has maintained its firmly authoritarian government. Other nations have criticized China for its autocracy and human rights violations. Tensions with the United States have repeatedly risen over regional power (including China's claim to Taiwan and territorial disputes with close American ally Japan); human rights abuses; and China's support for such regimes as that of dictatorial, militarist North Korea. But China and the West are now mutually dependent economically—which means that despite any ongoing disputes, at least some degree of cooperative coexistence is essential.

China's role in the world economy highlights the continuing importance of global economic interconnectivity. Modern telecommunication and the Internet have strengthened these ties even further. Workers in developed countries with high labor costs have been squeezed out of employment as many low- or semiskilled jobs move to less expensive overseas markets. Laborers in developing countries press in turn for opportunity and advancement, as pressure from foreign companies to keep wages low and productivity high often result in virtual slavery. Western popular culture—spread further by television and the Internet—has been embraced in many parts of the world, but it has also sparked backlash from cultural and religious traditionalists who feel threatened by what they consider to be decadent and immoral foreign ideas.

Cultural globalization has reinforced a sense of grievance in some Islamic communities, building on centuries of tension between the Middle East and the West. Opinions about pluralism and the wide circulation of diverse ideas have long differed: the first printing press did not appear in the Arab world until 1720, nearly three centuries after the first European press. Until the 1860s, independent newspapers were virtually unknown in the Arab world. But recently, Western technology, clothing, art, and music have been steadily embraced—and religious traditionalists have mounted significant resistance. The status of women, traditionally relegated to subordinate positions in Islamic culture, has prompted particularly serious clashes in some Muslim countries. Many women have pushed for greater social status, political rights, and equal employment, with widely varying success. The issue remains a difficult one, with women frequently facing social restrictions and even violent repression.

Conflict between Middle Eastern Muslims and the West mounted in the aftermath of the First World War, when the collapsing Ottoman Empire gave way to political and economic domination of the region by Europe and the United States. Even after direct colonial control of the region ended, Western powers continued to support dictatorial regimes to ensure their own access to vital oil supplies. Islamic militancy gained strength during the 1980s Afghan war against the Soviets, in which Islamic fighters, or *mujahedeen* (who were aided and equipped by the United States), were central. Some militant groups that were active in Afghanistan emerged as terrorist bodies with far larger aims—particularly Saudi billionaire Osama bin Laden's al Qaeda organization.

Although most Muslims around the world did not and do not endorse terrorism, the clash between Islamist militants and the West quickly emerged as one of the world's major post-Cold War fault lines. In the 1990s, terrorist groups turned their focus from Middle Eastern regimes to the West as they aimed to force the United States and Europe to withdraw entirely from the Middle East and end their support of Israel. In 1993, militants inspired by a radical Egyptian sheik detonated a truck bomb beneath New York City's World Trade Center. In the mid-1990s, bin Laden's al Qaeda established bases in Africa and plotted anti-Western attacks on U.S. embassies in Africa. Later, as the radical Islamist Taliban took control of Afghanistan, al Qaeda relocated to there. It launched attacks on New York City and Washington, DC, on September 11, 2001.

In the wake of the 9/11 attacks, the United States and several allies took military action to dislodge al Qaeda from its Afghan base. In the following years, enormous resources would go toward hunting down the organization's leaders and blocking further attacks. Meanwhile, hostilities widened. In 2003, the United States invaded Iraq after it claimed that Hussein was gathering weapons of mass destruction to use against the West. The charges against the Iraqi dictator proved inaccurate, and the war caused controversy across the United States and around the world. A resurgent Taliban continues to pose a threat in Afghanistan as U.S. forces begin to withdraw, and Pakistan—where many resent America's military presence in the region—has become increasingly radicalized.

Repeated efforts to restart Israeli-Palestinian peace talks, which had stalled, have resulted in little progress despite wide international support for a two-state peace arrangement. Palestinian groups have continued to launch terrorist attacks and deny Israel's right to exist, while Israel has continued to expand settlement in the occupied territories that are seen by supporters of a two-state solution as belonging to a future independent Palestine. The Middle East was further roiled by the Arab Spring revolts of 2010 and 2011, as protesters across the Arab world—avoiding government censorship by using the Internet—rose up against several dictatorial regimes. The outcome of those uprisings remains a great unknown, as pro-democracy activists struggle for influence against powerfully entrenched Islamist parties seeking to impose Islamic rule.

As it moves into the new millennium, the evolving global community faces challenges: terrorism and peace, ethnic conflicts and border disputes, pollution and global climate change, resource management and population growth, the global status and rights of women and regional minorities, and democratization and its opponents.

POSTSCRIPT: RECENT EVENTS (1992 TO PRESENT)

The 1990s

After decades of government expansion that began with the New Deal and continued in the Great Society, twelve years of Reagan Republicanism had significantly challenged post–New Deal assumptions about federal power. Views over the appropriate role of government in American life greatly differed as Bill Clinton took office as president in 1993. Although he secured a small increase in upper-income tax rates in 1993, Clinton fashioned himself as a new kind of Democrat—a more centrist politician who openly challenged the basic assumption of 1970s and 1980s Democrats that increased spending and government expansion were the default answers to social problems.

Rising health care costs and limited access to health insurance were recognized national concerns, however, so Clinton's administration pressed for comprehensive reform on this issue. Marking the first time a president's wife had taken a public role in policymaking, Hillary Clinton spearheaded the administration's health care efforts. But the complex, cumbersome plan that emerged drew considerable political and public opposition and was rejected by Congress. The aftermath only deepened the country's divisions over the direction of government.

In the 1994 midterm elections, disillusioned voters broke away from decades of rarely interrupted Democratic dominance in Congress and handed both houses to the Republicans. The voters clearly intended to issue a call for more limited government—a balance between Clinton's health care activism and Reagan Republicanism. But the new congressional majority interpreted its victory as a mandate for drastic spending cuts, in some cases aiming well beyond Ronald Reagan's positions and seeking to roll back New Deal protections Reagan had defended.

In 1995, the new Congress briefly shut down the federal government, denying funding in an attempt to force dramatic spending cuts. The political fallout damaged the new majority's standing, leaving the country even more divided and Washington in deeper partisan turmoil. Clinton compromised with Congress to reform the national welfare system; spending was reduced, and requirements that recipients of public assistance actively pursue work were tightened. He also helped lead the government to a balanced budget for the first time in decades, fulfilling a core tenet of Reagan Republicanism—one that had eluded Reagan because of the burden of soaring defense spending and revenue-sapping tax cuts. By the end of Clinton's second term, the country had a budget surplus.

Despite such examples of productive bipartisan cooperation, partisan hostility remained alarmingly high. The Republican Congress had quickly launched aggressive investigations of potential corruption in Clinton's background, although lengthy, controversial, and expensive inquiries yielded few results. In 1998, it emerged that Clinton—who had been accused of sexual harassment before his election—had lied under oath in a civil lawsuit about an affair with White House intern Monica Lewinsky. House Republicans impeached the president but fell well short of a conviction on any charge in the Senate. The impeachment, which was only the second in American history, was unpopular and contributed to a reduced Republican majority in the 1998 midterm elections.

The Clinton years, which marked the first post–Cold War presidency, witnessed an unstable international situation—one with fresh diplomatic opportunities alongside new threats and challenges. The world was no longer divided between two stable superpower-led camps. Freed from such control, regional nationalism surged, combining with religious and ethnic separatism that had been forcibly contained for decades. Nationalist uprisings and ethnic mass killings in Bosnia drew U.S. and NATO military intervention. Islamic militants—who resented America's powerful role in the Middle East, its backing of dictatorial governments in the region, and its long-standing support for Israel—strengthened and expanded their influence.

Radical Islamic militants had gathered in Afghanistan in the 1980s, trying to expel an aggressive Soviet invasion and relying on U.S. aid to do so. As Gorbachev pulled back from military confrontation and withdrew Soviet forces from Afghanistan, militants—particularly Osama bin Laden—turned their hostility to the West, determined to provoke Islamic religious war aimed at unifying the Islamic world under their own brand of religious rule. In 1993, Islamic militants inspired by an Egyptian cleric detonated a truck bomb beneath the World Trade Center in New York, killing six and injuring dozens.

Bin Laden and al Qaeda, his network of followers, moved to Islamist-held territory in Africa to develop their anti-Western plans. They returned to Afghanistan as that country fell to the Islamist Taliban movement. In 1998, they launched bloody bombings of American embassies in Kenya, and they planned further attacks. After the Kenyan bombings, Clinton launched a cruise missile strike on bin Laden's base that narrowly missed the terrorist leader. Yet the U.S. response to al Qaeda was haphazard: members of the intelligence services were unsure of America's overall goals and often failed to share and coordinate information.

As the century ended, America remained politically, socially, and economically divided. Although the economy had boomed under Clinton, manufacturing jobs were now moving to cheaper developing labor markets abroad. Increasing economic globalization, including NAFTA, which linked the United States with Canada and Mexico, further altered the domestic economy and complicated employment prospects, forcing many Americans to retrain for new types of jobs. Changing views on religious and social issues—especially among younger Americans—increased divisions on such controversial topics as abortion, gay rights, and immigration. Further, rapidly changing demographics shifted the racial and ethnic identity of the country: as America became more urban, more racially diverse, and more secular, many Americans—especially older people from more rural areas—feared that the traditional America they cherished was disappearing.

The 2000s

In the 2000 presidential campaign between Al Gore, Clinton's vice president, and Republican George W. Bush, a closely divided country yielded a controversial, contested result. Gore narrowly won the national popular vote. The Electoral College was decided by a disputed result in Florida, where Bush's brother was governor, and where the federal Supreme Court, on a five-to-four party-line vote, stopped the state's recount with Bush leading by only five hundred votes. Later analysis suggested that the limited recount Gore had sought—focused on specific counties with Democratic majorities—would not have changed the outcome. But controversy continues over the full statewide count, the role of state Republican officials in handling the vote and the recount, the Supreme Court's role, and the legal efforts launched by both campaigns after the election.

During Bush's first year in office, al Qaeda continued to orchestrate its long-planned efforts for a major attack. American intelligence services continued to misinterpret important evidence, and the new administration—presented with only fragmentary data—did not appreciate the seriousness of the threat. On September 11, 2001, al Qaeda terrorists hijacked four American airliners, flying two into the Twin Towers of New York City's World Trade Center and collapsing both buildings, and flying a third into the Pentagon in Washington, DC. The fourth plane crashed in rural Pennsylvania after passengers rallied to overpower the hijackers. Three thousand Americans died in the attacks.

Bin Laden viewed Americans as weak and cowardly, and fully expected the United States to collapse after the 9/11 attacks. But Americans united in powerful resolve. President Bush declared a "global war on terror" as he unleashed an attack on al Qaeda's base in Afghanistan. Central Intelligence Agency officers and Army Special Forces helped anti-Taliban Afghan militias retake the country. Although bin Laden and many other al Qaeda leaders escaped, the terrorist movement had lost its haven; targeted attacks over the coming years would deprive bin Laden of most of his top deputies. Although the organization and its loose-knit community of sympathizers would manage major attacks in coming years in such cities as London and Madrid, its capacity as a global threat had greatly diminished. Several attempts to wage another attack on the United States were thwarted.

Most Americans had supported the Afghan war. More controversially, the Bush administration now shifted its focus to Iraq. Bush argued that the Iraqi dictator, Hussein, was still pursuing chemical, biological, and nuclear weapons. In fact, Hussein had abandoned such programs after the 1991 Gulf War. But, wanting to intimidate his enemies, particularly Iran, he resisted UN weapons inspections. Neoconservatives had also gained influence in the wake of 9/11: they pushed to increase America's security and remake the dangerous Middle East by creating pro-Western, democratic regimes—by force, if necessary. Bush and his neoconservative advisors pressed for an invasion of Iraq in 2003, effectively eroding the unity America had enjoyed after 9/11. The Iraqi invasion was met with opposition from most foreign nations and limited support from Arab allies. Although Hussein's government quickly fell, the predicted weapons of mass destruction were not found. The situation in Iraq rapidly decayed as sectarian conflicts, long suppressed by Hussein's brutal regime, burst into chaos.

Critics charged that the Bush White House had failed to plan for realistic postinvasion scenarios, instead hoping to remake and democratize the region with little cost or difficulty. Iraq was soon teetering on the edge of religious civil war. Despite the heavy costs of the wars in Afghanistan and Iraq, Bush pressed for new rounds of tax cuts, particularly for upper-income Americans; the budget surpluses Clinton had left soon gave way to massive deficits. Many Americans distrusted Democrats on national defense, and Bush narrowly won a second term in 2004. Public discontent with Bush's policies grew, however, and the Republicans lost Congress in a 2006 midterm election landslide. A fresh American military effort restored some order in Iraq, but the new Iraqi government insisted on a solid timetable for U.S. withdrawal. Iraq remains riven by sectarian conflict, corruption, and ethnic divisions.

In 2007, the U.S. economy began to falter—and it slumped into serious crisis by early 2008. Government oversight and regulation of businesses had slackened since the late 1970s, and risky financial practices had become more common. Banks offered subprime mortgages (at higher-than-standard interest rates) to high-risk, low-income buyers. Both major political parties encouraged the practice: Democrats urged loans to low-income and minority buyers as a matter of social justice, whereas Republicans looked to bolster home ownership and the important housing market. Because those mortgages were backed by the homes themselves, and because the housing market was soaring, many saw them as sound investments. Financial institutions bought up these mortgages with enthusiasm, expecting to repossess the valuable houses if the borrowers defaulted on their loans. But many potential home buyers lacked the money to meet ever-rising prices, making the housing market a bubble ready to burst.

By early 2008, falling home prices had begun to erase the value of the subprime mortgages. Having overinvested in these assets, financial institutions were suddenly in grave danger. Business and consumer confidence fell, and major financial institutions failed. Financial lending was drastically curtailed, and economic growth was stifled. As businesses closed and jobs were lost, consumer spending plummeted, forcing still more businesses to shut down. As the unemployment rate rose even higher, consumer spending dipped even lower. And as the crisis rapidly escalated, opinions on the most effective response differed drastically. Despite conservative opposition to federal intervention, the government moved to bail out failing institutions and prevent a full collapse of the fiscal system. Nevertheless, the nation plunged into the worst recession in decades.

Both Bush and the Republican Party had been unpopular even before the fiscal crisis, and Democrats were favored to win the 2008 election. Indeed, that fall, Democrat Barack Obama was elected as the nation's first African American president. Despite his solid electoral win, however, Americans were still sharply divided on spending, regulation, taxation, and the president's push for a health care reform law. Conservative Republicans retook the House of Representatives in 2010, but their uncompromising small-government agenda also proved divisive and controversial, helping propel Obama to a second term—in spite of the nation's slow economic recovery.

As Obama's presidency unfolded, manufacturing jobs continued to move abroad, and the economy continued to shift. Many workers were unqualified for available positions, as was the case in the high-tech sector, in which many job positions went unfilled because there were not enough qualified applicants. Deep political, social, and religious differences persisted, and America's white majority shrank as its minority presence grew. Islamic terrorism and global instability continued to pose constant threats, even after a 2011 Special Forces raid in Pakistan killed bin Laden. Americans continued to battle over the nature and proper extent of the fight against terror, balancing security against privacy and due process. Inspired by their shared national heritage, many Americans were left searching for common ground and a new political center—while others clung fiercely to their own visions of America's past and future.

Who Is Common Core

Common Core is a nonprofit 501(c)3 organization that creates curriculum tools and promotes programs, policies, and initiatives at the local, state, and federal levels, with the aim of providing students with challenging, rigorous instruction in the full range of liberal arts and sciences. Common Core was established in 2007 and is not affiliated with the Common Core State Standards (CCSS).

Common Core has been led by Lynne Munson, as president and executive director, since its founding. In six short years, Lynne has made Common Core an influential advocate for the liberal arts and sciences and a noted provider of CCSS-based curriculum tools. Lynne was deputy chairman of the National Endowment for the Humanities (NEH) from 2001 to 2005, overseeing all agency operations. NEH is an independent agency of the federal government that funds scholarly and public projects in the humanities. Lynne was the architect of Picturing America (http://picturingamerica.neh.gov/), the most successful public humanities project in NEH history. The project put more than seventy-five thousand sets of fine art images and teaching guides into libraries, K–12 classrooms, and Head Start centers. In 2005, Lynne led the first postconflict U.S. government delegation to Afghanistan to deal with issues of cultural reconstruction. In 2004, she represented the United States at UNESCO meetings in Australia and Japan, where she helped negotiate guidelines for cross-border higher education.

From 1993 to 2001, Lynne was a research fellow at the American Enterprise Institute, where she wrote *Exhibitionism: Art in an Era of Intolerance* (Ivan R. Dee, 2000), a book examining the evolution of art institutions and art education. Lynne served as a research assistant to NEH chairman Lynne Cheney from 1990 to 1993. She has written on issues of contemporary culture and education for numerous national publications, including the *New York Times*, the *Wall Street Journal*, *USA Today*, *Inside Higher Education*, and National Review Online's *The Corner*. She has appeared on CNN, Fox News, CNBC, C-SPAN, and NPR, and she speaks to scholarly and public audiences. She serves on the advisory board for the Pioneer Institute's Center for School Reform. Her degree in art history is from Northwestern University.

Learn more about Common Core at commoncore.org.

Acknowledgments

On behalf of Common Core (CC), I would like to thank those whose time, knowledge, and passion created this invaluable resource for teachers. There are many who deserve heartfelt thanks; without their contribution, the Alexandria Plan would still be just an idea in our minds. My first thanks are to Kate Bradford and Lesley Iura at Jossey-Bass/Wiley, who advocated for publishing a new education series on history, despite the subject's having been marginalized for decades. They share our confidence that history is on its way back into classrooms.

Much of CC's Washington, DC, staff played—and continues to play—a significant role in shaping, shepherding, and promoting this work. Staff members include program manager Sarah Woodard, program assistant Lauren Shaw, and partnerships manager Alyson Burgess. Barbara Davidson, CC's Deputy Director, was fearless in her leadership of this effort.

Special thanks to the more than one hundred teachers who piloted the Plan in their respective classrooms. We are particularly grateful to Susan Hensley, elementary curriculum specialist for the Rogers Public Schools in Arkansas, for her lead role in the piloting effort. The piloters' enthusiastic and insightful feedback was an essential ingredient in our work. Also, recognition needs to go to CC's Alyssa Stinson for arranging the pilot project. Thanks also go to Russ Cohen of Schoolwide, Inc. Russ provided review copies of the more than eight hundred titles we considered for inclusion in the Alexandria Plan.

Many experts were involved in informing, shaping, and ensuring the accuracy of this work. Historian Harvey Klehr exhaustively reviewed our U.S. history era summaries to make sure we had our facts correct. CC trustee and past president of the National Council of Teachers of English Carol Jago reviewed and improved our text studies. Lewis Huffman, social studies education associate for the South Carolina Department of Education, provided keen, real-world guidance that was instrumental in making the Plan of service to teachers. Susan Pimentel and her team at Student Achievement Partners provided invaluable early advice that shaped the rigor of the Plan.

Research assistant Jennifer Foley's review of this work was incredibly beneficial. Our Plan was meticulously edited by Allison Lawruk to ensure that it was error-free and of maximum use to teachers. The materials were painstakingly copyedited by Shannon Last. Betsy Franz and Rebecca Hyman helped obtain the images that appear throughout the Plan. And Natanya Levioff drove our project deadlines to completion.

We are grateful to Ed Alton and his team at Alton Creative for their ingenious design of our website, commoncore.org. We are indebted to branding expert Christopher Clary, illustrator Amy DeVoogd, and copywriter Peter Chase for work that enhances both the website and this book.

There are three people who worked tirelessly for months on the Plan and who are most responsible for imbuing the Plan with heft, utility, and joy. Historian Jeremy Stern is not only our nation's foremost expert on state social studies standards but also a thoughtful, trenchant scholar who has the gift of writing the kind of history we all want to read. Jeremy brought extraordinary care and devotion to the crafting of each of the thirty-six era summaries that form the basis for the Plan and from which the topics for our text studies are derived.

Education policy consultant Sheila Byrd-Carmichael served as a writer and Common Core State Standards (CCSS) expert on this project. Sheila worked to ensure that the text-dependent questions and performance assessments for each suggested anchor text would allow students to meet, indeed surpass, the standards. She also brought forward essential academic vocabulary in each text study.

Lorraine Griffith is a teacher at West Buncombe Elementary in Asheville, North Carolina. She is also lead writer of all of CC's CCSS English language arts–based curriculum materials for grades K through 4. Lorraine identified the essential historical content in each of our anchor texts and made it the focus of the series of text-dependent questions that form the spine of our text studies, and of the Plan itself. Her uncanny ability to translate her passion for how great literature, history, and art can transform the learning experience for students is a gift to CC and to the teachers who use our curriculum materials.

Jeremy, Sheila, and Lorraine's depth of knowledge and passion for bringing quality resources to teachers inspired everyone involved in this project. We hope and expect that their enthusiasm will be evident to you as you begin to work with the material contained in this book.

It was a privilege for me to work alongside these inspired experts. I look forward to our next project together!

December, 2013

Lynne Munson
President and Executive Director
Common Core
Washington, DC

Index

D

Y

Z